Redemptive Connection

**A FRAMEWORK FOR MENTORING TEENS & YOUNG
ADULTS INTO A THRIVING ADULTHOOD**

Pam Parish

FOREWORD BY: ANDY CROUCH

PRAISE FOR REDEMPTIVE CONNECTION

Redemptive Connection is more than just a book; it's a journey into the depth, beauty, and insight of healing and hope. As someone who has experienced the harsh realities of orphanhood, adoption rejection, abuse, and the complexities of biological family reconnections, I can attest to the transformative power nestled within these pages. This book provides practical, personal, and biblically-rooted solutions for anyone navigating the rocky waters of broken families and trauma. I was 18 when I joined my family, stepping into a relationship filled with its own set of challenges. Yet, through the grace of our greatest Redeemer, our Heavenly Father, what was once vulnerable and fractured has flourished into a thriving, redeemed connection. This book acts as a beacon of light, illuminating the dark crevices of past traumas and guiding readers toward sealing their wounds to foster richer, stronger relationships. The tools offered here are not just impactful— they're life-changing. For anyone longing to turn their pain into purpose and their trials into triumph, *Redemptive Connection* is an essential read.
Katya Grace Parish, *Daughter*

From the Author: Katya was the first daughter to come into our family at the age of 18. She was the seed that God planted for the birth of an entirely new direction in our family's life and in the trajectory of my life's work. As she indicates in her endorsement, the relationship hasn't always been easy and has fractured and repaired time and time again. That is redemption at work. To say that I'm honored by her words and her desire to read this book in its entirety and write this endorsement is an understatement. I'm humbled and moved by the GRACE of God in her life and mine. I'm blessed to be her mom.

Redemptive Connection—what a powerful phrase, and book title. In this book, Pam delivers. Andy and I have been around the foster care block as foster parents, and also as support to foster families in our local churches. We've fallen in love with a handful of kids who've navigated the world of *dis*connection. We've seen the deep need for healing that comes from genuine, compassionate, and authentic connection—redemptive connection. *Redemptive Connection* is a profound and essential guide for individuals and organizations guiding families in the important work of fostering and mentoring youth who've experienced trauma. Please don't miss this amazing resource!

Sandra Stanley, *Fostering Together*, North Point Ministries

I admire Pam deeply as a friend and as a CEO, and it's a delight to feel her joy and wisdom on every page of *Redemptive Connection*. She writes with authority because she's earned every word; and she's a great teacher because she's been a voracious learner. As you work through the depth of the practical help here—my favorite is the dozens of descriptions of healthy and unhealthy practices and responses to every kind of situation—you realize that you're in the hands of a real master at this high-wire craft of parenting. I'm able to see myself and my own kids (now young adults) in such poignant ways through the words of this book. Pam uncannily names everything we did right, everything we did wrong, and in this book I hear—in her own voice— the grace, consolation, and "well done" that I know Jesus offers me in my journey as a father.

Scott Kauffmann, *Partner*, Praxis

I recently had the privilege of reading *Redemptive Connection*, and I was profoundly moved by its timely insights. As a trauma professional and a parent currently navigating personal challenges, I found the book incredibly affirming and enlightening. Pam's vulnerability breathes life into every page, making complex concepts relatable and actionable. Particularly impactful were the discussions on maintaining a healthy balance of vulnerability with our children, the innovative concept of harmful felt safety, and the practical G.R.A.C.E. Response, which deserves a spot on every refrigerator. This book is a must-read for caregivers eager to understand their own stories and how these influence their caregiving. It's a comprehensive, honest, and deeply necessary resource that promises to make a significant impact on its readers.

I'm grateful for the opportunity to endorse this work and hope it reaches everyone who needs its wisdom.

Pam Taylor, *Co-Founder,* **Watch Me Rise**

Through *Redemptive Connection*, Pam emphasizes the importance of meaningful and intentional relationships that can transform the future of youth aging out of foster care. The book offers a step-by-step guide through a "redemptive framework" to equip families and service providers with effective tools for impacting the trajectory of the youth they love and serve. Pam's dedication to the work of Connections Homes is inspiring. She is changing lives and inviting others to participate in the stories of young adults.

Robyn Smith, *Board Chair,* **Connections Homes;** *Chief Human Resources Officer,* **Jackson Healthcare**

Pam Parish writes with an exquisite blend of honesty, humility, expertise, humor, and profound experience. In *Redemptive Connection*, she masterfully guides readers through the complexities of trauma experienced by young adults, offering a supportive pathway toward a thriving and joyful adulthood. The book meticulously unpacks the trauma stemming from abuse, neglect, and unstable childhoods, providing step-by-step insight that encourages introspection and the capacity to foster healing in others. As I read, I found myself engrossed, revisiting sections, and wishing I had access to such a resource earlier in my career with vulnerable children and families—and even while parenting my own children. *Redemptive Connection* is an indispensable read for anyone in the helping professions, whether they are novices or seasoned experts.

Lynn A. Johnson, *Former Assistant Secretary,* **Administration for Children and Families, U.S. Department of Health and Human Services,** *President and Founder,* **ALL IN Fostering Futures**

As a therapist specializing in adoption and foster care, I found *Redemptive Connection* to be an essential read. Each chapter eagerly unveils a model rooted in grace, compassion, and love—a blueprint that all parents, especially those parenting, mentoring, or working with young adults, should embrace. Over my years in practice, I've witnessed many parents reach the brink of despair. This book not only offers fresh insights but also instills a hope that many might think unattainable. I urge therapists and family service professionals to not only read but also integrate and teach the principles laid out in this transformative guide.

Amy L. Curtis, PhD, *Senior Director of Counseling Services,* **Buckner Children and Family Services**

Redemptive Connection is a profoundly insightful guide for parents navigating the complexities of children transitioning into adulthood, especially those with trauma histories. As an adoptive mom and a mentor to others on this journey, Pam's words deeply resonated with me, addressing thoughts I have long grappled with. Her book offers wisdom for loving our adult children with *Redemptive Connection,* mirroring the example set by Jesus. I wholeheartedly recommend this book to any parent seeking to cultivate healthy and connected relationships with their children throughout their lives. This is a book I will revisit for years!

Tera Melber, MA, *Founding Director,* **Resound Trauma Education, LLC.**

In *Redemptive Connection,* Pam Parish lays out a compelling vision for healthy relational growth - for ourselves and those we love and serve. Pam shares a wealth of hard-earned wisdom for mentors and parents of teens and young adults. Read this book, and you will be inspired by tenacious commitment. You will gain a sturdier understanding of love's simultaneous tenderness and firmness, its gentleness and continual call toward growth. Most of all, this book illuminates Christ's persistent invitational way with each of us - teaching us, bit by bit, to increasingly respond **to** "the upward call of God" in our lives. (Philippians 3:14)

Rachel Medefind, *Director, Institute for Family-Centered Healing &*
Health, **Christian Alliance for Orphans (cafo.org)**

ACKNOWLEDGMENTS

I want to acknowledge my husband, my rock, and my best friend, Steve. Not a single word of this book or the story that inspired its words would have been possible without your steadfast love and deeply compassionate heart. You truly are "Saint Steve." I love you to the end of time. You have my forever "yes."

To our daughters, sons-in-law, and grandbabies: you are the inspiration behind it all. Your courage, strength, humor, stubbornness, vulnerability, trust, and love are blessings that fill every day of my life with joy. Candie, Katya, Tae & Kelsey (Juan, Jayden, Adrianna, & Junior), James & Elizabeth, Tyree & Seara, Charlee, Paul & Kristan (Wesley), and Heather- I love you all deeply

To my Board of Directors and the team at Connections Homes, thank you for being a part of this story with me. Every part of this work has been lived out in your day-to-day interactions with our youth and families. You've wrestled through the concepts alongside me as we've tested, tweaked, and refined them. I'm proud that you're not only my team but also my friends and co-laborers in Christ. Thank you.

To my friends at Praxis (praxislabs.org), I am humbled to know you and have the privilege to learn and be inspired by you. This book began at a Praxis gathering and the framework was born during a mentoring hour. The intentional ways that your team works with founders gave space and fertile ground for this seed of an idea to be planted, watered, and come to life. The result of this will be countless youth and families healed and *redemptively* restored. Thank you.

There are literally hundreds more whom I could thank for the words on the following pages, but I'm excited for you—the reader—to dive into the content. So, to all of my friends, pastors, co-laborers in this world of foster care and adoption, and all of our family, I love you, and I'm so grateful that you're in my life. You are all little lights of joy and inspiration in my path.

Choose joy every day.

A published work of *Ready or Not Resources*

Scripture quotations are taken from the *Holy Bible*, New Living Translation, copyright © 1996, 2004, 2007, 2013 by Tyndale House Foundation. Used by permission of Tyndale House Publishers, Inc., Carol Stream, Illinois 60188. All rights reserved.

Where quotes are used, credit is given to the originator. The author has tried to give credit where credit is due. However, due to extensive exposure to reading, training environments, and relationships within the foster care and adoptive community, a phrase may be used that originated elsewhere. If this may occur, please don't hesitate to contact the author via her blog at pamparish.com.

Editors: Jeni Nitzel, Kristan Bhandari
Cover Art: Canva
Cover Design: Pam Parish
Author Photo: Selfie ☺
Inspiration: Every vulnerable youth who ever had the courage to embrace family time and time again despite brokenness and loss. And every family in the trenches alongside them as *redemptive connections*.

ISBN-13: 978-0-9964928-1-2

DEDICATION

This book is dedicated to every young person who has the drive to overcome their obstacles and thrive in life. The most courageous of those are the young adults 18 – 24 coming out of our foster care system who've been broken time and time again by the idea of "family" yet have the courage to risk it again for healthy belonging. I'm in awe of you.

Redemptive Connection

A Framework for Mentoring Teens & Young Adults into a Thriving Adulthood

Written By:
Pam Parish

Foreword By:
Andy Crouch

Table of Contents

FOREWORD

Andy Crouch

Books are not just meant to be read—they are meant to be lived. Every worthwhile book is an invitation to a different way of living. And this is a worthwhile book, offering a beautiful and truthful picture of what it means to accompany young people into a life of real thriving. It describes in emotionally powerful and refreshingly practical detail what that kind of life requires.

I'm especially grateful for this book because, as you'll learn in the first pages, Pam Parish has grasped and lived out the vision of one of my own books, *Strong and Weak,* in a way I'm not sure anyone else has—better, I am quite sure, than I have grasped or lived it myself. She had the crucial insight not just to see how the framework of authority and vulnerability from that book could apply to her experiences and the work of Connections Homes, but also to realize that it actually *didn't* apply in a crucial way. That led to the dual frameworks described in this book—authority and vulnerability, on the one hand, combined with belonging and self-efficacy, on the other hand—which together give powerful insight into one of the most dramatic and delicate dances of life, that of families with emerging adult children.

Pam and the families she equips through Connections Homes apply these frameworks alongside young people who have had to walk an incredibly tough road. I did not make it through this book without pausing many times to clear the tears from my eyes. But not all my tears were prompted by the stories of exceptional resilience and rescue that you will encounter here— stories that, if you are one of the people brave and fortunate enough to join Connections Homes' work, you will have encountered firsthand. I also found the insights in this book deeply moving in clarifying my own experiences parenting two biological children of our own, and indeed in understanding my own coming of age decades ago—even though my children's lives and mine have had a fraction of the hardship that others have known.

Indeed, the insights here touch on such deep and universal themes that I'd consider this book essential reading for anyone who wants to be a wise and courageous parent cheering on their children as they take the field of adult life. Reading this book gave me a renewed empathy for my own kids as they navigate emerging adulthood, and a renewed sense of my calling in this new phase of parenthood.

It also, as any worthwhile book should, caused me to revisit and wrestle with the question of whether I have lived life as fully as I should—whether I myself have settled for isolation, survival, and what Pam calls "harmful felt-safety," instead of the thriving connection for which we are all designed. While these questions were and are challenging, among Pam's greatest gifts to her readers is her utter confidence in grace. The diagram on the last page—which I won't spoil by describing, and which you'll only fully grasp if you take the journey of this book before you arrive at it—is a powerful reminder that no matter how far we wander, love will have the last word.

This is a book to be lived—indeed, in Pam's family and countless other families who have chosen the way of redemptive connection, it is a book that has been lived. I'm so grateful it is in the world, one more signpost on the way to the life that really is life.

Praise the Lord, my soul; all my inmost being, praise his holy name. Praise the Lord, my soul, and forget not all his benefits— who forgives all your sins and heals all your diseases, who redeems your life from the pit and crowns you with love and compassion, who satisfies your desires with good things so that your youth is renewed like the eagles. The Lord works righteousness and justice for all the oppressed.
Psalm 103:1-6

INTRODUCTION

This isn't a religious book. It's a book focused on walking alongside and mentoring youth and young adults who've experienced trauma. As the author, my personal relationship with Jesus Christ served as a steadfast anchor for me throughout my journey. I will occasionally make references to scripture in the context of its personal significance to me as I navigated through challenges, learned from mistakes, and developed the skills necessary to fulfill the roles of a mother and mentor to our daughters, as well as to lead an organization focused on recruiting, training, and connecting mentors with young adults transitioning out of the foster care system. My relationship with Jesus has undoubtedly shaped how I've developed these frameworks and tools, which will be apparent as you read. However, I believe wholeheartedly that even outside of a faith context, the principles and tools in this framework can be of help to any family seeking to connect deeply with teens and young adults with trauma histories as they transition to adulthood. I also make no apology for ending this book with a reminder of who Jesus is in our own redemptive story and that He is the ultimate model for us as we journey into *Redemptive Connection* to the teens and young adults we care for. Feel free to skip that last chapter entirely if it's not central to your belief system.

"*...who redeems your life from the pit and crowns you with love and compassion...*" I love those words from Psalm 103:4 because they uniquely encapsulate my story of parenting teenagers from hard places who had experienced more heartache and misery by their teens than I had in my entire life. I came into this journey wholly unprepared to parent through a trauma lens and, as a result, found myself and our family in *a pit* of chaos, hurt, and dysregulation. Gratefully, the Lord led me on a path toward learning about trauma-informed care and discovering how my unresolved childhood issues were impacting our family situation. In this process, I became *crowned with love and compassion* not only for my girls and their trauma histories and associated behaviors but also for myself, my husband, and a host of foster and adoptive families, kids, teens, and young adults. This book and its contents are a culmination of nearly two decades of immersion in trauma-informed learning and applying the principles I learned—and having to adapt many of them to my teenagers as they aged into adulthood.

I don't hold a degree in psychology, trauma, or counseling. I'm simply a mom who, at the very bottom of *a pit* of despair, was desperate for help and devoured every resource that I could get my hands on to find answers. At the end of this book, you will find a resource library full of many books, speakers, and training that saved our family. Many of these authors, trainers, speakers, and therapists are dear friends of mine today. I'm so grateful for their impact on this world of trauma and, I can say without hesitation, that I wouldn't be penning these words today without their influence.

My journey into trauma-informed learning came at a conference, The Christian Alliance for Orphans (CAFO) Summit—an annual conference that brings together nonprofit leaders, church leaders, parents, and experts to learn about best practices in foster care and adoption and to receive training in areas where they would like to grow and learn. This particular summit was being held in Nashville, TN and I was attending as a church staff member to look at ways that we could implement a foster care and adoption ministry within our church—and all of the sessions that I chose to attend were on this topic area. Back home in Georgia, I had left my husband with our three daughters, two of whom had severe trauma histories. Here I was attending a conference hoping to implement a ministry at our church for others to do what we were doing as a part of my job, while on a personal level, our family was coming apart at the seams because all of the ways that had succeeded for us in parenting one child from birth were failing miserably with our new daughters.

As the Lord would lead (or fate would have it), I couldn't find one of my sessions. As I was walking through the conference facility searching for the room that I had planned to be in, I walked past a large room that was full of people—packed, actually. On the stage was a thin white-haired woman speaking, and everyone in the room was giving her full attention. I decided to give up my search for my other planned session and slip into a chair at the back of the room to see what this session was all about. The speaker's name was Dr. Karyn Purvis. That session changed the direction of my life forever. So much so that after it was over, I sat silently with tears streaming down my cheeks, wondering how it was that I didn't know what I had just learned and regretting how much damage I had done in my own family, specifically with my girls with trauma histories, by not knowing it.

Dr. Purvis is the co-author of a fantastic book, *The Connected Child,* and helped to develop, in my opinion, one of the best trauma-informed approaches to parenting children from hard places, *Trust-Based Relational Intervention (TBRI).* Immediately after hearing her speak, my husband and I purchased the book and signed up to become trainers through a training curriculum called *Empowered to Connect* based on TBRI principles. We didn't just learn. We dove into the deep end to save our family. The Empowering, Connecting, and Correcting principles we learned and began to teach other families were game-changers in our household. From the very beginning of using these principles and applying this understanding, we experienced major changes. Yet, there were definitely areas that we struggled to adapt to teenagers as opposed to younger children. For us, the struggle in balancing the connection and correction often hit a roadblock in areas that were necessary to help our girls learn to take personal responsibility and become prepared to be well-functioning adults in a society that isn't always going to slow down to *connect* before *correcting.* It was absolutely necessary for us to connect with them deeply while also disconnecting with them enough to allow autonomy and growth. There were many times that the need for both caused difficulty for us—and especially for them—the older they got.

One of the early ways that my husband and I would phrase this push/pull conundrum was in terms of *the monkey on their back.* I'm not sure where we first heard the phrase; it's certainly not one that we made up, but it stuck with us. Our girls were no different from most teenagers making the transition to interdependence often expecting us as their parents to solve their problem/issue for them rather than accepting ownership of it for themselves. When these occurrences would arise, we would say, *"That's not my circus and not my monkeys,"* as a way to let our girls know that we didn't create the problem and it wasn't ours to solve. It was effective, but it wasn't always connected. We struggled greatly with this balance and failed way more often than we succeeded. We longed for an effective way of practicing trauma-informed TBRI principles in the older years of teenagers and early years of young adulthood with our girls.

Even as I launched Connections Homes, an organization that I founded to help match youth aging out of foster care to Mentoring Families who commit to being a safe and stable support system for them, my team and I would find ourselves searching for ways to guide our families in connected ways around issues that involved the need to remain attached in meaningful ways to their young adult while at the same time not stepping into problem-solving *for* the young adult. Letting someone you love struggle, hurt, or fail doesn't always feel like love or connection—to either of you. Sometimes it's necessary, and sometimes it's a mistake. The problem is that the lines are gray, and the resources available to navigate that tightrope in a trauma-informed way are difficult to find. The distance between helping and enabling is often minuscule, and finding a way to differentiate the two was difficult. For our work and my family to truly be successful, I really needed to figure it out.

How can we help an older teen/young adult with a trauma history feel connected and secure in our relationship while also giving them enough independence and autonomy to make good decisions and handle the consequences of bad decisions? As a mother and as a leader this was a central question for me and one that for almost five years of our organization's life, was asked regularly in our training and support of our Mentoring Families. I knew instinctively that both connection and personal responsibility were critical to moving our girls and our organization's young adults into an adulthood where they could thrive. I just couldn't find a resource to meet both of these goals at the same time while also considering a trauma history that makes connecting difficult and hasn't provided the key foundational framing for real personal accountability.

As the Lord would lead (or fate would have it), I once again found myself sitting in a learning atmosphere that would change my whole trajectory related to trauma-informed care. This time, it was unrelated to foster care and adoption and instead focused on nonprofit leadership and building a redemptive organization. If Karyn Purvis and TBRI were the greatest things to happen to me as a parent of teens with trauma histories, then Praxis, a business and nonprofit accelerator focused on a redemptive approach to leading ventures, was the greatest thing to happen to me as a nonprofit leader for an organization focused on connection and belonging for young adults with trauma histories. The foundational framework of this book began on a September day in 2019 in Los Angeles, CA. As the founder of Connections Homes, I was honored to be selected as a 2019 nonprofit cohort member in the Praxis Labs nonprofit accelerator. There's no way that I could have ever imagined the impact that the Praxis team and accelerator would have on me as a leader and, ultimately, on our organization. It was truly transformational. As transformational as the entire year process was for our organization, this day in Los Angeles would be one of the most transformational.

On this day, author and Praxis partner Andy Crouch was leading a session on authority and vulnerability, a powerful teaching based on his book *Strong & Weak*. In the teaching, Andy drew a 2x2 graph on the board with Authority at the top axis and Vulnerability on the right axis, describing a flourishing life involving both the ability to meaningfully act and take a meaningful risk. Immediately, I resonated with the premise and could see many ways in my life that I was required to balance what I knew (my expertise, experience, abilities, etc.) with what I was willing to put at risk (money, love, comfort, security, etc.) and in doing so was rewarded with an outcome that I would describe as a flourishing moment—getting married at 19, taking a job out of state away from everyone I knew, adopting a child from foster care.... all these things and more in my life had required both authority and vulnerability. As Andy continued teaching through the other quadrants of the 2x2, I continued to resonate with all of them—control (all authority and no vulnerability), suffering (all vulnerability and no authority), and withdrawal (neither authority nor vulnerability). As I reflected on the teaching with my own story, I could see where I had been in each of these places at one time or another and, not just me but every foster and adoptive family I've ever worked with and counseled. This simple tool was meaningful and helpful as I thought about my struggles and successes as a parent and how we could better support our families at Connections Homes. I took copious notes and was exploding with ideas of how we could use this information and this tool to provide greater support to families in our work. I couldn't wait to return to Georgia and share this with my team. Then a problem arose. A problem that kept me up all night.

The problem came later that evening as I continued to think through Andy's 2x2. I kept thinking about the suffering quadrant and how, for most of the youth we serve, this was the quadrant they fit in—by no fault of their own. They were truly victims—vulnerable to the decisions and actions of others with no real authority to act on their behalf. Our youth didn't fit on this 2x2 at all, and to get them beyond the suffering quadrant was, quite simply, the problem that I've been trying to solve for years. I couldn't sleep *at all* that night. The next morning, we each had the opportunity to spend an hour with one of the Praxis core team members or a mentor we had heard from during our time there. I went to the team and asked for an hour with Andy because I desperately needed to solve this problem.

That hour with Andy Crouch is the foundation for this entire book. It was in that conversation that, together, we wrestled through what it meant for the youth we serve. Being vulnerable and unable to take meaningful action in their childhoods because other adults and systems had done it for them had put our youth at a disadvantage in achieving a flourishing life. So, we began to unpack and dissect the question: How could we help them thrive in life and give them the tools to get onto their path toward a flourishing life? The result of that conversation was a 2x2 graph encompassing all that I had struggled with both as a parent and as the leader of our organization. This 2x2 grid and its quadrants have proven to be a game changer in our organization as we train and equip families to walk alongside their young adults as mentors, guides, and support systems. To get youth onto their path toward a flourishing life, we must first help them to *thrive* as an interdependent, connected, and fully functioning adult. From this thriving life, a young adult can begin to take meaningful actions and choose meaningful risks to live a flourishing life.

We call this 2x2 and the trauma-informed approaches surrounding it the *Redemptive Connection Framework (RCF),* and it's through this framework that our team works with Mentoring Families and our youth to achieve our vision of helping young adults thrive in life through connection to a safe, stable support system. The concepts in this book have been a game changer for our organization. They have also been a game changer in my own family as I've had more concrete trauma-informed tools and understanding to truly help our girls become all that God has created them to be.

It's my sincerest prayer that as you learn about the *Redemptive Connection Framework* through this book, a new approach to understanding and helping older teens and young adults who've experienced trauma will be unlocked for you and that every young adult you serve will thrive. This framework results from more than five years of hard work, training, refining, and research. I'm thankful to have the opportunity to share it with you finally.

Because everyone deserves to belong,
Pam Parish

Also, the following two pages include the primary 2x2 matrixes foundational to this book. I encourage you to bookmark these pages and refer to them throughout the book.

Authority

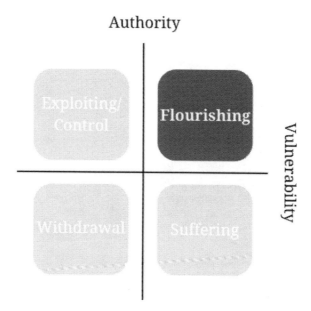

Andy Crouch's Authority/Vulnerability Matrix

Authority – The capacity for meaningful action
Vulnerability – The capacity for meaningful risk

- **High Authority / High Vulnerability – Flourishing** This quadrant represents the balance between the power to act (authority) and the willingness to risk (vulnerability), which leads to growth and flourishing.
- **High Authority / Low Vulnerability – Control** Here, individuals or entities exert power without opening themselves to risk or harm, potentially leading to domination, manipulation, and exploitation.
- **Low Authority / High Vulnerability – Suffering** This quadrant is characterized by exposure to harm without the means to protect oneself, leading to oppression or victimization.
- **Low Authority / Low Vulnerability – Withdrawal** Represents the disengagement from meaningful interaction and risk, leading to isolation, detachment, and withdrawal.

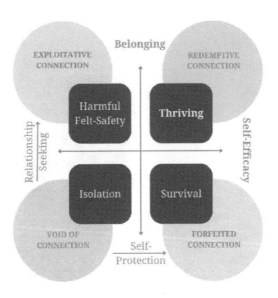

The Redemptive Connection Framework

Belonging – To be a member or part of a group or family
Self-Efficacy – Confidence in the ability to exert control (authority) over one's own motivations, behaviors, and social environment.

- **High Belonging/High Self-Efficacy – Thriving (Redemptive Connection) -** This ideal quadrant represents a young person who feels a strong sense of belonging and possesses high self-efficacy. They are able to thrive, forming deep connections with others and engaging effectively in building their own life, dealing effectively with both challenges and successes.
- **High Belonging/Low Self-Efficacy – Harmful Felt-Safety (Exploitative Connection) -** This quadrant represents a young person who feels a sense of belonging but has low self-efficacy. Their emphasis on relational needs without the capacity for personal growth or independence can lead to harmful relationships and fractured identity structures.
- **Low Belonging/High Self-Efficacy – Survival (Forfeited Connection) -** A young person in this quadrant has developed self-efficacy but lacks a sense of belonging. They may be highly independent and capable but struggle with forming or maintaining meaningful connections, operating in survival mode.
- **Low Belonging/Low Self-Efficacy – Isolation (Void of Connection)** A young person in this quadrant lacks both belonging and self-efficacy, leading to disconnection, isolation, and a sense of helplessness.

"As you move outside of your comfort zone, what was once the unknown and frightening becomes your new normal."
Robin S. Sharma

CHAPTER ONE

JOURNEY INTO THE UNKNOWN

It was November of 2006. I was resting on my couch watching a PBS channel documentary about The Heart Gallery, an organization birthed by professional photographers who wanted to take better photos of children in foster care who were available for adoption. The photos allowed the kids to show off their passions and personalities much better than a case manager placing them against a blank wall and taking a photo. The work of the Heart Gallery increased adoption rates because it allowed potential families to see a little more of the child's personality. I was stunned by the beauty of this idea and blown away that I was a full-grown adult who didn't have a clue that children in foster care sometimes didn't get to go home. It broke my heart and lit a spark in my mind. I walked out to our garage, where my husband was tinkering on something, and said, "Did you know that there are hundreds of kids right here in our state available for adoption from foster care? Kids the same age as Kristan (our eleven-year-old biological daughter)?" He looked up and said, "No, I didn't. Why is that?" I launched into all my newfound Google education about parental rights termination and how older kids languish in foster care without adoption sometimes because so many people want babies and toddlers. After my mini-lecture, Steve said, "That's terrible. I wonder what happens to them?" That's when the spark in my mind turned into a fire in my heart, and I said, "Do you think we could look into the process of becoming an adoptive family through our state?" He looked at me briefly and said, "It doesn't hurt to find out what it takes. Sure."

We had talked about adoption for years, but the structure of our life just wasn't suitable. Now that Kristan was eleven, we didn't particularly want to start over in parenting a much younger child. This new avenue felt like the perfect fit for our family. We knew Kristan deeply wanted a sibling, and we could never provide that for her medically. Adopting an older child was something that we all felt confident that we could and should do. I went to work gathering all the information I could on the process, and by December, we were in classes to become certified as foster parents in Georgia. By May of 2007, we were approved by the state, and on 7/7/07, we identified an eleven-year-old girl that we thought would be a perfect fit for our family. She moved into our home in September. We had no clue how much our lives would change over the next few years.

We had a good life. A charmed life. We had recently moved to Atlanta from Raleigh, NC, where I had spent several years as an executive for a mobile technology company. We were taking on new roles at a rising multicultural megachurch, creating a new community of friends, and getting to spend time with old friends we had missed in North Carolina. Kristan was eleven and had recently traveled to England and Scotland with the U.S. Student Ambassador program; she was intelligent, well-behaved, and overly responsible for a kid her age. Life was beyond blessed for this small-town Kentucky girl from a coal mining & factory-worker family.

It hadn't come easy, though, or without its challenges. Married at 19 years old, my high school sweetie and I had spent our fair share of years scraping by. We'd lived in trailers with holes in the floor and had our electricity cut off for nonpayment. If it hadn't been for our state's WIC provisions when Kristan was a baby, we wouldn't have been able to keep up with groceries, and I vividly remember having to buy groceries for an entire week with only $11 to our name. We ate a lot of hamburger helper, eggs, potatoes, and ramen noodles.

Before having Kristan, we had suffered two miscarriages; our doctors had told us that they were concerned I might not be able to carry a pregnancy to term. It was devastating. I wanted to be a mother so badly. We were 24 when we finally got pregnant with Kristan and made it safely through the first trimester without incident. She's a miracle; her middle name, Faith, reflects that miracle in our lives. When it came time to deliver her, I was battling gestational diabetes and preeclampsia. And once she arrived, I nearly bled to death on the table. She ended up in NICU for a week with Group B Strep, and I battled a uterine infection with a blood count of three. Our miracle child was here, but medically, I would be unable to have further children.

I share all of that to say that we felt grateful beyond measure to have a child and financial stability and purpose in our lives. None of those things are things we achieved quickly, and we tried hard never to take them for granted. Among those things, being parents was our top priority. We read the books, listened intently to sermons on biblical parenting, studied developmental stages, and applied everything we could to our parenting to ensure Kristan had the best shot at her best life. We were proud to be parents and devoted to doing whatever we needed to get it right. So, on that 2006 day, when we decided to find out how to become a permanent family for a child from foster care, it wasn't something that we decided lightly. We knew we would devote as much conviction and care to this child as we had to

Kristan because this child would be just as much of a miracle. We had always wanted more children, and Kristan had dreamed of a sibling for most of her life.

The training classes that the state required us to take threw a lot of information our way. We learned about trauma, about attachment, about behaviors that we had never even considered a child could have, and about the rules and regulations of fostering and adopting through the state. It was a bit overwhelming and sometimes a lot scary. Yet we never wavered in our decision or confidence that we could do this. We had made it eleven years in this parenting thing and had a pretty good dynamic in our home—we were pretty confident, to say the least.

Once we were approved and it was time to wait for our case worker to present us with a child, there was plenty of time to discuss how we wanted to handle this process. We decided to look at as many kids as possible—*on paper*—but we would only meet a kid in person if we were 100% committed to bringing that child into our home. Our phrase was, "We're not used car shopping." This human being has God's innate value, and we would treat them as such. That meant all the calls with case managers happened before a meeting, our questions were asked, and all the paperwork was reviewed. Once we decided to meet a child, it wasn't a visit "to see"—we were already committed. And just like there's nowhere to "send Kristan back to," we decided we would never walk away from a child, no matter what. Our yes would be yes—completely. We were confident we could provide our new daughter with a good family environment, love, and a happy life. The problem was— she didn't want any of it.

In all our devoted learning and careful walking out of the process, it had never occurred to either of us that a child whose parental rights had been removed wouldn't *want* to be adopted by a family who wanted them. Our idealistic thinking met reality on my birthday when we were scheduled for our first face-to-face meeting with our new daughter at her group home. As we drove to the meeting, her case worker called and said, "I just want to set your expectations that she's not too thrilled to meet you." We told her it was okay, and we were committed. After arriving at the group home, we waited patiently for her school bus to arrive. It did. She saw us and walked right past us without saying a word. We were off to a brilliant start.

Not once did we change our commitment to our adoption, no matter her reception of us. The challenge for us was that the state had made permanency through adoption part of her case plan. So, the truth was—she didn't have a choice—someone would adopt her. Why not us? So, we remained committed and brought her home as a permanent part of our family a month later. We were thrilled to add another daughter to our household. She felt like she was being kidnapped. And, in hindsight, I really can't blame her.

She adapted and grew to love and trust us, but it wasn't without its challenges—many that we didn't understand or have the capacity to handle well. The main underlying complication for her was a feeling of betrayal of her biological family and loss of her identity. Even though there were things that we didn't know yet about parenting with a trauma-informed approach, this one piece of the puzzle I specifically understood deeply. My upbringing was deeply broken, and I didn't know my biological father. I loved both of my parents despite their many flaws, and I understood that if I ever had a chance to know my biological father, I would take it—and that taking that chance wouldn't mean that I loved my dad, who raised me, any less. I just wanted to know another part of myself. It was important. So, I also knew how important that was for our daughter. Many times, we let her know that although we were her legal parents, that did not mean that her birth parents weren't just as important to her. We understood and respected it. We wanted her to have a relationship with her birth parents as she got older, as long as it wouldn't put her at risk of any harm. As much as we could, we always tried to tell her we were thankful for the parents God used to bring her into this world. Without them, we wouldn't have her. We prayed for them and one day hoped to know them. And we meant it.

Although there were many ways that we fumbled and failed our way through before adopting a trauma-informed parenting style, we were deeply committed and had a grace-based approach all along. It's the glue that holds us together. I also had the privilege of working closely with our adoption agency through support groups and additional training. Eventually, I became certified to teach our state's foster care curriculum. I would teach alongside a case worker from our agency to help other families become approved to foster or adopt through the state. A basic lens of trauma and its impact on the developing brain was formed through these things. Yet knowing and understanding behavior is one thing; having a toolset to address the behavior adequately is another.

Learning to parent children who've experienced trauma and loss became a central focus in our home because God, in His divine plan, led our family to grow again and again through various circumstances: foster care, aging out of foster care, homelessness, trafficking survival, and adoption disruption. Over the next six years, we would grow from having one daughter to having seven—changing nearly everything about our lives, including me having to trade my Mercedes for a Minivan.

There are many times in the Bible that right before performing a miracle to relieve someone's suffering, it says Jesus was "moved with compassion." Compassion is sometimes confused or substituted for the word empathy. They aren't the same thing. Empathy feels another person's pain without the necessity for action. Compassion is moved to find ways to alleviate the pain of others. I had a deep empathy for the broken families that children without families come from because I, too, had come from a broken family background. Steve had a deep compassion for them—not wanting to see anyone suffer if we had it in our means to help, and we did. God hadn't brought us to this place for our comfort. He brought us here to be of service to our world. To put it in the words of one of our previous pastors, Danny Chambers, "We were blessed to be a blessing." The specific way that doors were opening for us to become aware of the suffering of others in our world was through our eyes being opened to the plight and outcomes of children without a family. He brought deep compassion to our household for the suffering of kids, teens, and young adults who would have gone into their adult lives without someone stepping into their story. We couldn't ignore it.

Yet, every "yes" we gave to God and a new daughter along the way brought a new set of opportunities and challenges to our family. Things as simple as needing to find a new place for someone to sleep, bed shuffles, and general integration within the family dynamic. From things as complicated as typical teenage behaviors to trauma-related responses—eye rolls, not doing chores on time, needing to be driven here and there, food issues, lying, running away, sexual identity, sexual behaviors, drugs, alcohol, sneaking out, raging behaviors, shoplifting, fussing, and fighting, lots and lots of tears/emotion, and more. Whether a typical teenage behavior or a behavior developed by years of neglect and abuse, we were overrun at times and outnumbered.

Over time (as described in the Introduction), we became trained and certified in a trauma-informed parenting approach called *Trust-Based Relational Intervention (TBRI)* through an Empowered to Connect training program. Not only did it change the atmosphere in our home because it gave us a toolset to use as we were walking through challenges and helped us to begin to focus on maintaining a *connection* amid challenges rather than jumping straight to *correction,* but it also allowed us to work with and train other families—increasing our community of trauma-informed friends who understood our journey. God also moved me to write three devotionals for foster and adoptive families, which can be found on Amazon.

God was blessing us in our chaos, but the journey was more complex than we imagined. We lost friends, people that we thought would understand didn't, friends we trusted passed judgments on us without having a complete picture of what was going on in our home, some of our family didn't get it or fully accept our new daughters, and our capacity to hang out with friends and have fun was severely diminished. Amid that, we had some great relationships and a core group of friends who rode the chaos rollercoaster alongside us, and we developed new friendships that we treasure. They were genuinely refreshing in the midst of the storm. Even so, I would be lying if I didn't say that there were so many times that we thought back on our life and wondered what it would be like if we had never said "yes." We would certainly be more comfortable. But would we be more fulfilled? Doubtful. About the temptation and desire to return to "normal," my friend Elizabeth Styffe says, "Normal is just a setting on your washing machine." While that quote always makes me chuckle, it's true. There is never a "going back." Nothing would be the same if we could. It would be sad. There is only going forward into the new normal—over and over again.

One of our biggest challenges along the way was the need to adapt many of the trauma-informed tools to teenagers and young adults. Connection was critical but there were many times that tools fell short. For example, puppet play was one of the favorite tools for working with children in trauma, letting the puppet recreate the behavior you want to enforce—finishing your dinner, keeping your seatbelt buckled, being nice to your sister, etc. Play relaxes the brain and helps kids retain concepts their survival brain might otherwise never allow them to retain and repeat. Well, 16-year-olds wouldn't tolerate working and reworking a behavior using puppets. Yet, in one of my funnier and more desperate moments, two of our daughters had been arguing (there was so much arguing!), and I had reached my limit. I wanted to scream at them to go to their rooms and not speak to anyone the rest of the day, but that would not have been a connected response. I needed to find a way to deal with the behavior while maintaining connection and harmony in our home. As a trainer for *Empowered to Connect,* I had a bin full of hand puppets I used with families in training. I grabbed a panda puppet and a monkey puppet, handed one to each, and said, "I don't care how much longer you argue. But from this point forward, your puppets are the only ones that can speak, and you must have the argument in their voices." Gratefully, it worked. Within five minutes, they were giggling.

Figure 1 Two of our daughters, Kristan (left) and Heather (right), practicing "puppet play" to end an argument.

Compromise, giving voice, choice, sharing power, fidgets, 'time in,' saying 'yes,' and many other tools were excellent tools that changed everything in our home. In using many of those tools, we sometimes came to a situation that required our daughter to take responsibility for the behavior or choice, and we needed to take a step back to let them experience their autonomy and consequences for her choice or behavior. This didn't feel connected, and many times, it wasn't. It was a huge struggle for us to balance helping vs. enabling, and sometimes, the connection tools felt more like enabling for a teenager with potentially life-altering consequences from their behaviors. It often felt like a failure on our part. Yet, even with the struggle and our imperfect use of the tools, I can unequivocally say that these tools saved us. It's worth it for any parent on this journey of parenting children from hard places to gain a deep understanding of trauma and the tools available to help you. This book and our framework aren't a departure from them at all. It's simply building on a solid foundation of trauma-informed approaches that many amazing people have developed. For us and many other parents of late teens and early young adults, we've had challenges adapting good trauma-informed approaches to our young people, especially our older teens who are transitioning to adulthood. I knew something was missing, and I was continually searching for tools and resources to help me be a better mom to our girls and a coach to the amazing families we serve. That search would eventually carry into the work that I began to do through an organization that I founded, Connections Homes.

A New Unknown
In the fall of 2013, our pastors, Dennis & Colleen Rouse, challenged us to ask God what He was doing in our story and family. Is there more that God is opening the door for us to do? We were undoubtedly at capacity in our home and lives with seven daughters, all transitioning into adulthood simultaneously. God had uniquely brought all of these stories together and under our roof. So, what was He doing? Four of our daughters had come into our family at 18, which is unusual in and of itself. The question from our pastors was, "What if God is doing something bigger in your story?" We needed to pray about that and ask God what He was doing. We started by trying to understand why four girls entering young adulthood had shown up in our family's story without family.

The statistics were shocking. 21,000 youth age out of foster care every year across the U.S. without safe, stable support systems to help guide them into an interdependent adult life. That number was about 700 a year in our home state of Georgia. 81% of boys[1] will end up serving some time in jail—mostly for survival crimes (if you're hungry, you're going to do what it takes to eat), 71% of girls[2] will end up pregnant within the first year after foster care, up to 50% of their children[3] will have interaction with the child welfare system, and 97% of youth aging out of foster care without a safe, stable support system will end up in chronic poverty, or worse[4]. It was a heartbreaking reality, and God gave me compassion for this problem.

Through this season of prayer, realization of the problem, and the support of our home church, Victory Atlanta, I left my position at Victory to launch Connections Homes in June 2014. Connections Homes' mission is to prevent poverty and homelessness for youth aging out of foster care or homeless without a family by connecting them to Mentoring Families who commit to being a part of their life for life. Our vision is to empower youth without family to thrive in life and impact the world from the security of a healthy connection. We accomplish this through our *Choice-based Matching Model,* which works with churches and our community to identify connection-ready youth and families. Each youth and family undergo a certification process to be approved for our program. Families must go through our Connection Training, which is built around a trauma-informed understanding. We then complete a Discovery Profile on each youth and family. Those profiles are shared with families and youth, who can each say yes or no to the match. At the core of this process is *choice*—we believe every youth should be given *a voice and a choice* in their permanent family-like relationships. We work hard to ensure that choice is baked into everything we do. Once matched, our Mentoring Families commit to being a part of their youth's life for life.

Over and over, as we were growing our program, we would run into families facing the same struggles that Steve and I had faced in our home—the battle to maintain a healthy connection while also taking their hands off and allowing their young people to experience the consequences of destructive behaviors and poor choices and knowing when to make that decision and understanding how to go about it lovingly and connectedly while dealing with their fears and anxieties. My team and I knew these

---

[1] https://www.young.senate.gov/newsroom/press-releases/young-include-older-foster-youth-in-implementation-of-family-first/

[2] https://www.young.senate.gov/newsroom/press-releases/young-include-older-foster-youth-in-implementation-of-family-first/

[3] https://imprintnews.org/research-news/study-parenting-foster-youth/31352

[4] https://www.young.senate.gov/newsroom/press-releases/young-include-older-foster-youth-in-implementation-of-family-first |
https://duckduckgo.com/?q=aging+out+of+foster+care+less+than+3%25&atb=v239-1&ia=web - here's a search link to many articles on that stat. We use the 97% because it brings into sharp reality that without a secondary education or skilled trade, these youth will live in chronic poverty or worse.

challenges needed to be solved. Still, a framework was missing on how to do all that with a young person who is a full-grown adult, possibly not even living in your home, and can move in and out of the relationship at their will. It's not an easy dynamic to navigate for anyone.

God, in His great providence, had taken what He did in our home and led me to my life's work. Everything I knew about parenting well had been strained, shaken, broken, rebuilt, and had grown. I was different; our family was different. My whole life was different. Along the way, I learned that the most critical aspect (outside relationship with Jesus) determining the success or failure of relationships forged through brokenness is the simple yet complex concept of *connection*. I would anchor all of our work on the healing nature of connection.

"Connection is why we're here. We are hardwired to connect with others, it's what gives purpose and meaning to our lives, and without it there is suffering."
Brené Brown, *Daring Greatly*

CHAPTER TWO

REDEMPTIVE CONNECTION FRAMEWORK

We all need people in our lives that we can trust. We need people as friends, counselors, challengers, coaches, teachers, antagonists, and guides throughout all of our lives. At many points in my life, I've had individuals who've shown up in my story in all those ways. I wouldn't be the person I am today without them—and neither would you. Connection is not only healthy for us but also essential. Without it, we wither away in loneliness and live in a world void of the beauty of relationships. Connection is the foundation for emotional well-being, trust, and healthy communication within the family and the world. From the earliest eye contact and sleepy smiles between mom and baby to a father teaching their young adult the art of negotiating better pay before taking a job. Connection is designed to undergird us as we launch into a healthy life. To give us the confidence to jump, knowing that if and when we fail, strong connections will still help pick us up, dust us off, and send us back out again.

The struggle for our young people who find themselves without a family through no choice of their own is that the connection is broken. The very relationships designed to provide us with the most security have been the ones that have failed them the most: the parental relationship. That is a wound that isn't so quickly healed. Yet, a healthy and consistent connection is needed for our youth to have a thriving life. Karyn Purvis, co-author of *The Connected Child* and co-founder of *TBRI,* says, *"What was broken in relationship can only be repaired in relationship."* It is with this understanding that early on in our work, I knew that connection had to be central to all that we do and that putting a lifelong relationship into place for a young person without a safe, stable support system could be the essential ingredient for ensuring that they could attain a thriving life.

Whether it's a Mentoring Family through Connections Homes, a foster or adoptive family, or a natural family, our role as our teens and young adults transition into adulthood is to maintain a healthy connection while allowing our young person to separate from us to establish healthy interdependence. I often use the analogy of tetherball to describe this relationship (See *Figure 2*). It is our young person's role to leave the nest of our home and their dependent relationship with us to go out into the world and form their connections and establish their own life—to find a purpose, to find relationships, to have relationships break, to find jobs, to lose jobs, and all of the many parts of building a resilient and thriving life. In the tetherball analogy, we are the pole to which the ball is attached. The ball (our youth) will go away from us and explore and sometimes get beat around by life. Yet we are always there, never moving, for them to wrap themselves back around for guidance and love as they prepare to go back out and try again. Another analogy that we use to help families understand this concept is "Lighthouse Parenting"—we are a lighthouse on the shore of our young person's life. We are reliably there to shine a light warning of dangers, but don't jump offshore to save them. We allow them to ride out their storms.

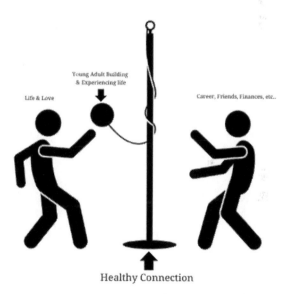

Figure 2 Drawing of the Tetherball Analogy for connection to young adults transitioning to adulthood

Neither the tetherball pole nor the lighthouse are in a position to solve the problems for the young adult, but they both serve as a solid connection to help guide the process. This is the challenge we face as individuals coming alongside an older youth or young adult navigating the transition to adulthood, especially if we don't have the benefit of years of relationship as they've grown from infancy. Yet our young people must learn autonomy and independence from the safety of healthy connections. This conundrum was my biggest unresolved hurdle as a mom and an organizational leader. How do you build a meaningful connection with a young person who was a stranger to you only a short time ago while balancing the need to guide them to self-efficacy and autonomy? Even if we can slow down to help them heal, the world will not. Bosses aren't typically trauma-informed, future relational partners aren't likely to be trauma-informed, and when deciding on whether a law was broken or not, the police don't traditionally use a trauma-informed approach. To complicate it further, many of our older youth with histories of trauma, some of my girls included, reject our attempts at connection and view our attempts at guiding them toward self-efficacy as abandonment, unfairness, and rejection. As a parent, I felt the burden of these truths and often vacillated between pushing my kids too far away and taking my hands off too much or overcompensating on their behalf to keep them from failing and experiencing the inevitable pain that would follow. I sometimes still struggle with this. Additionally, for our families at Connections Homes, the young people they are matched with are already living life "on their own" because we don't move young adults into the homes of their Mentoring Families. So, learning how to develop a strong connection while supporting the already complicated and complex reality of young people who aren't fully equipped for interdependence was a complicated support we needed to prepare our families to navigate well.

At the end of the day, as safe and stable connections in the lives of our young people, to not fail or falter in our commitment to stand firm in healthy connection with them, we have to learn to see what is going on in our young person's life as they inevitably fail and falter in their transition to an interdependent adulthood. Our ability to stand firm requires a balanced approach of empathy and compassion—understanding where they are coming from and what they might be feeling while being intentional in our decision to act or not act on their behalf. The foundation of our Redemptive Connection Framework is an understanding of where our young people are as they balance their connection to us and others and their feelings of worthiness and confidence to go out into the world "on their own."

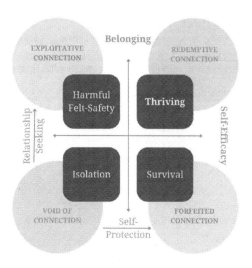

The Redemptive Connection Framework

Belonging – To be a member or part of a group or family
Self-Efficacy – Confidence in the ability to exert control (authority) over one's own motivations, behaviors, and social environment.

- **High Belonging/High Self-Efficacy – Thriving (Redemptive Connection)** - This ideal quadrant represents a young person who feels a strong sense of belonging and possesses high self-efficacy. They are able to thrive, forming deep connections with others and engaging effectively in building their own life, dealing effectively with both challenges and successes.
- **High Belonging/Low Self-Efficacy – Harmful Felt-Safety (Exploitative Connection)** - This quadrant represents a young person who feels a sense of belonging but has low self-efficacy. Their emphasis on relational needs without the capacity for personal growth or independence can lead to harmful relationships and fractured identity structures.
- **Low Belonging/High Self-Efficacy – Survival (Forfeited Connection)** - A young person in this quadrant has developed self-efficacy but lacks a sense of belonging. They may be highly independent and capable but struggle with forming or maintaining meaningful connections, operating in survival mode.
- **Low Belonging/Low Self-Efficacy – Isolation (Void of Connection)** A young person in this quadrant lacks both belonging and self-efficacy, leading to disconnection, isolation, and a sense of helplessness.

The Redemptive Connection Framework

With this understanding and these challenges, I sat in a room full of nonprofit leaders in 2019 as Andy Crouch plotted Authority and Vulnerability on a 2x2. I found myself and many families I had worked with on the grid. As he taught us this simple framework for living a flourishing life (described in the book's introduction and more detail in the next chapter), I had difficulty finding our youth on this grid. They were victims of a family system and government system that made decisions on their behalf—many of those decisions had led to their harm and not to their good. Many of our youth had been bounced from home to home, from potential connection to broken connection, again and again. This profoundly impacted their ability to connect meaningfully and trust as adults after adults had made promises that weren't kept and, worse, were broken without remorse and repair. On Andy's 2x2, this put them squarely in the quadrant of suffering. This understanding led me to the crux of a problem I needed to solve. Little did I know that solving this problem would lead me to a framework that would help the problem I had been grappling with for years. In finding a way to frame the journey to a thriving life for a young person who has experienced trauma and brokenness, I would also find a way to help families walk alongside their young people in meaningful connection while allowing them to experience autonomy and independence.

As Andy and I sat to unpack what a youth stuck in the suffering quadrant meant and figure out how to move a young person to a flourishing life, he asked the question, "What would you say are the two primary factors of youth you've seen who achieve a flourishing life?" We discussed the essential things I had seen in our thriving youth and ultimately arrived at "Belonging and Self-Efficacy." We ultimately agreed that our youth are on their journey to what our organization's vision statement called *thriving*. Youth can't move to a flourishing life with personal *authority* and *vulnerability* until they have a safe and supportive community of people where they feel they *belong* and have developed confidence in their ability to design their own life and *self-efficacy*. From this conversation, our *Redemptive Connection Framework* was born, a 2x2 similar to Andy's but designed as a simple guide to a thriving life for our young people built on the youth's need for both Belonging and Self-Efficacy. In the nearly five years since that initial conversation, my team and I have refined and expanded this simple 2x2 into a framework that is a crucial part of our training and support for families stepping into the story of young adult lives through our Don't Go Alone (DGA) program at Connections Homes.

In this chapter, we will provide an overview of the framework, explaining each quadrant from the connection perspective. Later in this book, each quadrant will have its own chapter, with a section solely devoted to tools that families can use to work with youth.

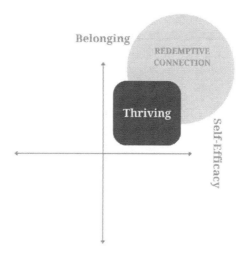

Figure 3 The Redemptive Connection Framework illustrates Thriving as Redemptive Connection

To truly thrive in life, a young person must balance healthy *belonging and self-efficacy*. In this balanced place, these young people from hard places likely have a *Redemptive Connection* to one or more individuals in their lives with whom they feel comfortable being their whole, authentic selves and who challenge them to believe deeply in themselves and their ability to achieve their hopes and dreams despite inevitable setbacks and disappointment.

Belonging – *to be connected as a member or part of a group.*

There was no doubt that the most critical aspect of *thriving* was connection and belonging. I remember being a young adult myself, and I can't imagine what I would have done or where I would have been without a safe and consistent family. My husband and I married young, and there were so many decisions, mistakes, emergencies, and life events in our early 20s that, without our family, we would not be where we are today. To have someone to call, somewhere to go for the holidays, a place to do laundry, someone to help you figure out why your car is making that ticking sound, somewhere that your picture hangs on the wall, and so much more. When you've been parented consistently from birth to adulthood, these are the things that we can take for granted. Many of us can't imagine not having someone to call if we have a question or not having a name to write on the "emergency contact" line of just about every form you must fill out. These are struggles and hardships for many of our young people. For these youth and the precious girls that came into our family, this kind of connection and belonging is not easy to obtain and sometimes even more challenging to feel comfortable with—but it's the most critical need to live a *thriving* life.

In a 2016 study of 43 former foster youth from the School of Social Work at the University of Victoria in Canada, findings revealed that while approximately half of the youth reported having support from family, most did not have family whom they regularly relied upon for emotional, practical, and financial support. Further, while nearly all youths indicated that having support made a difference, many also noted that they were on their own for daily living. The study's findings are an important reminder of the gap between youth from care and parented youth regarding their access to support during their journey to adulthood.[5]

For almost all of the youth we serve, including my daughters, biological family relationships are critical to them. However, the study above found that those relationships may need to become more stable and supportive to help them achieve their dreams and goals. Having an external community of trusted individuals with whom the youth can feel safe and have a sense of belonging is critical to their long-term success and the development of self-efficacy.

Belonging is a fundamental human need, and it is essential for young people who've experienced trauma and loss in their family systems. These young people have often experienced multiple disruptions, from being removed from their families to bouncing from foster homes to group homes numerous times. As a result, they can often feel disconnected and isolated, significantly impacting their ability to maintain confidence and achieve their goals.

We can provide youth with various life skills, from cooking to budgeting, learning to drive, and learning how to interview well. Still, without a safe, stable, and consistent support system to believe in them, encourage them, and challenge them to use those skills to build the life they dream of, they will often fall short of achieving their dreams. We can provide a young person with a true sense of belonging, which is the foundation of self-fulfillment for human motivation[6]—see Maslow's Hierarchy of Needs in the diagram (See *Figure 4)*. After our basic needs are met, the most important aspect for achieving our full potential is *belonging and love—connection.*

---

[5] 2016 Elsevier Ltd. *Is anybody there? Informal supports accessed and sought by youth from foster care.* Deborah Rutman, Carol Hubberstey

[6] Maslow's Hierarchy of Needs. Maslow, A.H. (1943). "A Theory of Human Motivation". In Psychological Review, 50 (4), 430 - 437

Maslow's Hierarchy of Needs

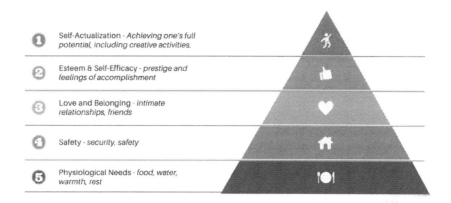

Figure 4 Maslow's Hierarchy of Needs, developed in 1943

Self-efficacy – *belief in their capacity to meaningfully act.*

As we wrestled through what the second most crucial aspect was to live a *thriving* life for our youth, we tossed out words like agency, self-worth, and personal responsibility. While all of them are necessary, none felt entirely correct because they all required an inner belief that I had seen many of our youth struggle with. Many of our families have often expressed concern about their young person's low self-esteem and inability, or even refusal, to complete or even try simple tasks. When explored, we discovered that the youth didn't believe they could do a good job and didn't want to embarrass themselves or be disappointed. This went beyond a fear of failure, which most of us struggle with occasionally. It was an almost paralyzing sense that even with their best effort, they wouldn't even come close to succeeding.

Self-efficacy is an individual's belief in their capacity to act in the ways necessary to reach specific goals[7]. In other words, they need to believe in their ability to meaningfully act in ways that can move them toward accomplishing their goals and doing whatever they set their mind and practice effort toward. This is an essential trait for all of us, especially for young people transitioning to adulthood who need to establish a healthy, autonomous life. These young adults have had a disrupted educational history, inconsistent and unhealthy social connections, and little to no support and guidance that other young people have from their families.

---

[7] Bandura, A. (1977). *Self-Efficacy: Toward a unifying theory of behavioral change.* Psychological Review, 84(2), 191-215

Believing in one's ability to meaningfully act to build the life one dreams of is foundational to developing all the other characteristics necessary to achieve Andy Crouch's definition of authority—*the capacity for meaningful action.*

- When youth have a strong sense of self-efficacy, they are more likely to take the initiative and make healthy decisions rather than rely on others to think for them. This, in turn, helps them develop a sense of agency, or the ability to act independently and make choices that affect their lives.

- When youth have a strong sense of self-efficacy, they feel more confident in their abilities and are more likely to value and respect themselves. This sense of self-worth helps them feel more capable of positively contributing to their community and world.

- When youth have a strong sense of self-efficacy, they may be more likely to take responsibility for their own decisions and actions and understand the impact these have on others—good and bad. This sense of personal responsibility helps them to develop accountability and commitment to living up to their responsibilities and owning their actions and the consequences that result from them.

Redemptive Connection – *Thriving.*

Healthy belonging and self-efficacy lead a young adult to a *thriving life.* A thriving young adult is strongly connected to a supportive and caring family where they feel accepted and valued for their true selves. Additionally, they believe deeply in their ability to take meaningful actions to achieve the life they aspire to lead. This combination of healthy belonging and self-efficacy empowers them to confidently navigate challenges, pursue their dreams, and lead a fulfilling and purposeful life—a *flourishing life.*

We call this type of connection a *Redemptive Connection* because it is a connection to an individual or family who doesn't just see the youth for who they are in the moment—through the lens of their brokenness—but sees them for all that they can be as things that were once broken are healed and redeemed in their life. It's not a connection that tries to restore what was lost; that's an unwinnable goal. We can't ever restore a broken childhood to the teens and young adults that we love. The only thing within our power is to help them see the redemptive path before them so that out of their brokenness can emerge beauty.

Void of Connection – *Isolation.*

It's rare that a young person with a history of trauma, abandonment, and loss enters our lives to parent or mentor as a *thriving* young person. Most of our youth enter our lives in the opposite position—alone, isolated, and void of connection. This is the next quadrant on our *Redemptive Connection Framework* that we will explore (See *Figure 5*).

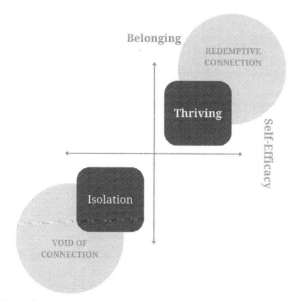

Figure 5 The Redemptive Connection Framework illustrates Isolation as Void of Connection

Isolation and loneliness are a pervasive problem for older teens and young adults in foster care or aging out. Without belonging and stable connections to supportive adults and lacking the stability to develop healthy self-efficacy, these young adults are highly vulnerable to suffering. Having been "raised" in a system built on dependency, few have developed the confidence and skills for true independence. Their lives are void of meaningful connection; many articulate feelings of being invisible and unimportant.

The image I think of when I consider how these young people feel is the image of someone lost at sea without an orange safety flag or large life preserver. There could be a thousand planes flying overhead, but no one can see you in the expanse of the ocean. In feelings of extreme loneliness and isolation, many of our youth describe being a part of a vast world, yet no one truly sees them—no one who would pick out their face in a crowd or know their voice from a distance. Void of connection, their deepest desire is to be seen and find anyone who will let them be a part of their tribe, which often moves them into the next quadrant.

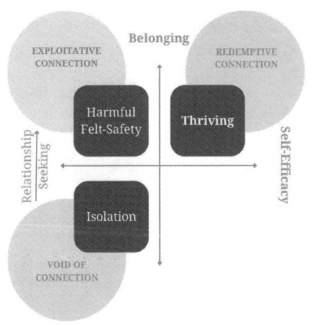

Figure 6 The Redemptive Connection Framework illustrates Harmful Felt-Safety as Exploitative Connection

Exploitative Connection – *Harmful Felt-Safety*

Felt-Safety is the sense of emotional security and comfort in a particular environment or situation. For most of us, our family is the most essential place of felt safety in our lives. Felt-Safety goes beyond physical safety and involves how we perceive our surroundings and the level of emotional well-being that we feel when we are in those surroundings. Because belonging and felt-safety are something every human innately seeks, they are the primary drivers in many decisions. We move to specific communities to be close to felt-safety of friends, good schools, a church community we belong to, like-minded neighbors, and more.

Youth without a history of healthy family or consistent felt-safety will often pursue Harmful Felt-Safety to meet their belonging needs and escape isolation (see *Figure 6*)—seeking relationships that provide them with a sense of belonging, comfort, and protection, even if those relationships or environments are detrimental to their well-being in the long run. These relationships may offer a perceived sense of safety or belonging, even if they are ultimately harmful or exploitative.

Exploitative Connection environments exploit the young person's vulnerabilities, emotional needs, and desires for belonging to further the goals and interests of the group or relationship, often at the expense of the young person's individual well-being, safety, and long-term goals. Rather than finding the true safety and belonging they crave, young people often find themselves trapped in lifestyles and situations that are difficult to escape.

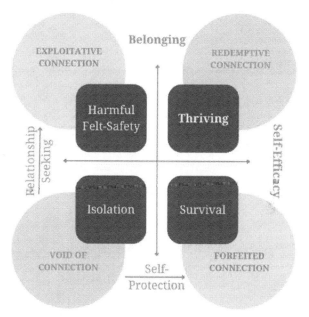

Figure 7 The Redemptive Connection Framework illustrates Survival as Forfeited Connection

Forfeited Connection - *Survival*

If you touch a hot stove once, you're unlikely to do it again because it causes pain. Relationships, especially family or parental ones, have caused our young people pain—many times repeatedly. For some young adults, the idea of getting hurt again in family-like or trusted relationships, especially with adults who want to 'help' them, is just too much of a risk to take. As a result, they move into the survival quadrant (see *Figure 7*) to *forfeited connection* and choose to tap into an internal sense of self-efficacy and forge their adult life on their own.

Tapping into internal resilience structures and messages of relational brokenness, young people in the *Survival* quadrant decide that there's no one else to depend on or trust. Rather than suffer, they pull themselves up by their bootstraps and "make it on their own." To self-protect, they forfeit the possibility of healthy connections and choose instead to "get by" on their limited resources.

Putting the Framework to Work

We will explore each of these quadrants in more depth in later chapters, including tools that families can use when they can identify which quadrant their young person is in. In the meantime, I want to tell you how I've used our framework to guide a Mentoring Family toward a connected and continued relationship with their young person.

After years of being connected to a young lady who was attending college and doing exceptionally well in life, a Mentoring Family reached out to me because they were beginning to experience some challenging behaviors and pull-back from their young lady—behaviors such as drug use, promiscuity, and choosing not to see them over several months. We began to explore triggers and stresses that might exist in the young person's life. All these behaviors were out of the character that they had known from this young lady over the years of connection, so they were at a loss. Unfortunately, in her biological family, both of her parents were deceased. So, the Mentoring Family was a source of family-like connection and support for her. We explored all the avenues of school, work, friends, and more. Nothing stood out except that she had moved away from healthy friendships and relationships to hang out with poor influences who coerced her into behaviors and choices that were outside of her norm. I honestly dug deep to try to figure out what was going on. There had to be a "why," I knew this young lady didn't just wake up one day and decide to turn her life upside down.

Finally, the Mentoring Family said that one of the biggest things that happened to her recently was the loss of an adult friend who had mentored her for many years before they came into her life. Lightbulbs went off, and I quickly pulled out a sheet of paper and drew the RCF. This young lady had lost yet another significant person in her life, and her feelings of *isolation* were triggered. She was grieving and, in her grief, was feeling incredibly lonely and afraid of losing others who meant something to her. So, she distanced herself and instead sought out *harmful felt-safety*. Feeling vulnerable to a life alone without *belonging*, she put aside her *self-efficacy*. Instead, she gave herself to friend groups and choices that gave her a sense of belonging while casting aside hopes and dreams that had been her top priority months before. In her grief, she had bounced back to isolation and sought relationships with harmful people and activities. We worked on a plan to schedule time with her intentionally, give her time for healing, and help her to find additional support. As a result, this young lady made considerable strides to get her life back on track. The Mentoring Family had the patience and understanding to walk her through this without feeling personally offended or walking away.

This worked well for this family with my guidance and the support of our team. However, I can promise you that I would have been a disaster if I had been handed just this framework before I had received training on my need for self-awareness. After years of work, I know enough about myself to know that I would have tried to control my kids by constantly informing them of the why behind their behaviors. Tapping into my potential as a gold-medal status lecturer, I would have plenty to say to them about what *they should do* to get out of the place they are and move toward *thriving*. We can't effectively help our young people until we're willing to first look at ourselves.

"Pursue authority by itself and you will not only end up without the authority you seek but plunged into the very kind of vulnerability you hoped to avoid. But the reverse is not true. Because God is for us in our vulnerability, because "all things are ours," because even the ultimate vulnerability of death cannot hold us in its grip—the pursuit of vulnerability actually leads to authority and to the flourishing that comes when authority and vulnerability are combined."
Andy Crouch, *Strong & Weak*

CHAPTER THREE

FINDING ME

"In the event of a sudden drop in pressure, an oxygen mask will drop from above. Secure your own mask first before assisting others." If you've ever flown, you've heard this standard flight attendant instruction as the plane is taxiing toward takeoff. The same applies to us as we work with our young people from hard places. There will be many times that your triggers, traumas, and tragedies will cause you to overreact or underreact to behaviors and situations with your young person. It's a truth that I wish that I had known much sooner in my journey than I did. It could have saved a lot of heartache—both mine and my daughters'.

I first became aware of the impact of my own story on my chaotic family environment while going through Empowered to Connect. We were going through a module on Adult Attachment[8], and as our trainer described the various attachment styles, I had a revelation for the first time in my life that my childhood was playing out as I was parenting my girls from hard places. Their behaviors and complex issues were triggering my trauma, and my unhealed attachment response was a dismissive one. I began to put a lot of work into becoming aware, noticing my brain and body responses, and taking intentional action to respond appropriately rather than reactively. I also learned about the impact of Adverse Childhood Experiences (ACEs)[9] and took the quiz—my score is a 9 out of 10. Individuals with a high ACE score (2 or more) are much more likely to experience mental health issues, depression, drug and alcohol issues, chronic health conditions, and suicidality

---

[8] To learn more, you can start with reading Adult Attachment Theory and Research, A Brief Overview by R. Chris Fraley at labs.psychology.illinois.edu/~rcfraley/attachment.htm

[9] To learn more, visit cdc.gov/violenceprevention/aces/index.html

than those scoring two or less. There was no question that I had a childhood that needed dealing with and that my own "stuff" was getting in the way of a solid and nurturing relationship with my girls. Listening to Andy teach from his Authority and Vulnerability 2x2 unlocked clarity for me even further.

In Andy Crouch's book *Strong and Weak*, he presents a vision of a flourishing life that embraces both our strengths and our fears. The book's full title is *Strong and Weak: Embracing a Life of Love, Risk, and True Flourishing*. What I love about that title is that it almost perfectly articulates how I felt when our family entered the foster care and adoption world. We had a deep desire for a flourishing family, we had love to give, and we felt we had weighed the costs and determined it was worth the risk. I wish I had read Andy's book before our journey began. It could have helped me see my actions and reactions more clearly along the way. As I listened to him teach, my whole journey as a mom flashed through my mind. Example after example of how my authority or vulnerability had come to bear on my greatest mistakes and successes.

We started this journey into foster care and adoption, where many families start. We have room in our home and hearts for another child. Some children don't have families. God tells us to care for the orphan and the widow. We are good parents. We have a sound support system. We have access to all the good things: schools, churches, doctors, etc. Surely, even with our flaws, our family is better than not having a family at all, and any child coming into our lives and home will fit in and be grateful to have a family that loves them. Naivety, blind faith, reckless hope, ego, privilege, or whatever other descriptor you want to put on it—that's where we were. Andy would call it all authority without recognizing our vulnerabilities.

What I have learned since 2007, as our family grew from one daughter to eight, makes the last paragraph hard to write and even harder to read for me. Our courage and confidence would keep us going and almost drown us simultaneously. Our love was without question, and we took our responsibility as parents seriously because we wanted to give our girls the best chance at a great life. Yet, early on, we failed to recognize that we didn't know what we didn't know about parenting in the context of trauma and the impact of my trauma on our family dynamic. We were blind to our blind spots and fighting hard to make the way we had successfully parented up to that point (our authority) work. It took a chance encounter at a conference in Nashville (also described in the Introduction) to open my eyes and bring us to our knees in vulnerability. By then, we had added another teenage daughter to our family, older than our other two. Our parenting skills were under fire, and we didn't understand why because we hadn't recognized our limitations and lack of understanding.

All these thoughts and more came to mind as I listened to Andy teach on his Authority and Vulnerability 2x2 (pictured on next page). Through a simple presentation in a room full of nonprofit leaders, Andy unpacked a concept that helped explain and clarify things in our home that I had struggled to find words to explain for years. I scribbled notes as quickly as I could. For the rest of this chapter, I'm going to try to the best of my ability to bring you into my mind and heart as I learn these concepts and begin to apply them to my successes and failures and to the successes and failures of other families that I've worked with along the way. I will in no way teach this as well as Andy can. Nor will I even come close to the beauty of his words in *Strong & Weak*. I can't encourage you enough to pick up a copy of his book and dive in for yourself.

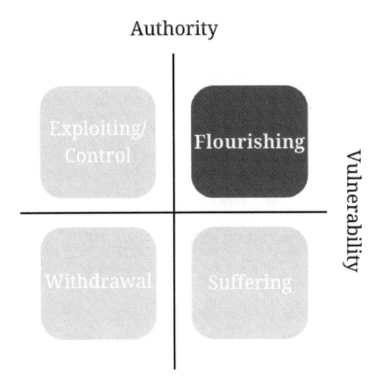

Authority

Exploiting/Control

Flourishing

Withdrawal

Suffering

Vulnerability

Andy Crouch's Authority/Vulnerability Matrix

Authority – The capacity for meaningful action
Vulnerability – The capacity for meaningful risk

- **High Authority / High Vulnerability – Flourishing** This quadrant represents the balance between the power to act (authority) and the willingness to risk (vulnerability), which leads to growth and flourishing.
- **High Authority / Low Vulnerability – Control** Here, individuals or entities exert power without opening themselves to risk or harm, potentially leading to domination, manipulation, and exploitation.
- **Low Authority / High Vulnerability – Suffering** This quadrant is characterized by exposure to harm without the means to protect oneself, leading to oppression or victimization.
- **Low Authority / Low Vulnerability – Withdrawal** Represents the disengagement from meaningful interaction and risk, leading to isolation, detachment, and withdrawal.

As a parent of an older teen or young adult, it is our responsibility and privilege to take a step back from our kids and allow them to move into interdependence with a healthy amount of autonomy to begin designing their own lives. In a typical parenting situation, we should move from parenting through control to parenting through influence naturally over time throughout the teenage years. Letting go is built upon a foundation of trust and love cultivated over the years, starting with healthy attachment and bonding in infancy and continuing through every developmental stage into adulthood. Giving us the *authority* to set boundaries, provide correction, speak wisdom, problem-solve, and guide decision-making in big and small ways over the years. It also challenges us in areas we don't have all the answers to, which, in a healthy, flourishing life, gives us insight into our *vulnerability*—our limitations—pushing us to reach beyond ourselves into a broader community of support.

If you could travel back in time and ask "2007-2010 Pam" if she wanted her family to flourish, I can promise you that you would receive an emphatic "Yes!" And if you were to dig a bit deeper, the descriptions of what that flourishing would look like for the family would be along these lines:

- Our family has a deep love and respect for one another.
- Our children honor us as their parents.
- Obedience and good behavior.
- Shared love for Jesus and commitment to Christian values.
- A spirit of gratitude for family.
- A happy home environment.
- Family fun and enjoyment of one another.
- Good grades, good college & career choices, good partner choices…

This list could go on and on, but you get my drift. Not only would I probably say these things, but I also firmly believed that for those things to happen, I needed to show up every day and do all the right things to be a good parent. Any hint of them not shaping up with my idea of flourishing meant that I wasn't doing a good job. None of these are bad things to have in a vision for your family. The problem wasn't in what we wanted flourishing to look like. The problem was our belief that our sole job was to control it. Our family had grown from one daughter in 2006 to seven by 2013—four of whom came into our family at 18. There was so much going on, and so many things felt so out of control that my response to the chaos was to organize and *control* it.

Exploiting / Control

There's no way that I would have ever conceded to the description of exploiting my children. It's beyond comprehension to me that anyone would exploit their children for any personal gain. Yet when Andy began to unpack this quadrant in terms of *control,* I found myself guilty and could look back at some of my biggest parenting failures and find control among many of them.

In many ways, so much of our parenting journey is in the quadrant of control by design. If we didn't control the feeding schedule for our newborns, they might starve. If we didn't control television time and bedtime, our kids might not get a good night's sleep and perform poorly in school. If we didn't control the serving of healthy meals, our children might become malnourished on a Cheez-Its and Fruit Loops diet. In a *flourishing* family, there is a healthy balance of control and grace—boundaries that are well-intentioned and seasoned with grace to give kids the ability to have freedom within a structure of safety and accountability.

For me, and for many families that I've worked with, it moves from healthy boundaries to unhealthy control when fear comes in. When I become afraid that the 14-year-old with an F on their report card will never graduate high school and live on my couch forever, or the 16-year-old caught partying with her friends will ruin her entire life, never find a husband, end up on the streets, and be in and out of jail. For sure, there are bad things that happen because of poor choices as teens, but by and large, actual catastrophes from those decisions are rare. Yet my propensity as a parent was to continually catastrophize everything into a future of doom and gloom. Then, based on those fears, I jumped headlong into *control* to immediately ensure that the 14-year-old came straight home from school and spent time on schoolwork—regardless of the siblings playing freely in the cul-de-sac. Or the 16-year-old being grounded from all interactions with friends because now her "friend choices couldn't be trusted." Neither of these responses deepens the relationship with the child.

On the contrary, it invited bitterness and resentment to have a seat at our family table. God, in His great mercy, led me to learn trauma-informed approaches, which helped me to grow in so many ways and quite literally saved our family from disaster. I wish that I had been given Andy's 2x2 along with those trauma-informed tools so that along the way, as I was seeing the child, I could also *find me*. Since learning this information, I've learned to stop and ask myself what I'm afraid of, which is making me feel like I need to *control*. Often, identifying those fears is enough to help me take the time to figure out a better approach that balances *authority* and *vulnerability*.

Through a better understanding of my children's trauma, I began to shift my parenting style and balance grace with authority. Which, as Andy's diagram so beautifully reveals, made me feel vulnerable and came with an element of risk. But it also opened the opportunity for me to deepen my relationship with my girls and begin to understand that many times, the reasons behind any given outcome or behavior weren't as black and white as I would have previously categorized them. Disrespectful tones weren't always because they wanted to show disrespect. Sometimes, it was simply because of irregulated emotions grappling with their triggers and just needed a minute to calm down and refocus. A simple tool like keeping my calm and asking in a level and often playful tone, "Would you like to say that again with respect?"[10] allowed my girls to rephrase without me jumping to immediately correct or escalate the emotions by adding mine to the mix.

It was a valuable insight as I worked on developing an understanding of my childhood experiences. Because I had never really dealt with it, I was unknowingly triggered. Learning about my attachment style and propensities was a critical insight for me. In a house full of emotionally dysregulated teenage girls, my response to emotion was to dismiss it, solve it, fix it, move past it quickly, ignore it, engage with it, or run from it. Sit *in* it? Sit *with* it? Walk *through* it? Nope. It was a huge lightbulb moment for me in my understanding of why I reacted the way I did to my girl's moods and emotions. If I couldn't solve the problem or if they didn't accept my wise counsel on the issue, I would have to move away—sometimes both physically and emotionally—from the issue (and the child) because fixing it, sucking it up, getting over it and moving on were the only tools that I had in my survival arsenal. Gratefully, I have a wonderful friend, Amy Curtis, a trained attachment therapist specializing in adult attachment. As I navigated this season, I often called her for advice. Nearly every conversation resulted in her asking me to quit talking about what the child had done and focus instead on my reactions. She challenged me to *find me* and approach the issue with grace *for* the child and *me*. Nine times out of ten, my response had been to

---

[10] Many of the techniques that I used, including this one, to become a better parent are a result of the trauma training that I received through *Empowered to Connect*. I encourage you to read *The Connected Child* and visit *empoweredtoconnect.org* if you're interested in learning more.

control the situation through discipline, fixing the problem, or lecturing (I'm a world-class lecturer –ask any of my daughters!). Leaning into *control* is a natural response for me. It still takes a lot of internal dialogue to remind me to allow *vulnerability* to have an equal voice in my responses.

Here are a few tips to help when you find yourself in the *exploiting/control* quadrant:

- Listen and validate. Take time to listen to your child's feelings, thoughts, and experiences. Validate their feelings. This fosters a sense of trust and shows that their voice is heard and respected.
- Be flexible and adaptable. Be willing to adapt and adjust your parenting strategies to meet each child's specific needs.
- Share power & allow choices. Involve the child in decision-making when appropriate.
- Examine your expectations. Make sure that what you expect your family to look like isn't standing in the way of letting your family form in a new way.
- Practice patience and empathy—with both your child and yourself.

Withdrawal

I've had the honor and privilege of working with hundreds of foster and adoptive families as they navigated the new and challenging landscape of trauma. During almost two decades of living this work and training and supporting families, I've seen my fair share of families completely breaking down and being unable to continue their journey because of the amount of secondary trauma that they've experienced. It's always the saddest thing in the world to me for a child to go back into the foster care system because of a family breakdown. There have been a handful of cases in which I agree this is the best decision for both the parents and the child. This should always be respected by the family's support team, which hopefully includes therapists, social workers, doctors, and other trusted advisors. However, many times, I've simply seen fatigue, lack of support, improper training/education on trauma, fear, and unmet expectations move families into the withdrawal quadrant where the best way forward is out. Almost every family I've walked with has spent extended time in the control quadrant before making the heart-wrenching decision to withdraw, so I'm moving to this quadrant next.

Moving into the *withdrawal* quadrant often comes after an extended period in which the family feels like the behaviors of the child(ren) are beyond their *control*, that their efforts to get help are coming up dry, and the changes to their family are more significant than they are willing to *risk*. They feel incredibly *vulnerable* to the future and don't believe they can make a difference. I would encourage anyone finding themselves moving toward *withdrawal* to get a good network of support around themselves.

Unfortunately for many families, this is easier said than done as most of our churches, schools, friends, and family are also ill-equipped to provide understanding or assistance to families deep in the mire of navigating life with a child who experienced more trauma in their young lives than many of us experience in a lifetime. Yet, many resources are still available from reputable organizations that can help. Please see the Trauma Resources Addendum at the end of this book for a list of examples that can help. You are not alone.

One example[11] that I will never forget is from a family that I once worked with who were in the process of adopting a nine-year-old little girl from foster care. This little girl had gone through many homes in her short nine years. Adapting to a forever home would be challenging for her from the start. For months, the family had tried to teach her the family rules, boundaries, and rhythms. Some she adapted to quickly, and others were a struggle. She was a very strong-willed child, and it felt like every day was full of power struggles between what the parents felt were acceptable choices and behaviors and the control that the little girl wanted to have over her own choices. As I did many times in my parenting, the family often leaned on their role as parents to *control* the situation through "I'm the parent, and I said so..." tactics. I frequently counseled them to allow choice and to share power with the child, which they found problematic because it wasn't how they had raised their other children. Allowing choice and sharing power felt like a weakness to them. I understand; I struggled in some of the same ways. After months of power struggles, the proverbial straw that broke the camel's back came down to the difference between a red shoe and a grey one on one chilly school morning. It was time to catch the bus, and the mom sent the little girl upstairs to get the shoes she had put out on the bed for her. She didn't want to wear real shoes; she wanted to wear flip-flops. The mom told her it was cold and that she had to wear the shoes. She went upstairs and came down with red shoes from the closet, not the grey ones that mom had laid out, which matched her clothes. Mom told her to go back upstairs and put on the grey shoes. She refused. The situation escalated to Mom standing in the doorway of her room, blocking her from exiting until she changed her shoes. The little girl refused and pushed Mom out of the way to run downstairs and out the door to the bus. This was the last straw for the family, and they asked the case manager to pick the girl up and close their home to future children. They walked away from their adoption and any future adoptions. Feeling *vulnerable* to the fear of potentially raising a child who might resort to physical violence, unwilling to *risk* it, and unable to *control* her behavior and obedience in their home, the family *withdrew*. In this instance, I understand why they felt the way they felt. Yet, in their determination to parent how they felt worked for their

---

[11] This story and its circumstances have been modified to protect the identity of the parties involved.

other children, they rejected good advice from not only me but also therapists and case managers who encouraged them to lessen the weight of rules and expectations long enough to let the relationship and bonds form. Rather than building healthy boundaries filled with grace, they opted for inflexible rules, sitting heavily in the *control* quadrant. They didn't want to feel *vulnerable* to learning new parenting tactics that might stretch them to *risk* giving up a little power. In the end, when all the efforts of *authority* failed without the willingness for *vulnerability,* they abdicated both and *withdrew.*

The red shoes/grey shoes story is an extreme example of *withdrawal,* but it can come in many forms that aren't as final or as long-lasting. Truthfully, I've found myself in many of these quadrants multiple times daily, from being emotionally and physically distant to avoiding difficult conversations or being unwilling to seek help and advice because I don't want to change. We can bounce in and out of this quadrant— even while staying in the game. Often, when we are bouncing out of the withdrawal quadrant, it is because none of our authority is effective, and we're feeling overwhelmed, which puts us in the *suffering* quadrant.

Here are a few tips to help when you find yourself in the *withdrawal* quadrant:

- Establish routines. Create consistency and predictability in routines, especially relationship-building ones, to foster security and belonging and invite bonding.
- Be present. Actively engage with the child in fun activities that they enjoy, strengthening connection and trust.
- Practice emotional availability. Emotional availability allows you to tune into the child's emotions and respond with empathy and understanding.
- Practice self-reflection. Notice your feelings, motivations, and barriers. Self-awareness can help you make positive changes in your parenting behaviors.
- Communicate openly. Create a safe space for communication with your child and others who can help build you up.
- Educate yourself. Make sure you get a good education on your child's specific type of trauma so that you can learn and know the most effective ways of interaction and redirection.
- Take a break. Instead of quitting totally, take a much-needed break to allow your body, mind, and emotions to rest.

Suffering

I'll never forget driving on the interstate one Thanksgiving Day. After dropping off one of our daughters at her home following Thanksgiving with us; I was finally alone in the car and entirely exhausted. Not only had I cooked since very early in the morning, but I had planned, grocery shopped, and coordinated attendance—driving hours to pick up and drop off so we could all be together. In addition, we had four of our girls in varying degrees of challenges, from identity crises to drugs and failing grades to sneaking out. The general mood in the house was challenging, and *all our attitudes* showed it. On that drive back home, I lost it.

I went to a full-on pity party and had a very transparent and broken-hearted conversation with God about everything happening in my heart and home. I was *suffering*. Why is this happening to me? We are simply trying to do the right thing, and it feels like everything is falling apart. Nothing that I've attempted (*authority*) is working. I don't know what else to do. I'm tired—beyond tired. I don't want to try anything else. I don't want to *find me* or *change me* anymore. What good is going to do if I'm the only one doing all the work? I don't think I can do this anymore. You know that conversation. We've all had it in our heads and hearts. Some of it is true, and much is self-focused, exhaustion-driven hyperbole. At that moment, if someone had given me a few dollars and a plane ticket out of it all, I would have seriously considered it (*withdrawal*).

Parenting children and youth from hard places is incredibly challenging. Along the way, I found myself in the suffering quadrant when I began to feel overwhelmed with the breadth and depth of the needs present in my home, from the typical everyday challenges of a large family to the individual needs of each child from vastly different trauma backgrounds. No doubt it was a lot. The strain on our resources, time, and emotions felt overwhelming. It was tempting in those moments to run to my room and hide behind a locked door with a brownie and a glass of wine. Honestly, I might have on more than a few nights. The rubber meets the road in the decision to stay there or pick me back up and do what needs to be done to regain harmony and connection in our home. I needed to do that dance more times than I can count. In the *suffering* quadrant, I needed to find myself in the emotions and reactions I was experiencing to figure out what *authority* I had in the moment. Sometimes, the only thing I had was prayer. Other times, a conversation with a friend helped me see myself and figure out a plan moving forward. Every time, the first bit of *authority* that I needed to take was to make a not-so-simple decision—the decision to stay in the game and give it my all again and again. All I could *control* was me and my choices.

Sometimes, *suffering* comes to us because of the natural difficulties of parenting children from hard places. Other times, *suffering* comes to us because we've abdicated our *authority* out of fear of damaging the relationship. We don't set firm boundaries because we're afraid of making our child mad or because we don't know what we will do if the child fails to maintain the boundary. We don't like difficult conversations or dealing with conflict. Often, we feel like a doormat that others walk right over because we feel helpless to set boundaries and stick to them. Or we fear the worst and feel like a terrible person if we can help someone and say no.

Early in our organization, Connections Homes, we matched a young man experiencing homelessness with a Mentoring Family. This young man had some significant financial needs and needed the guidance of a strong mentor to help him navigate getting on and staying on his feet. One of the things we caution our Mentoring Families against in training is giving a lot of handouts—especially financial ones—because it can create an unhealthy dependency (you'll learn more about this later in this book). This particular Mentoring Family had a lot of financial resources available to them and found it extraordinarily difficult to say no to requests for help with rent, phone bills, groceries, etc., even with good counseling from us to pull back and direct the youth to other resources so that he could begin to use his abilities to meet his needs instead of relying on the Mentoring Family for rescue every time. Over time, the Mentoring Family started to express feelings of being "used" by the young man, and in many ways, they were. The pattern of their relationship had been developed based on crisis and rescue cycles. By the time they had been in a relationship for many months, the young man hadn't learned how to have a relationship outside of this cycle, and the family felt taken advantage of and not appreciated. Ultimately, that relationship ended. It was unfortunate for both the family and the young man. In this instance, the family was suffering because instead of setting healthy boundaries around financial resources (*authority*), they gave the money, and eventually, what felt joyful in the beginning started to feel hurtful toward the end, and they felt taken advantage of (*vulnerability*).

Here are a few tips to help when you find yourself in the *suffering* quadrant:

- Find a professional for trauma-informed support for yourself and your child.
- Build a support network of other families in similar situations. You can learn a lot through the successes and failures of others.
- Take time to think through your boundaries and how you will handle them when they are broken. Deciding this upfront will help you not feel pressured "at the moment."
- Educate yourself on trauma to better understand what the child needs from you and how your own story may come into play.
- Find out what community resources are available to help in critical areas of need.

Over the years, I would put our family and me on varying degrees of *flourishing, controlling, withdrawing, and suffering* through many challenging seasons. The one thing that kept me moving forward was an unfailing commitment to putting in the hard work to *find myself* amid whatever season, challenging myself to grow, learn, and lean into the moment. Andy's 2x2 gave me the language to put around the work we had done in our family, a framework for all our successes and failures.

In our Mentoring Family training with our families, we ask them to answer two simple questions:

- What do you hope to bring a young person you're matched with?
- What is it that you fear?

In this simple exercise, we ask them to unveil their authority and vulnerability. The chart below shows how that would look if someone had asked me these questions in the context of my earlier description of my dream of a flourishing family.

Authority	Vulnerability
Our family has a deep love and respect for one another	Our family has deep resentment and bitterness for one another
Our children honor us as their parents	Our children do not consider/want us as their parents
Obedience and good behavior	Opposition and bad behaviors
Shared love for Jesus and commitment to Christian values	Rejection of our Christian values and a disbelief in Jesus
A spirit of gratitude for family	Resentment of family
A happy home environment	A home environment full of chaos and anger
Family fun and enjoyment of one another	Not speaking or no relationship
Good grades, good college & career choices, good partner choices	Poor grades, bad career choices, and poor relationship choices

What would it look like if you mapped your capacity and fears on the same two questions?

I would be lying if I led you to believe that none of our fears ever manifested in our family. Quite the contrary, *they all did* to some degree in one season or another—some still are. The journey to *finding myself* was a journey of introspection and self-work. This is why Andy's 2x2 significantly impacted me as I listened to him teach it. Everything in my Authority column is something that I thought we could *control,* and when, inevitably, that was challenged, my fears were unlocked, and our family was *at risk.* And in those moments, the most significant *risk* to the family wasn't whatever the young person was doing—it was how I would respond to what the young person was doing. How would I react when what I thought I could *control* was out of my *control,* and I felt *vulnerable?*

Finding ourselves is critical to successfully walking alongside our children as they grow up and transition into an interdependent adulthood. Not only did Andy's 2x2 lay the foundation for the development of our *Redemptive Connection Framework,* but it also provided a powerful tool that we can use as families to find ourselves as we're navigating these sometimes-uncharted waters of relationship with a young person with a traumatic background. I still use this nearly every day to *find myself.*

Redemptive Connection

Let's go back and look at how our process of finding ourselves helps us navigate *Redemptive Connection* with our young people. We have achieved great success working with hundreds of families who support young adults who have aged out of foster care or are without family, using this framework. I've used this framework in my parenting as I've sought to see the "why behind the what" of some of the choices and behaviors that my girls are experiencing. The challenge we all face, including me, is thinking that the journey from Isolation to Thriving is up and to the right (see *Figure 8*).

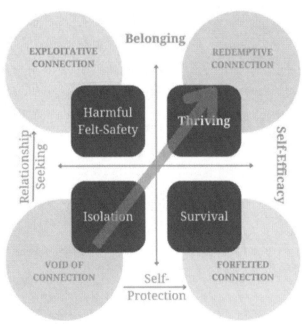

Figure 8 The Redemptive Connection Framework straight arrow "up and to the right" illustrates the unrealistic journey to thriving.

Redemptive Connection requires us to bring our authority and vulnerability to bear on behalf of our young people. It grants us the opportunity to experience true flourishing as we step forward with meaningful risk to meaningfully act on behalf of a youth who has experienced more trauma, grief, and loss than we might ever experience ourselves. The actual *doing* of this work is hard, and we want to see immediate results, but change happens over a lifetime. I didn't realize my own deep need for healing until late in life. There is no telling how many ways my trauma showed up in my early 20s and beyond without my understanding of it—likely impacting many people around me while I was completely unaware.

The journey for the young person and the family walking with them looks like a rollercoaster bouncing in and out of the quadrants (see *Figure 9*). This can happen all on the same day. Or, as with our example of the young lady who suddenly started having behavioral issues "out of the blue" in Chapter 2, our young person can be sailing along in a seemingly *thriving life* and suddenly be bounced back into another quadrant by life's circumstances. In these moments, we hold the axis of belonging— "I see you." "I love you." "I'm here for you." While guiding, prompting, and pushing toward self-efficacy— "You've got this." "You can do it." "I'm your biggest fan."

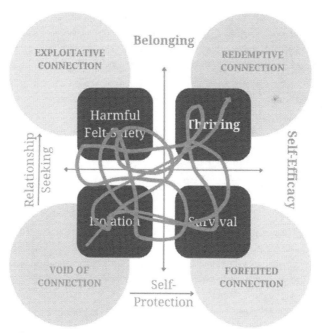

Figure 9 The Redemptive Connection Framework uses the random pathway to illustrate the realistically winding road toward thriving.

"The doctrine of grace and redemption keeps us from seeing any person or situation as hopeless."
Timothy Keller

CHAPTER FOUR

REDEMPTIVE PERSPECTIVE

Creaking bones, stiff knees, and back and shoulder pain simply from sleeping wrong on the bed—yep, I'm not a spring chick any longer. Getting older certainly comes with its pitfalls. As I write this, I'm in my early 50s and can't figure out where I put my phone yet again. Thankfully, I have an Apple Watch that will helpfully make my phone buzz so that I can retrieve it for the thousandth time today. These are just a few of the shifts we go through as we age; some would say they are annoyances, and others would say they are just what they are: aging. Yet, on the flip side of that, years of experience, wisdom, relationships, and insight are the priceless gifts of time. Perspective is one of those gifts. As we get older, we have the gift of looking back on our life and seeing how things we feared became the memories we treasure most, things that hurt us turned into tools that we could use in the future to help someone else, things that seemed to take forever as we were in the midst of them were only blips of time in the context of our whole life. Some of the hardest relationships became some of the deepest friendships. Redemption is like that. It is both perspective and hope. It's a perspective that understands that everything tends to work out and make us stronger and a hope that gives us the courage to continue right now because we know that even in the darkest nights, the light will eventually arrive.

The term redemptive is used in this book and our model on purpose. As with our entire framework, it was first inspired through my time as a part of the Praxis Nonprofit Cohort, where the Praxis team introduced us to a way of leading our organizations and lives through a Redemptive Frame[12]. Through the work of Praxis, I've come to think of redemption as a pattern of restoring glorious yet broken things to their rightful state, even at great cost. Or "creative restoration through sacrifice." That there is a component to our life and work that exists solely to challenge us to lay down our lives on behalf of others—to sacrifice so that someone else can win—is one that most of us aspire to, but few have a fundamental framework for achieving. And, if

---

[12] To learn more about Praxis visit *praxislabs.org*. To learn more about the Redemptive Frame you can look for their books on Amazon: *The Redemptive Nonprofit, Redemptive Investing, Redemptive Philanthropy, The Redemptive Business, and A Rule of Life.*

you're like me, before reading this book, you may not have given much thought to the word redemption and its power in your life and those around you.

I love Tim Keller's quote at the beginning of this chapter: "The doctrine of grace and redemption keeps us from seeing any person or situation as hopeless." This is perspective. It challenges us to see through the lens of hope and healing rather than catastrophizing. When we view life and circumstances through a redemptive perspective, we can see beyond the short-term pains and envision a redemptive future. When you focus on a redemptive positive amid the negative moment, it helps you to reject dwelling on the downside. It focuses your energy and mind on finding value, learning, and renewal.

I remember where I was sitting when my phone buzzed with a text from one of our daughters in her late teens. When I reached to get it, I realized she had sent a picture, so I clicked to open it. What greeted me was a photo of an ultrasound image with her name in the top left of the image. It was her way of telling us that she was pregnant. Not exactly how I had envisioned our first grandchild's announcement would occur. After getting over my shock and showing Steve the image, we pondered all the questions, "How is she going to afford this?" "Where will they live?" "How will she manage at such a young age?" All normal and relevant questions. Yet, in a moment of success, without having the redemptive language to describe it, we took a deep breath and handled the situation by "affirming the redemptive positive." We said to one another, "How we respond will be something she will remember forever. Let's talk about what we want to say first." And we did. We called her and asked her how she felt. She was happy. We asked her when she was due. And we let her know that we were excited to meet our future grandchild. We knew that being a mom was something that she dreamed about. She was just fast-tracking it more than we would prefer. And we also knew that school was not her thing, so college was probably an unreasonable expectation. She wanted to be a mom. I remember us discussing that one day, God could use this in her story to be there for other young moms (a redemptive positive). We also discussed how this would cause her to settle down and build a life (a redemptive positive).

All children are a gift from God, designed by their creator in their mothers' wombs. It was important for our daughter to experience our recognition of how this new life would bless all of us. From that point forward, we did all the usual things to celebrate our grandson's birth–baby showers, buying the stuff for Nana and Pop's (our grandparent names) house so that we could have them over comfortably, and waiting with bated breath for the call to come that she was in labor. Today, she is a wonderful mom, and it's apparent to everyone who knows her that being a mom to her kids is the number one priority in her life. That baby and those that followed saved her life, gave her purpose, and gave me a reason to buy more Christmas stockings! We're so grateful that we chose a redemptive perspective because our relationship with our grandkids could have looked different today if we had responded negatively.

Having a redemptive perspective doesn't mean that we ignore the issues or don't deal with or confront behaviors that need to be addressed. It also doesn't stop the consequences of the actions from taking place. In one such case, one of our girls went through a season of drug addiction, which led to her living in her car and eventually losing a job that she loved. We could have stepped in to give her a place to live, but our boundaries were drugs. I grew up with both a mom and a sibling who struggled heavily, and it was a massive trigger for me. I couldn't live with it and see it every day under my roof. And, it wouldn't have been wise for us to provide for her to live comfortably (and free) while spending her money and time in these ways. We also had a relationship with her employer and could have stepped in to ask for a reprieve from her being let go. We didn't. This was her choice and her consequences. What we *did* do was talk with her employer about the possibility of a "redemption period" (which was their idea) to give her 90 days without her job, and after those 90 days, if she could pass a hair sample drug test, she would be reinstated. It was excruciatingly hard to watch this play out. We loved her and hated to see her in pain. The only thing we could do was to maintain a relationship and encourage her as she walked it out. We believed in her ability to get clean and get her job back. And we could see the redemptive path in her story as someone who overcame. One day, there may be another young girl with the same issue, and she will have an opportunity to share her story. Still, in the immediate view, it was an opportunity to get her job back and to see her strength and resilience amid hard things, which she did. She made the choices and suffered the consequences, then put in the work and reaped the reward. This was redemption at work in her life.

Redemption vs. Restoration

Many families come into foster care, adoption, or being a Mentoring Family with the expectation that they have a part to play in giving back to a child or young person some of the things that they missed by not having a family. This is an unrealistic expectation for many reasons, not the least of which is that it puts us in danger of having a "savior complex" by thinking we—in all our goodness—are somehow better than everyone else in their lives previously simply because we can provide in ways that they couldn't. Restoration of all loss is a process that we can only partially influence. Some things can be restored—mental health, physical ailments, educational gaps, material belongings, and even shelter and food—through proper medical and mental health care and a community of support of which we might be one part. But some things can never be given back—a childhood full of good memories with parents who share their DNA, relationships full of trust that spanned their lifetime, a consistent education experience, a childhood home full of memories that they can return to as adults with their own family, and many more. These are lost and will have to be grieved to begin to heal. We cannot restore those things. And we shouldn't gloss over their loss by trying to provide pseudo-substitutes for them. All we have the power and influence to do is help our children and young adults see the redemptive positives that can one day come to pass.

While both a redemptive approach and a desire for restoration have their merits, a redemptive approach offers several advantages over a restoration approach, especially when parenting children and young people from hard places. Here are just a few important things that we intentionally do as we take a redemptive approach with our young people:

- **Emphasize a growth mindset:** With a redemptive approach, we emphasize growing and healing more than restoring what's lost. We use our influence with our young people to encourage *growing forward* rather than *restoring backward*. We work with our young people to help them understand that healing is a lifelong process and much of what has been lost can't be returned, but positive transformation can still occur, and they can live a thriving/flourishing life.

- **Validate childhood experiences:** Using a redemptive approach allows us to acknowledge and validate our young person's experiences, emotions, and struggles. We don't minimize or dismiss the impact of trauma, but we recognize that redemption can be found within the young person's unique story and ability to overcome adversity.

- **Nurture resilience:** By fostering resilience in our young people, we empower them to cope with challenges, build emotional strength, and adapt positively to difficult situations. Resilience is an essential skill that can benefit our young people throughout the rest of their lives.

- **Focus on strength and positivity:** We practice placing a greater emphasis on recognizing and affirming our young person's strengths and positive qualities. By focusing on their assets and encouraging their growth, they develop self-efficacy, allowing them to experience greater self-esteem and agency.

- **Support emotional expression:** Using a redemptive approach, we create an environment where young people feel safe expressing their emotions openly. This open communication fosters trust and enables them to process their feelings constructively.

- **Encourage collaboration and support:** We encourage our young person to seek support from a network of understanding individuals, such as therapists, counselors, trusted friends, or support groups. In adopting a collaborative approach, we aren't afraid to welcome relationships of others into our young people's lives—it truly takes a village. Others can offer multiple perspectives and resources to aid our young people in their healing process.

- **Promote positive relationship:** A redemptive approach focuses on growth, empathy, compassion, and healing. It fosters a more positive relationship between us as parents, mentors, and respected adults in our young person's life. This connection significantly impacts their ability to thrive and heal.

- **Reduce pressure for perfection:** We acknowledge that healing is not a linear or quick process, and setbacks are a natural part of the journey. It reduces the pressure on our young people to be "perfectly restored" and instead focuses on progress and growth—no matter how big or small.

A redemptive approach is a more compassionate and growth-oriented perspective that supports our young person's healing and well-being. Acknowledging their unique experiences and strengths can create a positive and supportive environment for their growth and transformation into a thriving adulthood.

Redemptive Connection

Redemptive Connection is entering into or remaining in a relationship with our young people to walk out a pattern of relationship that helps to restore their lives from brokenness to their rightful, purposeful, and meaningful state—thriving, even at great cost for us (personal healing work, trauma understanding, invested time, etc.). Or "creative restoration through sacrifice." The "at great cost" is my hardest part, and I've failed a lot. Maybe I don't want to put in the work on myself; I want to fix my kids. Sometimes, I don't want to look at a situation through the lens of trauma because it's so much easier just to chalk it up to disrespect, dishonor, disobedience, irresponsibility, etc. And it's simply easier to give the money or solve the problem because it *takes much less time* than trying to get to the bottom of the issue and come alongside our young person and help them grow. I could go on. The "at great cost" and "through sacrifice" parts of being a *Redemptive*

Connection to our young people are hard. On the other side of the "hard" is the hope of redemption: our young people experiencing a thriving life.

If our willingness to lay down our lives, pay a cost, and sacrifice as we walk with them through healing, failure, pain, and relational challenges helps them into *thriving adulthood,* isn't it worth it? As I was about to start writing these words this morning, one of our daughters called me to ask my opinion about her job decision. Right before she called, her sister had called to ask my opinion about a housing situation she was deciding. For both sweet girls of mine, getting to these decisions was years of healing in the making. I'm so proud of them. Walking with them as they shape their lives into their rightful, purposeful, and meaningful state—thriving—the cost and sacrifice have sometimes been a lot, but the payoff has been priceless. Life is long. Healing takes a lifetime. In the hard times, I've always asked myself if I still wanted to be in a relationship with our girls when they finally figure it all out. Do I want to be remembered as someone who helped and believed in them along the way? The answer to both has always been an emphatic yes. I know God will use other people along the way—friends, spouses, kids, bosses, counselors, pastors, and more, to help them whether I participate or not. I want to play a part in their story and sit on their sideline to cheer them on—to be their #1 fan. As a result, I stay committed and reach into my toolbox for one of my most frequently used tools—*grace.*

*"Grace is the voice that calls us to change
and then gives us the power to pull it off."*
Max Lucado

CHAPTER FIVE

G.R.A.C.E. RESPONSE

I love the Max Lucado quote above so much. It reminds me that grace isn't just a get-out-of-jail-free card. Instead, it's an intentional willingness to speak the hard truth while having the self-control to do it in love without harshness or punishment. This kind of grace comes alongside to empower and guide without judging or enabling. It's a grace that doesn't leave us alone in our mistakes and shortcomings or in repairing the rupture. True grace is authority and vulnerability working together on behalf of another.

One definition of grace is "unmerited favor"— not getting what you deserve. It's the teen coming home from school, throwing their backpack, shoes, and books in a pile at the door, and running straight to their room without talking to anyone and instead of making them come back down and pick everything up, put it in its place, and speak kindly to their siblings, we give them some time to themselves and prepare a saucer of cookies and a glass of milk to take up to them because we know that they failed a test that they studied hard for and probably just needed to cry. The problem is that it's relatively easy to extend grace in that moment because, in this example, we have foreknowledge of how they are feeling emotionally and why. What if that same young person came in the door like that without our foreknowledge of their emotional state? Would we have responded with grace? Many times, I did not. They *know better* than to leave their belongings in a heap, and they *know not to be rude by not speaking* to others in the home. They *deserve* to be disciplined to come back down and get it right. Grace is not something we earn—its definition says that we don't deserve it.

Extending grace is almost always a moment where we must take a deep breath and be purposeful in our subsequent actions, especially our following words. Nearly every time I've extended a graceful response to someone who didn't deserve it, I can promise you that I didn't *feel like* giving it. We extend grace not because someone deserves it or because we feel like it; we do it because it's the best and most redemptive path toward wholeness in our relationship and thriving for our young person. At the same time, grace isn't a wiping away of the wrong of another without requirement for repair. Quite the opposite, it's the holding back or lessening of the discipline, restriction, or punishment that might be deserved and responding with compassion while also providing structure for repairing and rectifying the situation. It's a *response* and not a reaction.

We Can Only Control Ourselves

You'll learn that I like acronyms if you've been around me for a long time. I'm perpetually finding easy ways for my brain to retain information and flows so that I can remember them and implement them later. The G.R.A.C.E. Response in our Redemptive Connection Framework is no different. It's an easy way to put action and flow to a concept of extending grace and empowering our young people. The first step of the G.R.A.C.E. Response sits outside of the acronym. It is *grace* itself: to be intentional in getting our own emotions, expectations, and desired outcomes in control with realistic expectations for the moment before we try to work through the conflict or problem with our young person. We don't have any control over our young person's emotions, actions, and thoughts—we can only control ourselves. I've found that I can respond rather than react to my girls by remembering that and taking a moment to survey my emotions, thoughts, and feelings. When I don't take a personal inventory, I find myself making mistakes and saying/doing things that I later regret.

My friend Lesli Reece has a phrase that has stuck with me for years. She says in moments of temptation to react or judge, "We should suspend judgment for a moment." I loved that phrase when I first heard her use it and have often used it to remember to slow down and let the whole situation play out entirely before jumping to hasty conclusions, actions, or words. "Suspending judgment" is step one.

Suspending Judgement/A Curious Approach

Central to the success of "suspending judgment" is to approach the situation from a position of curiosity rather than our preconceived opinions or judgments of what's best, what's harmful, and what's needed… curiosity chooses to operate with an investigative approach. This is something that I learned entirely too late in my parenting journey (if you don't believe me, ask one of my kids!). In most instances, when we're trying to help our young person move toward thriving, we will not have much control over their situation unless we're overstepping into doing things *for* them instead of *with* them. So, we must control what only we can control—our response. Through a curiosity mindset and approach, we can soften our reactions and better understand the situation.

Suspending judgment and taking a curious approach allows us and our young adults to shift our perspective and broaden our understanding. By modeling curiosity, we also set an excellent example for our young person to adopt this communication style in their lives, relationships, and careers. Curiosity puts us in a posture of discovery rather than confrontation. It's easier for young adults to respond to our genuinely curious questions than assumptions and preconceived certainties. It's really about our mindset as we enter the communication environment. By intentionally challenging our inner dialogue and adopting curiosity, we allow ourselves to step into their shoes and understand their perspective—even if we disagree with it. Here are examples to help you adjust your mindset:

Control / Judgement Mindset	Curious Mindset
They are only thinking about their own wants/desires without considering others.	Why is this important to them? How does this make sense to them?
If they would just do what I advise everything would be fine.	What might I be missing about the situation that's complicating their decision?
They are difficult to talk to and it always ends up in frustration.	How am I contributing to the difficulty? What can I change?
If they would just change _____	What can I do differently?
What is wrong with them? How could they do this?	What led them to this action? What did they need?

A G.R.A.C.E. Response

Steps two through five are an acronym for a G.R.A.C.E Response that gives us the ability to gain critical insight into what is going on while helping our young person to develop a plan and set of disciplines necessary to build self-efficacy and take personal responsibility for solving or repairing the problem themselves. The G.R.A.C.E. Response is both belonging & self-efficacy at play as we are *with* the young person as they think through the issue, experience the consequences, and create a resolution plan. This toolbox for redemptive connection keeps relationships at the center while encouraging confidence and agency in our young people.

The G.R.A.C.E. Response encourages a redemptive mindset and sees our young people through their potential for growth and healing, even in the face of inevitable adversity. We all fail; if we're honest, many of us staggered through young adulthood—I know I did. Too often, we're tempted to dismiss our failings as a young adult by saying things like, "But I didn't have the resources that my young person has available to them… if I had, I would have taken advantage of them." These statements and mindsets feel right, but they might not be because we're making them with the mindset of a much older adult, allowing us to take advantage of areas of our brains that are developed now but were *not* developed in our early 20s. So, faced with the same opportunity, you and I might have made the same decision as our young person. As we inventory our own emotions, thoughts, and feelings, we must also examine our expectations and ensure that we're not placing unrealistic ideals on our young people that we may not have been able to live up to ourselves at their age and their stage of brain development.

Below is a summary of each aspect of the G.R.A.C.E. Response:

REDEMPTIVE CONNECTION: G.R.A.C.E. RESPONSE

G: Get to Why
Understanding the motivations and underlying causes of the circumstance, behavior, and conflict.

R: Rally Around Realistic Goals
Set achievable and meaningful goals to address and improve the behavior while considering the young person's abilities and limitations.

A: Affirm Redemptive Positives
Recognize and affirm the positive qualities, strengths, and progress. Practice a hopeful vision of the future good resulting from the current hard circumstance or behavior.

C: Cultivate Resilience
Foster resilience in both you and your young person, helping them bounce back from challenges and develop coping skills.

E: Engage Supportive Community
Involve and seek support from a network of individuals who can help, guide, and encourage you and your young person.

Get to Why (G)
Family dinner was essential to our family routine when our girls were at home. On most nights, we would gather around a long table in our dining room over tacos, spaghetti, homemade pizzas, pot roast, or many other family favorites constantly in rotation, eating family-style from the bowls and plates in the middle of the table. One evening, our life-of-the-party daughter sat down to dinner and was snarly and rude almost immediately. It was extremely out of character for her, and throughout the next few minutes, everyone around the table was uncomfortable with the rudeness. Finally, I asked her if she wanted to leave the table and return to her room. She took me up on the offer and left the table. This daughter was also not a crier—she

held the epitome of a "suck it up and keep moving" attitude toward her life in general.

After dinner, I went upstairs and knocked to enter her room, shockingly finding her crying. In one of my rare moments of getting it right, I didn't engage in telling her just how disrespectful her behavior was, how uncomfortable it made us feel, or how ungrateful it was because I had cooked a big meal just for her to sit down and act that way—all ways that I've reacted from time to time. Instead, I sat down on the bed beside her and asked, "Can you tell me what happened?" She immediately burst into more tears and began apologizing for her behavior. After a few moments, between crying gulps, she said, "There was cantaloupe on the table, and it just made me mad." I searched the recesses of my brain to try and remember at what point she had told me that she hated cantaloupe and how I should have known that! I said, "I don't remember you telling me you hated cantaloupe." What she said next is something I will never forget. She said, "I don't think I've ever seen you have it here. I hate it because our mom used to push it into the carpet and make us (her sister and her) eat it out of the carpet as punishment." My heart broke for her, and I immediately understood the "why" behind her behavior at the dinner table. Without being able to put words to it at the moment, her brain reacted to the triggering smell of cantaloupe, and she "flipped her lid," and the resulting behavior came out as rude toward others at the table. Even though it felt personal to us at the moment, none of it was directed at us or because of us. A sudden trauma memory caused her rudeness at the moment. This is why it's essential to "Get to Why" when responding to our young person's behaviors, actions, or circumstances.

"Get to Why" aims to understand the motivations and underlying causes of the circumstance, behavior, and conflict. In almost every issue, behavior, and circumstance we've seen in our young people, there is a "why behind the what." Even further, there is a "why behind the why." The difference between the two is often nuanced and missed if we don't take the time to understand and develop a curious mindset.

One of the first places that we start when trying to understand the why behind the what of any issue is understanding trauma and triggers. In many cases, behavior (both ours and our young person's) can be triggered by past experiences and manifest in many ways. The best way to walk this out is through open-ended curiosity, such as the question I asked our daughter, "Can you tell me what happened?" In starting there, I intentionally put aside my assumptions about disrespect, ungratefulness, and dishonor and gave her a safe space to evaluate her emotions and reactions. The *why behind the what* (what they are/were feeling) for her was that the smell and sight of the cantaloupe "made her mad." To dig deeper, we needed to get to the *why behind the why* (what is causing them to feel this way), which was that it had been used against her in a punitive way in childhood, which created a trauma memory and response for her.

One of my favorite models for understanding the brain's response to trauma triggers is Dr. Dan Siegel's Hand Model of the Brain (see *Figure 10*). Our brains are uniquely designed to keep us alive, to help us understand the world, and to retain information. From early childhood, we learn that the stove is hot and that heat burns and causes blisters. From that point on in our lives, we're likely to respond to the smell of smoke, a red-hot glow, the sensation of eating, and the sight of flames by automatically backing up without giving it a second's rational thought. This is our brain automatically protecting us from perceived dangers.

The Hand Model of the Brain

Holding your hand straight up and pointing to your wrist is an example of the brain stem, which controls the most primitive and first response systems active in our developing brains—our flight, fight, or freeze responses. This **"Survival Brain"** automatically takes control when immediate danger is sensed. It doesn't operate in words – it only operates in action. Our heart rate increases, and instinct takes over: run, hide, fight, submit, shrink, etc. If you put your finger on the center of your palm, this is an example of the limbic system. The **"Emotional Brain"** controls all our feelings and emotions. It also stores memory and "feels" the bonds of relationship and attachment. The limbic system also has no words—just feelings. Sometimes, when we're feeling emotional and can't find words to convey our emotions, or we're feeling impulsive and can't stop the impulse— we are acting out of our survival or emotional brain, or a combination of them. Now, take your thumb and bring it in over the center of your palm. This is your amygdala or **"Smoke Detector."** The amygdala scans the environment for danger and screams loudly. When it screams, it throws the thinking parts of our brain "offline" and calls our Survival and Emotional Brains to the front so they can feel and act on the danger we face. Finally, take your four standing fingers and fold them down over your thumb. This represents your **"Thinking Brain,"** with your four fingers representing the cortex. Here, we have words, think critically, solve problems, be creative, plan, share our beliefs, and control our impulses because we can put language and logic to use on our behalf—this is where we develop and experience resilience. When our "smoke detector" sets off an alarm, our "thinking brain" disengages, and we have trouble retrieving data, organizing information, and processing what's happening. Dr. Siegel calls this **"Flipping the Lid."** If you bring your four fingers back up quickly—that's a flipped lid. If a car is coming at you at 60mph, your brain automatically flips the lid because it just needs you to feel the fear and jump out of the way. If your cortex stayed engaged in calculating the rate of speed, probability of impact, and seconds that you must move—you would likely die.

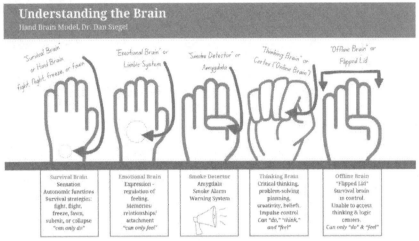

Figure 10 Dr. Dan Siegel's "Flipping the Lid" hand model of the brain.

The same responsive/reactionary brain system is activated in response to trauma and triggers from our past experiences. When triggered, the prefrontal cortex shuts down, and it's hard to think or talk; we're flooded with intense emotions and body memories. It takes time, relational connection, and walking *through* the feelings to settle the brain and help it feel safe. Once that happens and the cortex returns online, the brain can make sense of what happened, find words to explain, and even sometimes locate the trigger that caused the response. This type of reaction or "flipped lid" can occur over and over in our lives as the brain responds to triggers from our past. We often can't find the words or make sense of the trigger because our brain isn't ready to let go of the memory and repress it for our safety. This is why healing is a lifelong journey and why it's so important that the first step in our G.R.A.C.E. Response is to Get to Why.

In "Get to Why," here are a few other helpful tools that we can use:

- **Practice empathy & compassion:** take time to consider what your young person might be feeling, recognizing that their behavior might be a result of a flipped lid due to past trauma and triggers. Try putting yourself in their shoes and thinking about the most compassionate action or response.
- **Respond with non-judgmental curiosity**: ask open-ended questions and give them time to process and respond.

Remember that their perspective is theirs, and even if it's not entirely true, a curious approach can help unpack it more fully.

- **Avoid assumptions**: refrain from making assumptions about motives. Instead, seek clarification and keep an open mind and heart.

Using a redemptive approach, "Get to Why" involves compassionate and curious exploration of the underlying reasons behind what's happening. By taking time to understand your young person's perspective, emotions, and experiences, you create an environment where healing, empathy, and positive change can occur.

Rally Around Realistic Goals (R)

How do you eat an elephant? *One bite at a time.* This is the phrase that got us through the Senior year for one of our sweet girls who experienced extreme project and test anxiety. Teaching her to break down the project into a single step at a time and the test to a single question at a time was an every-week exercise. But she remembers and uses this phrase and set of actions even today. Setting achievable and meaningful goals helps us to address and improve sometimes frustrating behaviors like poor performance in school, perceived laziness in obtaining a job, etc. We must consider our young person's abilities and limitations to do this successfully.

As we continue to focus on progress and growth in our young people, we should celebrate small victories and provide the support they need to work towards positive change. I know it will sometimes feel like it's taking forever to see results, but small changes over time do add up. I promise. Remember that a redemptive approach acknowledges that healing is gradual and encourages a sense of accomplishment, even if it's only an inch forward.

There are so many tools around for setting goals, from planners to webinars to YouTube videos and so much more. I encourage you to talk to your young person about what works for them and find a pathway to work with them successfully. Or maybe they don't know how to set goals and prioritize, and you commit to working together to "try on" different types of goal setting to find something that works. For us, breaking goals into smaller steps was one of our most successful tools and seemed to work with our girls whether they had performance and project anxiety or not. The main thing is to help your young person define an objective they are trying to achieve (get a job, pass a class, buy a car, rent an apartment, etc.), and then help them think through the steps necessary to achieve that goal.

Here are a few tips and guides to help with goal setting:

- **Be realistic:** Consider that many of our young people who've experienced hard places have never learned to set goals. They didn't have the "piggy bank" experiences of saving for what they wanted so badly. But it's never too late to learn. Additionally, many of our young people struggle with delayed gratification because, in their experience, it would never happen if they didn't achieve it/get it/have it now. So, the concept of *small victories* can sometimes be complex, and we have to move the goalposts closer and celebrate them bigger than we might otherwise do.

- **Define clear objectives**: Clearly outline what they want to accomplish or envision. Tools like vision boards or SMART (specific, measurable, achievable, relevant, and time-bound) are good starting points. Many resources are available online to help you learn about these tools with your young person.

- **Collaborate**: Don't be afraid to sit with your young person and collaborate on potential goals and steps to achieve their dreams. Sometimes, just sitting with them and asking curiosity-based questions helps unlock things they haven't found words to describe.

- **Be adaptable**: Goals sometimes need to be adjusted over time. This is normal. You can help your young person learn to reset expectations and vocalize roadblocks by modeling and being adaptable. It's okay to reposition goalposts. We all do it.

- **Focus on effort**: Encourage your young person to reflect on their progress and acknowledge the effort that they've invested. Effort is often more important than outcome because it's in the effort that true self-efficacy is built, and it reinforces the importance of dedication and perseverance.

Affirm Redemptive Positives (A)

As I write this chapter, I've just returned from a work trip to Nashville to launch our Tennessee Branch of Connections Homes. While there, I spent an evening with our new Executive Director at an Artists Against Trafficking event where my friends Kyle and Allison Cruz performed. It was a wonderful evening in a beautiful country barn setting. Leaving the venue, I was still thinking about the fantastic stories and music that we had just experienced and how our organization's work intersected with the transforming work being done to rescue and redeem survivors, or thrivers, as they called them. I needed to use my phone flashlight to find my car in the middle of a grass and rock-covered field where we had all parked. It was pitch black outside, and we had all parked where we could with no real "parking spaces." I arrived at my car and started pulling out. Trying to avoid hitting the cars in front of me, parked tightly and close to where I was, I turned gently toward the right and pushed forward into the lane with only one tiny strip of gravel to navigate to the property entrance. As I paid attention to the cars in front of me, I failed to consider the car to my right and, within seconds, heard the horrifying crunch of metal as my passenger side doors slid down the back bumper of the car next to me. My heart dropped, and I came to a stop, trying to figure out which would cause less damage—continuing forward or backing up. I decided to back up and check out the damage. I had left a little early, so there was no one in the parking lot, so I took the time to jot down my information and leave a note for the driver. I maneuvered without a second incident and called my husband to tell him I had wrecked my car. After realizing it was a fender bender, he said, "Well, at least you're okay. The car can be repaired." At that moment, that was the *redemptive positive* that I needed to hear. I felt terrible and kept beating myself up for the mistake.

Recognizing and affirming our young people's positive qualities, strengths, and progress does the same thing that Steve did for me in that moment—recognizing that a mistake has happened, but it could be worse, and there can be a positive outcome. It is redeemable, and there are positive aspects (like me not needing medical attention from a different type of car wreck or worse). Another way that we *affirm redemptive positives* is to practice a hopeful vision of the future good that can result from the current hard circumstance or behavior—like the drug addict who can overcome and eventually help others out, the teen mom can help other young moms feel like they *can do it*, and so many more examples. *Affirming redemptive positives* means that we take a moment to think about sincere and specific ways that this momentary setback can be used for and seen in a good light.

Here are some other helpful tools for affirming redemptive positives:

- **Reinforce hope:** Highlighting the potential for continued growth and transformation. This helps to instill a sense of hope for the future in our young people. My favorite scripture is Jeremiah 29:11, which says, "For I know the plans I have for you, says the Lord. Plans to prosper you and not to harm you. Plans to give you hope and a future." For me, this verse has constantly reinforced the hope that no matter what happens, there can be redemption and, ultimately, a positive future ahead of me.

- **Offer constructive feedback:** Try to find ways that, even in the mistake, you see growth and improvement. They may have yet to get the job, but they applied, went to the interview, and took all the necessary steps.

- **Encourage self-reflection:** Asking curiosity-based questions about how your young person is feeling, what they learned, what they are proud of, and how they think this can be used in their future can encourage them to self-reflect and build on their skills, fostering self-esteem and self-appreciation.

Cultivate Resilience (C)

"Use your resources." I giggled as I wrote those words. Most of my kids, at one point or another, have heard me say that to them, and one may or may not still feel triggered and traumatized by that phrase (true story). It's not a phrase that I came up with just for them. It comes naturally to me because it's how I live my life. I've never been afraid to learn something new, try a new skill, or challenge myself beyond my comfort zone. I've always known that I could find resources to teach myself pretty much anything—and I've used them. So, it was necessary to teach my girls that they have the power at their fingertips (literally with smartphones) to find the answer to any question, develop any skill, and solve almost any problem because it's the secret to my success. It's also a great way to *cultivate resilience*.

Fostering resilience in both you and your young person by learning to bounce back from challenges and develop coping skills is a critical aspect of *redemptive connection*. Resilience is the process of adapting well in the face of adversity, trauma, tragedy, threats, or significant amounts of stress—such as family and relationship problems, serious health problems, workplace issues, and financial stress. It's simply "bouncing back" from difficult experiences and turning adversity into action that moves you forward. Being resilient doesn't mean you don't have trouble or distress—quite the opposite. Emotional pain, physical suffering, failure, and loss come to everyone. The most resilient people are those who've likely experienced the most significant amounts of distress, trauma, and loss. Resilience is also not a trait that people have or don't have. It's a set of behaviors, thoughts, and actions that anyone can learn and develop. I love the cartoon below that illustrates resilience in the face of the dragon of adversity[13].

Figure 11 Resilience & Adversity Cartoon

---

[13] I found this cartoon at monarchsystem.com/resilience-in-mi-work/

Becoming resilient starts with the realization that the adversity you experience—any pain, discrimination, or challenge—can be converted into powerful fuel that can bring opportunity[14]. So, let's redefine adversity from a state or instance of distress, calamity, hardship, or affliction to *fuel, energy, and our best friend.* When viewed through a lens of resilience, any adversity that we face can be seen as a teacher in our lives. Some of the worst bosses I've ever worked for are the ones I'm most grateful to have had. They taught me how *not* to lead—a valuable lesson I might not have learned otherwise.

This change of viewpoint is key to one of the most successful tools we've used in helping our families cultivate resilience in their young people. It's called the ABCs of Resilience[15], which stands for **Adversity, Beliefs, and Consequences.** Using this model helps our young people develop a healthy self-awareness of negative thought patterns and challenge themselves to respond with a resilient mindset. I'll briefly explain this concept. I encourage you to "use your resources" (giggle) to search more on this topic if you want to dive more deeply.

- **Adversity:** The negative situation or event.
- **Beliefs:** This is the story we tell ourselves about why it happened and what it means.
- **Consequences:** These are the feelings, behaviors, and actions that result from our beliefs.

In his book Learned Optimism, Martin Seligman adds a D, E, and F to Dr. Albert Ellis's original model.

- **Dispute**: Challenge the negative beliefs with alternative options.
- **Exchange:** Replace the negative belief with more positive and rational ones.
- **Feelings:** New feelings and optimism arise from taking a different perspective.

Not everyone reacts to adversity in the same way. It's not a specific "event" that drives a particular outcome; our thoughts and actions about that event predict it. When adversity happens, we first try to explain to ourselves why it happened—our beliefs about the cause of adversity set in motion our reaction, which produces a consequence. How we feel determines what we do.

Here are a couple of examples of **Adversity, Beliefs, Consequences, Dispute, Exchange,** and **Feelings** in action:

---

[14] Some of the content in this section can be found in The Resilience Breakthrough by Christian Moore—27 Tools for Turning Adversity into Action
[15] Ellis, 1996; Seligman, 1991 From Martin Seligman's book *"Learned Optimism"*

Example One:
    A. You sent a text to a friend but days later haven't heard back from them.
    B. You believe they are mad at you and are ignoring you.
    C. The friendship is likely over, or there will be a huge fight.
    D. You challenge your negative thoughts with another likely scenario in which they saw the text and forgot to respond or are overwhelmed with something else in life.
    E. You decide that the new scenario is more likely.
    F. Your feelings of anxiety are lessened, which allows you to send a new text and say that you hope they are doing well and just wanted to follow up.

Example Two:
    A. You get fired from a job.
    B. You believe it was unfair; they are just bad managers.
    C. You don't self-reflect or determine if you played a part; therefore, you may be at risk of repeating the same behavior at another job
    D. You challenge your tendency to blame others instead of performing healthy self-reflection and decide to acknowledge that you were late to work often and ignored your manager's warnings of poor performance. (Being resilient is also being honest with ourselves, especially when it's painful.)
    E. You decide that the firing was probably the right decision for the manager and resolve to work on your time management skills and perform your best at your next job.
    F. You feel like you learned a valuable lesson that will help you to be even more successful.

Cultivating resilience is about intentionally fostering emotional strength, adaptability, and the ability to bounce back from challenges in our young people, especially those who've experienced trauma. We provide the necessary support and strategies to help them turn their pain into purpose. Here are a few other ways that we can cultivate resilience in our young people:

- **Encourage healthy coping strategies:** Help your young person learn to cope with stress and challenges through adaptability and resilience as they learn to problem-solve, seek support, and engage in self-care.
- **Guide them to stress management techniques:** Help them learn valuable skills such as mindfulness, relaxation exercises, deep breathing, and more.

- **Encourage honest self-reflection**: Teaching our young people to view failure as a teacher and not through the lens of shame helps them to develop a willingness for healthy self-reflection.
- **Embrace flexibility:** Teach your young person the importance of being adaptable and open to change, which will help them develop the ability to navigate life's challenges more easily.

Engage Supportive Community (E)

It does take a village for all of us to develop into our most promising versions of ourselves, and it takes a village for our young people, too. The person that I am today in all my successes and failures is a mixture of all the people I've met along the way and their influences on my life—how I think, work, and learn. Early in my parenting journey, I recognized the need for an extended network of individuals to have input into my girls' lives and futures. That hasn't always been easy, and it hasn't always been helpful, but overall, it's helped way more than it has hurt. By involving and seeking support from a network of individuals who can provide guidance, assistance, and encouragement for both you and your young person, you are tapping into the knowledge and experiences of others that both of you need.

One of the most powerful outcomes of engaging in a supportive community is that you are helping your young person remove the stigma of seeking help by normalizing it. Seeking help is a sign of strength, not a weakness, and having others in your life to celebrate successes, give constructive advice, and be a listening ear is a huge benefit to the longevity and health of your relationship with your young person. We may think we want to "be there for everything" for our young people, but the reality is that we can't. It's okay to let go and let others have some input.

This has looked like pastors, family members, friends, counselors, teachers, and more for our family. We've worked hard at identifying and building relationships with trusted individuals in our girls' lives. Rather than feeling threatened by them, we've acknowledged and embraced them as vital parts of our girls' ecosystems to help them become the best version of themselves possible. Candidly, that hasn't always come as easily as I make it sound here, and it hasn't always proven helpful. Every story has three sides— your side, my side, and the truth—and sometimes the "others" in our girls' lives have heard just one side of the story and acted on that information, taking a stand against us. It's been hurtful when that happened, but almost every time, we've been willing to show up and work through it to the truth (not just our side). Yet, even with some speed bumps along the way, it is best for our girls to have these other amazing mentors, friends, and parent-like individuals as helpful guides and trusted advocates. We can't shoulder it all and don't have the best advice for everything our girls face. That's simply the truth. Recognizing that as parents and mentors is a huge step in helping our young people find the relationships that will move them forward and not leave them stuck.

I've also needed to engage my supportive community to help me navigate new areas with my young people. I've become involved in support groups, put myself in learning environments to develop new skills, practiced my learned skills, and sought counsel and advice from others. I had to be willing to accept that I'm fallible and make mistakes and listen to others as they share their perspectives, including my children!

Here are a few other tools to help as you walk with your young person to engage in a supportive community:

- **Professional guidance:** Encourage your young person to seek professional help, such as therapists and counselors experienced in trauma and healing.
- **Learn together:** Mutual learning creates a bond through a two-way exchange of information and perspective sharing. To take it even further in deepening your relationship, take time to intentionally let your young person learn about you. Don't be afraid to share your failures, hurts, and heartbreaks to help your young person see that you're not perfect and are learning, too.
- **Encourage open communication:** Promote open and honest communication between your young person and their supportive community. Always encourage them to be honest, even if it's about you.

By nurturing a supportive network around your young person, you are helping to provide emotional, practical, and educational support that contributes to their healing and positive change.

Along the way, as we seek a G.R.A.C.E. Response to our young person's challenges, we must remain humble and teachable. Learning to take stock of our emotions and expectations and accept advice and help from others will be one of the best keys to a truly flourishing relationship with our young person. From this heart posture, we can become helpful navigators in their lives as they learn, grow, and thrive.

"And the Lord answered me: Write the vision; make it plain on tablets, so he may run who reads it. For still the vision awaits its appointed time; it hastens to the end—it will not lie. If it seems slow, wait for it; it will surely come; it will not delay."
Habakkuk 2:2-3

CHAPTER SIX

THRIVING IN LIFE

In our work, we use the following description for what a thriving young adult looks like, "*A thriving young adult with healthy belonging and self-efficacy has a strong sense of connection to a supportive and caring family where they feel accepted and valued for their true selves. Additionally, they believe deeply in their ability to take meaningful actions to achieve the life they aspire to lead. This healthy belonging and self-efficacy combination empowers them to confidently navigate challenges, pursue their dreams, and lead a flourishing life.*"

Our vision is for a young adult to *thrive in life and impact their world.*

I've always been an avid believer in knowing where I want to go—what I envision for my life, work, family, faith, etc. As our scripture reference beautifully articulates, it's important to "write the vision and make it plain so that he who reads it can run with it." In other words, we won't hit the target if we don't aim the arrow. The mistake I've made along the way is often thinking that the target is a single precise destination instead of realizing that it's more likely just "in the vicinity" of where I think I'm headed and nestled among many other targets throughout my journey in life. I've learned that the things I set my vision toward often shift as I work to achieve them. I refine and redefine my direction as I gain more information and knowledge and engage more co-workers. More often than not (in my personal life), I find that when I arrive at the achievement of that vision or goal, a new door opens to expand my thinking and life, and, as a result, a new vision is born, and a new path is set before me.

Defining a "thriving life" isn't different from my journey and yours. There is a general goal to aim for, but the path to the goal, the achievement of the goal, and the trajectory it leads us on is different for each of us—even if we share similar dreams. The same is true for our young people, and much of what we would define as "thriving" is fraught with failure, struggle, boredom, tediousness, and trudging through the mud because all those things make us stronger and take us to places that we've never dreamed in our character, our friendships, our career paths, and our heart-passions.

Many know me at this stage of life and only know me as a foster care and adoption advocate, nonprofit founder/leader, and a voice for aging-out foster youth. What many don't know is that in my over 30 years of working, I've served in nearly 20 different types of roles: fast food cashier, Wal-Mart cashier, car dealership receptionist, executive assistant to the regional office director for a primary health insurance provider, office manager for a church, librarian, business co-owner with my husband, music artist manager, music artist pr & communications, corporate marketing vice president for a mobile technology company, women's pastor, youth camp producer, mega-church service producer, video producer, speaker, trainer, author, blogger, and now founder and CEO of a nonprofit. That averages about 1.8 years of focus per "specialty," even though that wouldn't be accurate for my journey as I've spent more time in some roles than others and there are quite a few overlapping roles. The point I'm making is that in my own life, I've "tried on" many hats along the way, and each of them has played a role in the knowledge, talent, character, and ability that I have today to help me achieve today's mission and vision. I've had the privilege of being fired from some of those roles, laid off from others, worked under terrible leadership, worked under excellent leaders, made mistakes, had incredible successes, and learned every step of the way. If it feels like I'm belaboring the point, I am. We often forget our path to where we are as we focus on guiding our young people to *where we think* they should be. If it was hard for us, do we believe it won't be hard for them? If we stumbled and failed, do we think they won't? If we struggled to find our purpose, do we believe it will be any easier for them? I know. I know. "I didn't have someone like me in my corner *when I was that age.*" That's what we all say. But, if we did, do we seriously think we would have listened any better at 21? Likely not.

Like us, our young people will "wander" and figure out who they are and what they are gifted at. They will experience many stops and starts along the way, and even though it's frustrating, it can ultimately be a vital part of the beauty of their life that leads them to flourishing. Yet, even amid it, there is a wandering that can be considered thriving and a wandering that would be regarded as a failure to thrive. Have you ever played a game of bowling with the 'no gutter ball' guards in place? You may not get a strike, but the ball also won't go into the gutter because the guards will stop it. We are the "no gutter ball" guards for our young people. We gently nudge and guide them but can't guarantee a strike every time. I hope I can provide some general guardrails in this chapter to help you determine where your young person is in terms of thriving.

Adulting is Hard

One of the most profound pieces of developmental research that I've come across during my time doing this work belongs to Dr. Jeffery Arnett, who defined an entirely new stage of development known as "Emerging Adulthood."[16] The truth is that over the last few decades, we've been living through a significant paradigm shift in how and when true adulthood begins. Through the work of Dr. Arnett, emerging adulthood is becoming recognized as an entirely new developmental stage that extends from around age 18 through the late twenties. In this section, I want to break down some of the most exciting and relevant pieces of this work to our goal of helping our young people to thrive in life.

As a self-contained developmental stage, emerging adulthood has risen in its development within the last few decades as a response to some interesting measures of societal change:

- Fifty years ago, the median age for marriage was 22 for men and 20 for women. *Today, it's 28 for men and 24 for women.*

- Before 1944 and the passage of the GI Bill of Rights, only a small percentage of high school graduates attended college. Today, young people get some college experience in one form or another. Women now make up a large portion of college undergraduates, choosing to build careers before marriage and children.

- Decades ago, young people got married rather than face the risks of pregnancy outside of marriage. Now, with birth control and the acceptance of sexual relationships outside of marriage, the commitment to marriage is later, if at all.

Marrying later in life and prolonging education & career profoundly impact a young person's feelings of independence and ability to thrive independently. Culturally, this development period is uniquely present in societies that allow young people a prolonged period of dependence in their late teens and twenties. There's no question that our American culture fits that definition.

The data shows that the world in which our great grandparents, grandparents, and even many of us grew up is vastly different from the world our young people are growing up in today. For the older generations, there was a more direct path from teenage adolescence to stable adult role-taking in society—entering love and career by their late teens or early twenties. My husband and I married in 1991 at 19, one year after graduating high school.

---

[16] Arnett, J.J. (2000). Emerging adulthood: A theory of development from the late teens through the twenties. American Psychologist, 55 (5), 469-480. Arnett, J.J. (2004). Emerging Adulthood: The winding road from the late teens through the twenties. Oxford University Press.

It was common in our small coal mining and factory working town, and neither side of our family questioned it. It wasn't easy by any means, but we grew up *together* very quickly, and by the age that many of today's young people are beginning to think about marriage (24), we were having our first child. So, you can bet that I've had to catch many *"when I was your age…"* comments before they exited my mouth!

Dr. Arnett's work describes five features of this new stage of development: The Age of Identity Exploration, the Age of Instability, the Age of Self Focus, the Age of Feeling In-Between, and the Age of Possibilities. I've found each feature to have great insights into what's happening with our young people today. We will briefly explore each, but I encourage you to purchase Dr. Arnett's book, Emerging Adulthood, if you want to dive more deeply into this information. There are also some good videos on YouTube where you can hear him teach this himself.

The Age of Identity Exploration: Young people are deciding who they are and what they want out of work, school, and love. Accomplishing this means knowing who they are, identifying their social roles, and being comfortable with that knowledge. It comes down to a feeling of learning to master life successfully. This takes a *struggle* to achieve over time. They also need to be allowed to make wrong decisions and learn from those decisions as an essential part of the process. Young people who fail to create their identity can become confused about their role in the world. As a result, they will either conform to others' expectations or rebel against them.

This can be especially hard for young people with histories of trauma and foster care. Being moved from home to home, parented by a multitude of families (some good / some bad), having a broken educational background, and having a moving target for where they may land to launch their adult life are all difficulties that add even more complexity to Dr. Arnett's work. His work isn't on young people from hard places; it's primarily on young people from average families. It's not hard to imagine for the young people that most of us are working with that finding their identity and who they truly are is an even lengthier process. In my experience, it lasts even into the late twenties and early thirties. This is why, with many of our formal governmental assistance programs ending between the ages of 21 – 24, it's critical to have a safe, stable support system that can be there for a young person as they continue to navigate into their 30s and beyond. And why it's critical for those of us already in the life of a young adult who experienced trauma to commit ourselves to remaining steadfast—no matter what—during this season of their life.

The Age of Instability: The post-high school years are marked by repeated residence changes as young people attend college or live with friends. For most, frequent moves end as families and careers are established in the 30s. Emerging adults rarely know where they'll be from one year to the next. They regularly shift their education choices, majors, and in-school/out-of-school decisions. They often boomerang back home several times due to financial instability and poor decision-making. Many of the moves emerging adults make are for some new period of exploration—in love, work, or education. Exploration and instability go hand in hand.

This feature of emerging adulthood reminds me of the importance of our tetherball analogy from Chapter Two. For most of our young people, instability is the definition of their entire life, and, like finding their identity, it can take much more time for them to discover a feeling of real stability with those of us who've stepped up to be their anchors (or tetherball poles) in life. We've found that for many of our youth, moving multiple times, changing careers, or even families don't feel like a heavy lift because they've done it all their lives. The challenge for our young people is creating a strong enough connection to keep them engaged in a relationship with us long enough for this feeling of stability to emerge later than it usually would.

The Age of Self-Focus: Freed of the parent (or authority) and society-directed routine of school, young people try to decide what they want to do, where they want to go, and who they want to be with—before those choices get limited by the constraints of marriage, children, and career. This is the most self-focused time of life. What to have for dinner? I decide. When to do laundry? I decide. When (or whether) to come home at night? I decide! Go to college? Work full-time? Combine work and college? Break up with a high school sweetheart? Move in with a boyfriend or girlfriend? Date someone new? Decisions. Decisions. Decisions. In making these decisions, counsel may be offered or sought from parents, mentors, and friends, but many of these decisions mean clarifying in their minds what they want, and no one can tell them what they want but themselves.

Being self-focused during emerging adulthood is normal, healthy, and temporary. By focusing on themselves, emerging adults develop skills for daily living, gain a better understanding of who they are and what they want from life, and begin to build the foundation for their adult lives. Yet, for us tetherball poles, it can be pretty tricky. We feel left out or brushed off. I remember sending one of my girls a text that read, "Hey! I forgot to give you the $20 that I owe you." I got an immediate response of, "Really?" To which I promptly replied, "Not really. I just wanted to make sure you're still alive since you haven't responded to any of my other texts in a couple of weeks!" She thought it was funny and responded with, "I know. I know, Mom! Sorry,

I've been so busy with work and friend plans that I just come home and go straight to bed." It's natural to miss our young person's companionship at this stage. Still, it is also natural and healthy for them to build their own life, and it is perfectly understandable to be too tired to text or call after a busy week of work and personal plans. I've been married since I was 19, so I don't have the context for what it's like to be single and looking for love in my twenties, and because I've been married since 19, I also don't have the context for having to make it on my own without a spouse's contribution to the budget and the household. As a result, I've often had to remind myself of the mental, physical, and emotional load that my young adult girls carry and that their self-focus isn't selfishness; it's survival.

The Age of Feeling In-Between: Many emerging adults say they take responsibility for themselves but don't "feel like" an adult. Between the restrictions of adolescence and the freedom/responsibilities of adulthood lie the explorations and instability of emerging adulthood. When asked if they've reached adulthood, most 18 – 24-year-olds answer with one foot in *yes* and one foot in *no*. In Dr. Arnett's research, 60% of emerging adults answered this way. Their criteria for "adulthood" were: 1) accept responsibility for yourself, 2) Make independent decisions, and 3) become financially independent. All three criteria are gradual and incremental rather than all at once. Consequently, although emerging adults begin to feel "adult" by age 18 or 19, they do not feel completely adult until years later, sometimes into their mid-twenties. By then, they have become confident that they have reached a point where they accept responsibility, make their own decisions, and are financially independent.

Interestingly, this research also coincides with brain research that tells us that the frontal lobe of the brain, our executive functions, doesn't fully mature until the age of 26. The frontal lobe plays a crucial role in a young person's ability to thrive. Its maturation can significantly impact their lives, such as executive functioning, emotional regulation, goal setting and persistence, social skills, risk assessment, stress management, time management (can I get an amen?), and self-awareness. As this area of the brain matures, young adults are better equipped to navigate the complexities of adulthood and work toward a thriving life. The hard part is getting there! I've often said that when we ask our 20-year-olds, "What were you thinking?!?" about a poor decision or action, they respond with, "I dunno." They're telling the truth. Long-term cause-and-effect thinking hasn't fully matured, so they haven't thought it through; for our young people who've experienced trauma, the process of maturing into the grey matter of their frontal lobe can take even longer.

Trauma can significantly impact brain development and functioning, including the maturation of the frontal lobe, which may result in delayed or altered development in some cases. Our young people may be dealing with:

- An **altered stress response** after being exposed to chronic stress can impact the development of the frontal lobe and lead to difficulties in emotional regulation, impulse control, and decision-making.
- **Impaired executive functions** such as planning, problem-solving, and working memory can cause our young people to struggle with tasks that require higher-level thinking and organization.
- **Difficulty regulating their emotions,** which can show up in mood swings, intense anger, or emotional numbness.
- **Reduced self-control** can lead to impulsiveness and a struggle to delay gratification, which can impact decision-making and risk assessment, two critical aspects of frontal lobe development.
- **Difficulty in relationships** because of impaired social skills. The frontal lobe plays a significant role in social cognition and empathy.
- **Delayed maturation** because the stress and emotional impact of trauma can divert brain resources away from normal developmental processes.

However, there is hope—there are still redemptive positives—just because it's a struggle doesn't mean it's impossible. It just takes a little longer. For our girls, I've seen some of this begin to set in during their early 30s. It's also important to remember that every young adult is unique; some may experience longer delays than others. Our role is to continue being supportive and point them in the right direction whenever possible. With all that's happening in their brain and development, it's no surprise that they feel "in-between."

The Age of Possibilities: In these years, optimism reigns in our lives. Most emerging adults believe they have a good shot at living a better life, finding a soulmate, and creating a life they love. This is the age of high hopes and great expectations, partly because very few of their dreams have been tested in the fires of "real life." The dreary, dead-end jobs, the family issues, the disrespectful children—none of them imagine this is what the future holds for them (and neither did we). More than any other period of life, emerging adulthood presents the possibility for change. For this limited window of time, fulfilling all their hopes seems possible. At this point in life, for most, the range of their choices for how to live is more significant than ever before and greater than it ever will be again.

Coach, Cheerleader, & Water Boy

As the gutter-ball protectors in our emerging adults' lives, it can be challenging to watch them bounce around, boomerang, fail, and falter. Yet a *redemptive* approach calls us to the sidelines of their lives as the ever-present cheerleader, the passionate and patient coach, and the sustenance-providing water boy. We can't cross the line onto the field in their game of life, but we can observe, advise, and provide what we can from our seats on the sidelines. We can remember our path to adulthood and how many setbacks and missteps we took along the way. And we can remind ourselves that *thriving in life* is a journey... not a single destination. It's a journey marked by self-discovery and growth. It involves embracing the uncertainty and occasional instability of the transition to adulthood. It's okay for our young adults to prioritize self-development, self-care, and self-reflection as they navigate the challenges of their identity formation and life path. And, even in their most confident moments, they often struggle with feelings of being "in-between," not quite adolescents but also not fully established adults. This transitional feeling is an essential part of their evolution. Despite the twists and turns, let's encourage their sense of hope and possibility because it's fuel to their resilience, and together, we can believe that their unique journey can lead to a future filled with accomplishment and purpose. Through a *redemptive connection* to meaningful relationships in life, our young adults can navigate their winding roads toward a thriving and flourishing life.

"Do not fear, for I have redeemed you;
I have summoned you by name; you are mine."
Isaiah 43:1

CHAPTER SEVEN

BELONGING

"We all are born into the world looking for someone looking for us, and we remain in this mode of searching for the rest of our lives." Dr. Curt Thompson, *The Soul of Shame*. Dr. Thompson is one of my favorite authors and a wonderful human being. I've loved the time I've spent with him personally, the opportunities I've had to hear him teach and share, and I have read every one of his books. His work on shame, belonging, community, and how our minds and souls are wired in trauma and rewired in healing have been transformative for me. Yet in all the books, talks, and conversations, the one phrase that keeps returning to me (I can close my eyes and visualize him saying it) is this quote about our search for someone looking for us. The first time I read it, I knew its truth deep in my soul. I didn't just read it. I felt it. Have you ever had a phrase viscerally reverberate through your body? This was it for me. My soul knew deeply that this was not just the story of the lives of the girls we have brought into our home or the story of the youth we serve; this was my story and my search. Growing up in a house that was marked with violence and quick mood swings due to drugs, alcohol, or yet another fight between my parents made me extremely hypervigilant about body language and facial expressions because knowing how to read them gave me all the clues that I needed to get my brothers and myself "out of dodge" to the safety of the backyard or woods behind our house. I learned to read my parents' eyes to know whether they were mad, sad, or glad. The look on their faces would tell me whether it would be a typical day with the family or our world would erupt into yelling, screaming, hitting, and cursing. The times when I could look into their eyes and see them seeing me were some of the moments that I treasured most, and still do. When I saw in their eyes that they saw my brothers and me and were present with us, caring for and concerned for our wellbeing, I felt belonging at its purest. The other times, the times when their emotions, addictions, and traumas clouded their eyes and swept them up in a vortex of dysfunction brought with it experiences of disconnection, fear, and pain—emotionally and physically—for my brothers and me. So, when I read those words by Dr. Thompson, I experienced a visceral reminder of what it means to be in a room with someone you deeply love whose eyes are searching for you as you're searching for them. And, what it feels like to be in a room with someone you deeply love whose eyes are clouded with anger, addiction, mental health issues, and more, who, rather than looking for you, are looking through you, or worse. To this day, I "feel" the looks in the eyes of others.

I sense when someone is upset or off-kilter, and it's difficult for me to stay engaged because everything in me wants to revert to the little girl protecting her little brothers and run. There's no question that I belonged to my parents when they saw me, and when they didn't, I was still their daughter. But the belonging that Dr. Thompson is writing about, the one we're all searching for, is more profound than what's on your birth certificate. The belonging we're all searching for is one in which we feel continually safe, accepted for our authentic selves, loved, and seen. Happily, I'll say that I did find that sense of belonging with my dad as I became an adult, and our relationship was restored and repaired. Yet, even as an adult with grown children, I still find myself searching in the eyes of those I love to be seen and known. We all do.

What is Belonging?

I love this definition of belonging given by Brené Brown in her book *Daring Greatly*, "Belonging is the innate human desire to be part of something larger than us. Because this yearning is so primal, we often try to acquire it by fitting in and seeking approval, which are hollow substitutes for belonging and often barriers to it. Because true belonging only happens when we present our authentic, imperfect selves to the world, so our sense of belonging can never be greater than our self-acceptance." Too often, especially as parents, we think belonging means "fitting in." We communicate that even if we don't believe that we are. We think that if our child rejects our religious beliefs or acts out in ways that aren't what we feel are appropriate or doesn't see eye to eye with us on some or most of our values, it means that we have to create hard lines and absolutes. We often phrase it as "boundaries," which can sound good and healthy and can be, but it can also be disconnecting and disruptive to true relational belonging. And let's be real… sometimes our "boundaries" are our way of operating in our authority and staying in the "control" quadrant because to do otherwise feels like more risk and vulnerability than we can muster. I get it; I've been there. It's so easy for us to carry the burden of our children's futures on our shoulders. Yet, our job is to hold onto the axis of belonging: "I love you," "I see you," and "I'm here for you always," while letting them walk their winding road toward their future. But real belonging is challenging work.

Make no mistake, my girls know exactly where I am in my faith, beliefs, and values. I communicate it clearly and openly. They also know the respectful behavioral expectations their dad and I hold them to when under our roof. It is, after all, our house. So, it's our rules. Yet, they also know I don't expect or demand that they come into complete alignment with me so that I can love them and show them they belong in my heart and our family. This is where flourishing and belonging come together. I can have my boundaries, beliefs, and values without hiding them from them or holding them back. They can have theirs without shame or hiding from or holding back from me. We can love each other, and that's okay. What that means for me is that I can have the authority of being able to say and stand on my values and beliefs while also exercising vulnerability in recognizing that it's not my role to force them to change who they feel they are in their authentic selves. In this place of both authority & vulnerability, our relationship can flourish, and they can, hopefully, experience true belonging as a part of our family. Both true belonging and flourishing leave space and time for *redemptive* work to be done in all our lives as we grow, change, adapt, reform, and realign our lives, beliefs, values, and priorities.

Before we move on from defining belonging, I want to issue you a challenge. I want you to think about the following statement: There's a big difference between allowing someone to *belong in your home* and allowing them to *belong in your heart*. I invite you to pause for a moment and consider how you feel about that statement in your journey. I'll share with you what this means to me personally. It means I can (and should) guard my heart daily from many things in this world—wars, rumors of wars, negative political discourse, lousy doctrine, news, shame, blame, etc. I should never guard my heart against the world that God has called me to impact. And the world He's called me to impact begins and ends in my home with my family on this road to redemption and restoration that we are all walking together. If I'm not careful, I can put up emotional walls that protect my heart from risk and keep my most important relationships on the surface. It's an area of my life and parenting that I must reflect on and evaluate regularly.

True belonging, the *I am yours and you are mine* kind of belonging is a redemptive love. Redemptive love is a possessive love. Not in an "I own you" sense but in a profoundly loving way, an "I am with you and for you" sense. And here's the most challenging part: **no matter what**. It's why I started this chapter with the scripture from Isaiah 43:1, "Do not fear, for I have redeemed you; I have summoned you by name; you are mine." That is redemptive love. As a Christian, my only response to the world around me is this: love has been shown to me, sacrifice has been made for me, and now I must go and do the same. When my kids reject me, I will pursue them. When my kids lash out, I will love them. When my kids turn away. I will stay. When my kids fight *with* me, I will fight *for* them.

How to Cultivate Belonging

Years ago, I came across a simple illustration of a "Belonging Cycle," which I have kept in my files and added to training throughout the years. In writing this book, I tried to find the original source but didn't have much luck. I will share it here because it helped me as I worked to create both a sense of belonging in our girls at home and a model by which we would train our Mentoring Families through Connections Homes. This Belonging Cycle (and there are many if you do a quick Google search) is designed as a virtuous cycle in which each part builds on and assists the other parts in a continuous growth cycle. Life and relationships are indeed like that. We move through year after year, season after season, growing, stretching, fracturing, repairing, and on and on across a lifetime to create a deep and meaningful life—a flourishing life.

There are four parts to this Belonging Cycle: Sense of Place (grounding), Sense of Identity (ego/worth), Sense of Values (soul/heart), and Sense of Responsibility (action). Along my journey as a mom and organizational leader, I've found ways to build practices and actions that align with these simple but critical aspects of belonging.

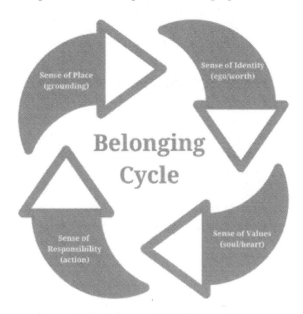

Figure 12 The Belonging Cycle Illustrated

Sense of Place[17] *(grounding)* – this one seems the simplest…it's what we call "home," right? Yes and no. It's not a single place. It can be, but most of the time it's not. My husband and I were both born and raised in Kentucky (Big Blue Nation!) Nebo for him and Nortonville for me. Together, we've lived in Madisonville, KY (the 'big city' nearest our hometowns), Clarksville, TN; Nashville, TN; Cary, NC; Lawrenceville, GA; Loganville, Georgia; and Conyers, GA. We consider Kentucky our "home," but we also feel at home in all the other places we've lived. Yet, at the same time, we have deeper attachments to and in some places over others. Jennifer E. Cross, in her paper, "What is Sense of Place?" describes six ways in which we relate to "place," and I've found them to help frame questions for myself and my girls on what the feeling "at home"—the sense of place—aspect of belonging means.

- **Biographical (historical & familial) – "What do you think of when you think of home?"** For me, the answer is, without a doubt, Kentucky. For each of my girls, that answer might differ depending on how much of their childhood was spent in any place. We must recognize this and celebrate what they think of when they think of "home." It's a core part of who they are, regardless of how many hurtful things may have happened there.

- **Spiritual (emotional, intangible) – "Tell me somewhere you feel at peace?"** Right now, that answer is at my desk as I look over the lake on our property. This brings me peace and comfort. That answer could also be *the mountains, the ocean, etc.* For my girls, it's my consistent prayer that my home is a place where they can feel at peace, especially now that they are adults with their own places. I work hard (meaning I'm highly intentional and put effort into it) to bring joy to them through holiday celebrations and fill them with comfort when they are with us here because I want to be a peaceful landing place for them. I also ensure they see themselves in my most sacred spaces through pictures on the wall, memories, gifts they've given us on display, and more. Even though, for most of our kids who come into our lives from hard places, we may never be considered their biographical "home," we can and should become a place where they feel a deep emotional connection. It's the big and small things along the way that help to

---

[17] Jennifer E. Cross, "What is Sense of Place?" (Paper presented at the 12th Headwaters Conference, Western State College, November 2-4, 2001).

encourage and solidify this aspect of belonging: making them a part of the traditions you have as a family (Christmas, Easter, Thanksgiving, July 4th, an annual festival that you "always" attend, Super Bowl Sunday, Friday Game night, Taco Tuesday, etc..), placing their pictures on the wall or your desk alongside other family photos, celebrating their birthdays, taking a vacation together or sharing a significant experience (running a marathon, going sky diving, getting your nails done, taking a painting class, etc.).

- **Ideological (moral, ethical) – "Tell me somewhere/someone you share deep values with?"** When I think of this question, I think of my faith community, my closest family members and friends, important organizations like the CAFO and Praxis communities that I'm privileged to be a part of, and the team that surrounds me at Connections Homes. People more than places; people who love what I love, share common values, and share my faith. For you, it might be a book club, a walking group, a game/card-playing group, or another. These are people and places that we don't have to pretend to be around; we can just *be*. Understanding this aspect of belonging in ourselves and our kids allows us to know one another more deeply, celebrate our differences, and acknowledge that it's okay to have other "villages" in our individual lives who meet this sense of place for us.

- **Narrative (mythical) – "Tell me your story. Do you have a sense of place in this world?"** This is the story we tell ourselves about "home" and "belonging." This can be based on truth, it can be based on longing/hope, and it can be based on our childlike views/memories. My aunt and uncle live in the house that belonged to my grandparents when I was growing up. My grandparents' house was an anchor in my childhood, and I remember the HUGE concrete back patio, the massive kitchen WITH AN ISLAND you could walk around, and the TWO living rooms—one for watching TV and the other for "sitting"—it was the nicest house I knew, and I loved it. As an adult, I still visit that house to see my aunt and uncle, and… guess what…it's just a house. Just an average house. I've lived in and owned bigger and smaller ones along my journey. Yet a part of my brain and heart will always see it as the biggest and best house ever because that's a defining narrative of my childhood. For many of us, it's been a struggle to watch our kids "romanticize" brutal and tragic parts of their birth and early life stories, to listen as they share beautiful memories of a childhood that we know was marked by extreme abuse or neglect, and to find ways to celebrate their early life without feeling like we're giving the trauma and tragedy a free pass. Yet, like my memories of my grandmother's *massive* house, our kids were kids, and it was home. We can't and shouldn't take that away. If later in life, as adults, they can see the truth and reflect on it, that's great. But it's their memory to sort out, not ours to argue with.

- **Cognitive (based on choice) – "Did you make the choice to be 'here'? | Dependent (lack of choice) – "Was the choice made to be 'here' by someone else?"** I put these last two together because this is the saddest one for most of the young people we work with and our daughters. Their childhoods have been distinctively marked by other people making choices on their behalf that impacted their lives in profoundly negative ways: addiction choices, anger choices, neglectful choices, abandonment choices, case managers choosing where they lived and who became their 'family,' families choosing to 'send them back,' and much more. This is why we designed a "Choice-Based Matching Model" in our work at Connections Homes. After watching so many of our daughters struggle with their lack of choice in becoming a part of our family, it became a strong conviction that every young person we work with deserves the dignity of a voice and a choice in their relationships. As we've walked alongside our girls into adulthood, nearly all of them have pulled away to some degree to find themselves, and we've tried to give them that freedom so that "coming back" into a relationship is their *choice*. It's hard because we've never stopped loving them and won't, but it's also necessary to allow them to define their own life and choose whether we should be part of it or not.

Sense of Identity (ego/worth) – We all gain our sense of identity over time. We evolve, especially as young adults. During this period of their life, it is natural to explore different aspects of identity and seek out belonging in various social or cultural groups. Finding a sense of identity and belonging is a crucial development task and is essential to the development of a healthy ego and sense of self-worth in several ways:

- **Validation & Acceptance:** Belonging to a supportive social group or community validates and accepts a young person's identity and worth. When others in the group affirm and appreciate who you are, it reinforces a positive self-image and contributes to a healthy ego. This validation communicates to our kids that they matter and that we value them for who they are.

- **Social Comparison:** Belonging to a group allows for social comparison, a natural process where individuals assess themselves in relation to others. Positive comparisons can boost self-esteem and ego development. When our young people perceive that they are valued members of a group and that they measure up compared to their peers, it bolsters self-worth. I sometimes call this "normalizing." This means that helping our young people see that others who've experienced their same life experiences are succeeding, making sense of their stories, and finding value in redemptive paths helps them to feel "normal" and to begin putting the pieces of themselves together (that they sometimes image irreparably damaged) into a purposeful identity with future hopes.

- **Support and Encouragement:** Belonging to a group or community typically comes with social support and encouragement. When our young people face challenges or setbacks, knowing they have a support system can enhance their self-confidence and self-worth. Encouragement and assistance from others can foster resilience and a positive self-concept.

- **Positive Feedback Loop:** Feeling a sense of belonging tends to boost self-esteem and self-worth, which, in turn, reinforces the feeling of belonging. This cycle of feeling like they belong as their authentic selves naturally leads to feelings of self-esteem and positive self-worth. This cycle promotes a strong sense of identity and healthy ego as it repeats itself over and over across time and over years of healthy relationships.

- **Psychological Safety:** Belonging to a safe, supportive, and committed community creates a psychologically safe environment where young people can feel comfortable being themselves and expressing their thoughts and feelings. This safety fosters self-acceptance and self-worth. It's an exercise in patience and humility for us as parents and mentors to allow our young people to be their authentic selves, especially when we disagree with parts of their identities that they are still working through. This could be across various spectrums: gender/sexuality (which automatically comes to mind when you say 'identity' these days) is just one aspect of one's identity.

Other elements could include political, moral, religious, geopolitical, and more ideologies. It's often difficult to watch our young people adopt viewpoints opposing ours, but for us, it's also proven to be some of the most engaging moments around the dinner table. Our rule is to say whatever needs to be said but keep it respectful, honor other viewpoints, and be civil. The world our kids are growing up in vastly differs from the one most of us grew up in, where our entire community shared similar viewpoints and ideologies. Those differences can be fought against or used to create deeper trust and bonds. We've chosen the latter in our family, or at least tried to as much as possible. As a society, we've lost the art of healthy debate and constructive "town halls." Our household has a ton of strong personalities, and it can be pretty fun to spar over differing strong opinions verbally. However, I also know that on a much deeper level, it helps to create a sense of safety for our girls from broken life roads to see that they have the freedom to break away from our tetherball pole and find themselves, even if we don't always agree with where they land. It's also a healthy reminder that it's their life to live, not ours.

- **Purpose and Contribution:** Healthy belonging also includes roles and responsibilities within the group. Whether it's "all hands on deck" to clean up after a big family meal or letting our young people teach us a skill that they have, it's healthy to be an active participant in the family dynamic. This type of participation in having "a role" provides a sense of purpose and creates opportunities for our young people to make meaningful contributions. Recognizing that you can positively impact a group creates and reinforces a sense of self-worth.

- **Respect and Dignity:** From within a group where a young person is experiencing true belonging, they are also more likely to be treated with respect and dignity. This respectful treatment communicates that they deserve to be treated well and adds to their self-worth.

- **Sense of Values (soul/heart):** Fostering a shared sense of values is integral to nurturing belonging in your relationship with your young person. It creates cohesion, shared purpose, and understanding. Finding shared values comes down to many things we've already discussed: open communication, shared experiences, and values exploration. Yet, it is also distinct in the Belonging Cycle because it requires us to help our young person truly explore knowing who they are by understanding their values and guiding principles for life. Along the way, we will find that we share many of these values and some that we don't. It's okay. For our young people to honestly know themselves, they need to figure out what they value and how they want to take their place in this world according to their values. Here's a few simple steps to help them along the way:

- **What are my core beliefs about how I want to live my life?** What are the words that come to mind? Examples might be *humble, open to others, curious, and embracing wisdom.* Hundreds of other words and values could be on this list. The intention is to find the four or five that truly embody who your young adult wants to be in the world.

- **How do I recognize when I'm living according to my values (what am I experiencing)?** I'll use a couple of examples from our list: **humble-** thinking about others more than myself, **open to others-** inclusiveness and broader network, **curious-** seeking understanding & asking more questions, **embracing wisdom-** listening to a broad range of opinions and experiences from diverse ages, cultures, or viewpoints.

- **What is the outcome of living out my values?**
  - **humble-** thinking about others more than myself; deep relationships & a life of service to others
  - **open to others-** inclusiveness & broader network; more expansive worldview, more open doors, large friends group
  - **curious-** seeking understanding and asking more questions; ability to shift perspectives, people trust me, etc.
  - **embracing wisdom-** listening to a broad range of opinions and experiences from a diversity of ages, cultures, or viewpoints; making better decisions and experiencing a flourishing life.

The fourth part of the Belonging Cycle, *A Sense of Responsibility (action)*, plays right into our next chapter on self-efficacy, so I've moved it there. As you can see, a concept as simple as "belonging" is complex and multi-faceted. It can take years to achieve, and that is why lifelong relationships are so critically important for young adults with traumatic backgrounds. It isn't easy to *thrive* if your whole existence is marked by temporary relationships that last a time, break, and never repair. Whether it's the youth's or the other person's fault, a series of non-committed relationships hinder growth and set our young people up for failure rather than flourishing.

The most important aspect of our ability to truly stick it out in achieving lifelong, healthy belonging for our young person is our ability to understand the complexities of their lives and create firm, healthy boundaries that allow us to show up consistently while also creating space for them to succeed or fail, fly or falter, come and go, and ultimately make life worth living for themselves with us as their biggest cheerleaders every step of the way.

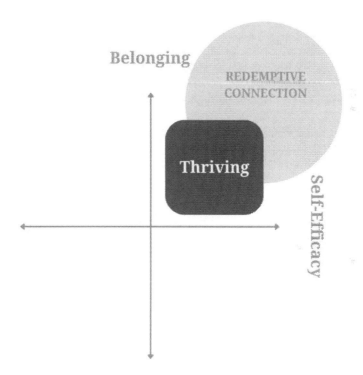

Figure 13 Thriving as illustrated in the Redemptive Connection Framework matrix.

"Have I not commanded you? Be strong and courageous. Do not be afraid; do not be discouraged, for the Lord your God will be with you wherever you go."
Joshua 1:9

CHAPTER EIGHT

SELF-EFFICACY

"You need to accept personal responsibility."
"You need to take ownership of your actions and their consequences."
"You need to set a goal and stick with it."
"The problem is that you quit halfway through."
"You can't just numb all of your problems and hide behind gaming."
"I don't know why you don't see your own worth."
"Can you just focus and stick with one thing at a time?"
"It's just one failure. Get up and try again!"

All these thoughts have been in my head at one point or another and many times came out of my mouth. As I've walked with my girls with histories of trauma and with hundreds of youths through Connections Homes, I've often been quite frustrated with their seemingly lazy and uncaring attitudes and actions toward what I would consider simple and expected young adult responsibilities, tasks, skills, and disciplines. The problem is that all too often, we not only have those thoughts but also rehearse them and, as a result, act poorly. Our authority and vulnerability can be tested during these moments. So, for a moment, before we dive into what self-efficacy looks like for our young people, we're going to make our way back to the Authority / Vulnerability 2x2 to take a look at how we would feel and act as a result of our young person's low self-efficacy and how we may be (without realizing it) contributors to it. When I feel like my young person is just not hitting the mark, I can easily take one of the three paths away from flourishing in the Authority/Vulnerability 2x2: control, withdrawal, or suffering. We'll start with *control:*

Authority

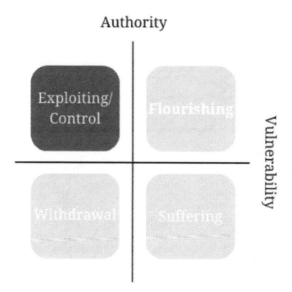

Figure 14 Exploiting/Control in the Authority/Vulnerability matrix from Andy Crouch's book, Strong & Weak.

In *control,* I choose not to take meaningful risks. Instead, I try to take charge of or fix the situation by issuing edicts, restricting privileges, or "helpful" lecturing (I have multiple gold medals in this parental sport). It's tough to watch someone you love flounder. You desperately want to help... to do it for them... to *make* them do it... or to *teach* them what they *should* be doing. However, when we operate from the *control* quadrant, we fail to build healthy self-efficacy in our young person by not letting them figure it out and find their path to success. Doing it for them reinforces an unhealthy self-efficacy belief that they can't do it alone. Trying to make them do it can often become a battle of wills, and very little stands its ground better than insecurity. So, it becomes a losing battle—for both of us. Lecturing to *teach* them what they *should* be doing also reinforces an unhealthy self-efficacy by using a negative/failure moment to unintentionally drive home the idea that *they can't/aren't* doing the right things. One of the most poignant learning moments in my parenting of teens into adulthood came when one of my daughters was around 16/17. I was on my way toward another gold medal-winning lecture series about what she should be doing when she quietly said, "Mom, when you tell me multiple ways how I should solve my problem, it makes me feel like you don't believe I can figure it out on my own." Ouch. She was right, and it was one of the moments that pushed me to begin to use more curiosity and G.R.A.C.E. Responses as an approach to "helping" my girls navigate their hurdles and roadblocks in life. I also learned a compelling question to ask in these situations that allowed me to share power and give up control, *"Would you like me to give you some ideas on how to handle this, or do you want me just to listen?"* But what if instead of controlling, we feel like they never listen, are always doing things to spite us, and taking advantage of us? What if we're in the *suffering* quadrant?

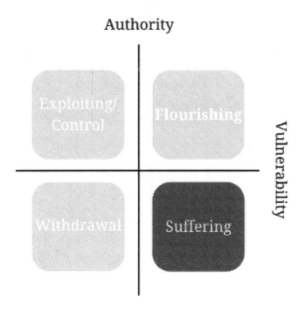

Figure 15 Suffering in the Authority/Vulnerability matrix from Andy Crouch's book, Strong & Weak.

In *suffering*, I would react out of helplessness either as a martyr or a victim by choosing not to take meaningful action through overcompensating for the young person at my own expense or by allowing the young person's low self-efficacy to erase my boundaries and steal my time in unhealthy ways. It would be easy to confuse *suffering* as a martyr with *control* because, in many cases, it manifests very similarly—doing *for* the young person instead of allowing them to do it for themselves. The difference is in the motive for doing it. In a control example, we do it because we want it done in a way that fits our timelines or expectations. In a suffering example, we do so because we want to be seen as good parents suffering and sacrificing to gain the admiration of our young person or others. Doing *for* the child instead of allowing them to accomplish, fail, try, or plan independently, whether from a place of control or suffering, has the same outcome: low self-efficacy for the young person. Allowing the young person's low self-efficacy to blur or erase our boundaries and steal our time in unhealthy ways results in a young person who has a false sense of control over their parent while also remaining stunted in their development of self-efficacy and capacity to take meaningful actions in their own life. There was a time in my parenting journey when I had six girls all in the home, five with trauma histories. Evenings had become a three-ring circus of begging for chores to get done, refereeing arguments, advising on school issues, helping with homework, and fielding an endless barrage of 'Can I please...', among other things. I was exhausted, my marriage was suffering, my work was suffering, and I had zero time for myself. All because of those meddling kids (imagine my best Scooby Doo voice) and their needs, wants, and whims. It was entirely their fault. Can you hear it? I was *suffering* as both a martyr and a victim. I wanted to be a good parent and keep the peace in my home, so it was easier to comply with every whim or need (both real and perceived). I also felt overwhelmed, taken advantage of, and unseen. Didn't they understand that I was laying my life down for theirs? Why didn't they care about my feelings? Why didn't they realize that I needed a break sometimes, too? Why are they making me stay up every night until nearly midnight when they know I have work to do? I felt like a victim.

One day, a good friend said, "Where are your boundaries?" I incredulously responded, "How can I possibly set boundaries for myself?" She just replied, "How can you not? Are you doing your girls a service or disservice by not allowing them to figure some stuff out on their own or with one another instead of by you?" Quietly in my Spirit, I thought, "Do they need me to show up the way I do, or does my pride need it?" That's the day I began to work with a personal trainer and took up running. I set a boundary for my well-being and started to put some structure in our home. Many of the self-efficacy tools that I will share in this chapter were born out of that season in my life where I figured out that the risks weren't all mine to take and that I had to stop my *suffering* and take some meaningful action to teach my girls to use their resources (I'm one of many resources but not the only one), that their life and success was their circus and their monkeys. What if, instead, I had decided to *withdraw?*

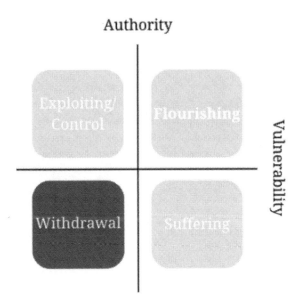

Figure 16 Withdrawal in the Authority/Vulnerability matrix from Andy Crouch's book,
Strong & Weak.

In *withdrawal,* I would choose not to engage in risk or action by becoming distant or indifferent from my young person's needs or breaking the relationship altogether. There's no question that it's draining and completely de-motivating as a parent or mentor to work with a young person who is stuck and keeps going around the same mountains repeatedly—never quite "becoming responsible for themselves." Being in this place makes us feel powerless or ineffective, and no one likes to feel that way. Most of the time, we arrive at *withdrawal* after exhausting all that we know to do (our Authority) and feeling taken advantage of over and over (our Vulnerability). Not only does *withdrawal* lead us away from a *flourishing* life and relationship with our young person, but it also hinders healthy self-efficacy and renders *Redemptive Connection* impossible. When we arrive at this place, it's helpful to go back to Chapter 5 and remind ourselves of the G.R.A.C.E. Response—especially in reminding ourselves that we can only control ourselves. We cannot control our young people. In taking a step back to suspend judgment and take a curious approach, we should look for the why behind the what of the behaviors that are exhausting us and explore some what-if scenarios for solutions. We will apply many of these tools in this chapter and the ones that follow as we begin to move with our young people around their quadrants on their path to *thriving*.

Our Perceptions of Self-Efficacy

As with many of the tools I'm sharing in this book, I also learned this one first-hand. One of our girls moved in with us at 18 after an extended time of couch-hopping and ultimately becoming extremely suicidal. After offering to let her move in and become a part of our family, she experienced a long season of what I deemed to be laziness and extreme disconnectedness. She slept most of her days away. There were times that Steve and I wondered if she might still be sleeping in her bedroom at 40! We often talked about the issue and how we could help her get up and move forward. She only got up and engaged in the world to go out with her friends and often stayed out terribly late. We experienced all the frustrations you can imagine, even though we loved her immensely. We worried that she would stay in her room away from family dinners and interactions because she didn't like us. Our other girls compared our 'hands-off' approach with her to the rules and responsibilities we had for them, and it seemed unfair, and in many ways, it was, but we were seriously at a loss. We worried that sleeping all the time was a sign of physical illness. As time passed and I had conversations with her about what she was experiencing, I realized that her physical body was responding to the *safety* she had in our home. She had spent 18 years fearing for her life many days and never feeling safe. Now that she did, her body was forced to sleep. She was healing. And, as simple as typing it now sounds, it wasn't simple to experience it. She slept for the better part of three months!

If you had asked us during those three months what her self-efficacy was, we would have absolutely said "low." We would have been wrong. After about three months of sleep, she got up, went to work one day, and has worked 60+ hours a week ever since. She is the hardest worker and most confident, self-made young lady I've ever seen. She's worked her way up to management in several companies and is a stellar employee, daughter, wife, and woman. Yet, for those three months, we could have easily made judgments (and did) that were utterly wrong, and had we not been trauma-informed at that point, we might have hindered her healing through our rules and expectations, and we would have certainly hindered our relationship.

I share that story as a reminder that other things can happen in our young person's life, body, and emotions that can appear as low self-efficacy. It's always a good approach to allow some time to pass, to have open dialogue, and to allow healing to occur—even if it sometimes feels like it's taking too long. Years ago, when our biological daughter was potty training, and I was stressing over whether she was ever going to get it or not, a wise older mom said to me, "I've never really seen a healthy five-year-old in diapers. All kids get it eventually, so don't be stressed. It will click when it clicks for her." She was right. I needed to seriously relax, for both of our sakes. The same is true with our young people who've experienced trauma. Almost all young people will eventually thrive and create a life for themselves from a loving, nurturing, safe, and stable support system. It just takes longer for some than others. It's okay.

What is Self-Efficacy?

It's worth revisiting our definition from Chapter 2: Self-Efficacy is an individual's belief in their capacity to act in the ways necessary to reach specific goals[18]. In other words, they need to believe in their ability to meaningfully act in ways that can move them toward accomplishing their goals, doing whatever they set their mind to and effort toward. This is an essential trait for all of us, especially for young people transitioning to adulthood who need to establish a healthy, autonomous life. These young adults have had a disrupted educational history, inconsistent and unhealthy social connections, and little to no support and guidance that other young people have from their families.

Believing in their ability to meaningfully act to build the life they dream of is foundational to developing all the other characteristics necessary to achieve Andy Crouch's definition of *authority—the capacity for meaningful action.*

- When youth have a strong sense of self-efficacy, they are more likely to take the initiative and make healthy decisions rather than rely on others to think for them. This, in turn, helps them develop a sense of agency, or the ability to act independently and make choices that affect their lives.

- When youth have a strong sense of self-efficacy, they feel more confident in their abilities and are more likely to value and respect themselves. This sense of self-worth helps them feel more capable of positively contributing to the community and the world around them.

- When youth have a strong sense of self-efficacy, they may be more likely to take responsibility for their own decisions and actions and understand their impact on others—good and bad. This sense of personal responsibility helps them to develop accountability and commitment to living up to their

---

18 Bandura, A. (1977). *Self-Efficacy: Toward a unifying theory of behavioral change.* Psychological Review, 84(2), 191-215

responsibilities and owning their actions and the consequences that result from them.

To that definition, let's now add what it looks like when a youth has low self-efficacy:

- Youth with low or weak self-efficacy are more likely to avoid challenging tasks because the fear of failure is overwhelming, and they don't believe they can do it. So, it's easier not to try at all because they don't have to experience the negative feelings accompanying failure.

- Youth with low or weak self-efficacy are likelier to believe that difficult tasks and situations are beyond their control. They stay focused on what they can't do instead of what they can or could learn to do.

- Youth with low or weak self-efficacy are more likely to view their failings as a reflection of their inability rather than as a learning experience that will help them in the future. They are also much more likely to give up early to avoid adverse outcomes instead of overcoming the challenges.

- Youth with low or weak self-efficacy are more likely to start something but give up when it feels overwhelming because they've lost confidence in their abilities to overcome the obstacles.

It is widely accepted that four sources empower the development of self-efficacy[19].

(1) Mastery Experiences (They must do it themselves)

Real self-efficacy requires us to fail and try again until we succeed. Even so, it's hard to feel unsure and clumsy when starting something new until we get the hang of it and feel comfortable. One of my favorite books is *Failing Forward* by John Maxwell. It's a book I paid my girls to read because its lesson is so profound. Every failure is a learning opportunity and ability to learn something new about us and our environment and develop a new skill. Actual skill and resilience don't come easy, and when we experience easy successes, we can become too quickly disappointed and thrown off by failure. On the other hand, when we experience success obtained the hard way, it builds self-efficacy in a way that teaches us that success is most often achieved through

---

[19] *A large portion of this chapter is a result of this research. I encourage the reader to dive deep into this Self-Efficacy tool if you'd like to know more.* Bandura, A. (1994). Self-efficacy. In V. S. Ramachaudran (Ed.), *Encyclopedia of human behavior* (Vol. 4, pp. 71 – 81). New York: Academic Press. (Reprinted in H. Friedman [Ed.], *Encyclopedia of mental health.* San Diego: Academic Press, 1998)

sustained effort. Sticking to things when they are hard strengthens us and develops an internal belief in our ability to overcome obstacles and do hard things. Easy success is why many successful high school students fail their first year of college. College is more challenging not just because the curriculum is more complex (it is) but also because it requires self-motivation, self-discipline, and time management that many of our young people haven't developed yet. When mom and dad aren't around to wake you up, take you to school, remind you of your assignments, or keep tabs on your grades, it's easy to sleep in and expect success to come the way it always has. This is why, as mentors and parents, we can't stand in the way of letting our young people do and experience hard things while being their biggest cheerleaders, even in failure, so they get back up and keep moving.

(2) **Social Modeling (They can learn from our failures, too)**
Seeing others succeed through sustained effort and bouncing back from failure helps to raise a young person's belief that they can do the same. This is why our vulnerability in sharing not just our successes but also our failures is so critical. For far too long, I felt I had to share my accomplishments only with our girls. It was only after one of my girls commented that they would never be as "perfect" or "successful" as me because it's "just not as easy" for them that I realized I was sending the wrong message. What might look easy on the surface has been anything but easy. I just have a "suck it up and move on with it" attitude (born out of my trauma responses) that makes it look like nothing ever bothers me or is challenging. To this day, I'm still consciously working on being more transparent and vulnerable with myself and my girls about how hard life is sometimes.

(3) **Social Persuasion (We must validate what they can become)**
It's incredible how good it feels to have someone tell you they believe in you—especially when you struggle to believe in yourself. Our young people possess capabilities they are unaware of because they may never have been allowed to build them. And if they know that we believe in them, it gives them a bit of borrowed confidence to dig deep and work toward mastery and sustained achievement. In an earlier chapter, I shared the story of our daughter who struggled with becoming overwhelmed with projects and tasks. I still remember one of our first conversations about breaking down the task into smaller pieces, I asked her, "How do you eat an elephant?" She looked at me like I had suddenly lost all my marbles and said, "Um… I have no clue. Why would you eat an elephant?"

I said, "The only way to eat something that large would be to start with one bite at a time. Eating an elephant is like doing this project. You're not going to do it all at once, but if you start with the first thing and get that done, it's easier to move on to the next. After a while, you'll have done it." To this day, when she's overwhelmed with something, she says, "I know. I know. One bite at a time." It was an effective way for us to say that we believed in her while at the same time helping her break the accomplishment down into smaller bite-sized pieces so that she could be successful.

(4) Mental State (How they perceive setbacks & pain matters)

For me, working with a trainer and taking up running was an excellent outlet, but I had never been an athlete and didn't think I would be a runner. Even so, I set a goal to run a half marathon and began a diligent training regimen. It was hard. Going from never even walking consistently to running for hours at a time was a growing experience. I was sore. I was tired. It wasn't easy to stay motivated. I would pass my house several times to get my miles in during my runs. It was so tempting to stop and go in to sit down. In running circles, there is something called "the wall." It's the moment that you feel like you can't go on—every ache is detrimental, every staggered breath might be your last, your lungs are burning, and your heart can't pump any harder. The thing is, none of those physical things are going to be what takes you out of the race; your mental attitude about those things is what does it. You're already out of the race when you begin entertaining "I can't finish" thoughts.

In the same way, a young person's mood, state of mind, and stress reactions can determine their success or failure. If they perceive pain as an indicator of failure, they are more likely to give up, whereas if they perceive pain as a part of the process, they can build the resilience to keep going because they know they can eventually do it. And I did end up completing several half marathons. I still hold onto those precious metals to this day!

How Self-Efficacy Impacts Outcomes

Whether we have parented our young person for a while (birth or otherwise) or stepped into our young person's life as a mentor, we have high hopes and desires that our impact and influence will produce good outcomes. There is no question that the sense of belonging that we can provide will go a long way in helping our young people feel safe and seen. However, belonging alone cannot achieve the outcomes we deeply desire for our young people. We must also understand how *self-efficacy* impacts their ability to accomplish the *thriving* life we want. Here are a few aspects of functioning that are affected by *self-efficacy* that, when paired with *belonging,* can indeed lead a young person into a *thriving* life:

Cognitive Processes (How they think)

Many of our purposeful human behavior is driven by forethought based on our emotions, which reflect our embodied goals. Our self-appraisals of our capabilities highly influence personal goal setting *(... as a man thinketh in his heart, so is he... Prov. 23:7)*. Most courses of action are first organized in our thoughts. We don't just experience success or failure without imagining success or failure. Anticipatory scenarios are something that we all experience. We construct them, and we rehearse them. It's no different for our young people. Those with a high sense of self-efficacy will visualize success scenarios. Those with low self-efficacy will visualize failure scenarios and rehearse how things can go wrong. It is tough to achieve much while fighting self-doubt. Thought is one of the primary ways we predict and learn to control events in our lives. Our thoughts draw from our experiences, so if you've never experienced success or positive thought, what imagination do you have to draw on? Mastery Experiences are critically important because it's only through the experience of success that you can build future thought processes that lead you to more success or resilience.

Motivational Processes (How they self-regulate)

"She's just not motivated to get a job." "He's just not motivated to do well in school." "I can't seem to motivate them to do anything to move their lives forward."

As parents and mentors, we've all said or felt a version of this occasionally. When working with young adults who've experienced trauma, it can seem like they are entirely unmotivated to move forward with their lives. They often seem stuck. And they are. Yet we tend to misunderstand that motivation isn't something you're just born with or not. It's something that is developed and is often impacted by our ability to self-regulate—a challenge that many youths with trauma histories experience. The same parts of the limbic system used in our more commonly known trauma responses—fight, flight, freeze, fawn—are also used in emotional processing and self-regulation. Almost all our motivation is generated in our limbic system through our cognitive processes that govern how we feel about ourselves, envision and experience others, and form beliefs (self-efficacy) about what we can or cannot do. It's through addressing these self-limiting thought patterns and beliefs that motivation is developed. A healthy self-belief will envision successful outcomes and generate helpful planning with forethought, resulting in actions designed to realize a future goal, accomplishment, or dream.

There are three forms of cognitive motivators and theories: attributions, expectancies, and goals. Self-efficacy beliefs operate in each of these three distinct ways:

- **Attributions:** "I attribute my success or failure to......" A high self-efficacy young person who believes in themselves and their ability to put in the effort to accomplish whatever is in front of them will attribute their failures to insufficient effort: *"I didn't study enough...," "I was late to work....," "I didn't put in the practice."* A low self-efficacy young person who struggles with their own belief in themselves will believe they can't and attribute their failures to low ability: *"I'm just not good at math...," "I just wasn't good at flipping burgers...," "I just can't play the sport, instrument, etc."*

- **Expectancies:** We do or don't do many things in life because of our belief about (expectancy) of the outcomes. Many youths choose not to enter our program because they expect that connection to another family will hurt them, just like every other connection that came before. Yet we've served hundreds of youths who enter our program because they believe and expect that not every family is the same as their past experiences, and it's possible to have a different outcome. I believed I could complete a half marathon, so I trained, practiced, and pushed through the pain because I had an expectancy of success. I've never entered a weightlifting competition because I've never liked lifting weights and, therefore, am aware that I lack the capability for it. Our belief in the outcome often drives our decision-making. The same is true of young adults. If they believe the outcome will fail, they will often self-sabotage, lack motivation, and avoid things.

Attribution and expectancy can be helped by helping our young people have a growth mindset[20] rather than a fixed one. A young person with a fixed mindset believes that their intelligence, talent, and qualities are fixed and they can't change anything. In contrast, young people with a growth

---

[20] "What is Growth Mindset?" renaissance.com *Renaissance EdWords*: https://www.renaissance.com/edword/growth-mindset/#:~:text=Growth%20mindset%3A%20%E2%80%9CIn%20a%20growth,Dweck%2C%202 015)

mindset believe their intelligence, talent, and qualities can grow and develop with hard work and dedication. A few examples of the difference in thinking are listed in the following table:

Fixed Mindset	Growth Mindset
I'm either good at it or I'm not.	I can learn anything I want to learn.
It's frustrating so I gave up.	It's frustrating but I kept going.
I hate failing it just proves I'm not good.	I don't like failing but I do know that I can learn from it.
Don't tell me how I can get better. It just makes me feel bad.	Please tell me how I can improve because I want to do better.

- **Goals:** Evidence shows that explicit, challenging goals enhance and sustain motivation. Being able to articulate and write out a goal accompanied by a strong belief that (even if it's in bite-sized pieces) they can accomplish it is a powerful motivator for young adults. It's also a practice many of our young adults are unfamiliar with. Goals give us incentives to align our behaviors, so even if it's something small like making a goal for the young person to initiate a call to you at a particular time each night, it's a helpful practice that can be celebrated and builds self-efficacy and motivation in the brain. Learning to goal set goals is like building a block tower—you start with one block and one layer at a time, and eventually, you make it to the top.

One of the easiest ways to help teach a young person goal setting is with S.M.A.R.T. Goals. It's a strategy used across business and education to help break down something big into achievable goals and objectives. S.M.A.R.T. is an acronym: *Specific*—a focused area for improvement. *Measurable*—a progress meter to measure your goal. *Achievable*—specifically, how/by whom it will be done. *Realistic*—the results that are possible with your current resources. *Time-bound*—a target date or time frame for achieving the results. Here are just a few examples (you can find lots of other examples and info about S.M.A.R.T. Goals by doing a quick Google search):

A S.M.A.R.T. Goal for Being More Active

- *Smart*: I will spend 30 minutes purposefully active time each day.
- *Measurable*: I will walk a minimum of 10 minutes each day, either indoors or out, and finish the 30 minutes by walking or by completing other activities such as gardening, stretching, or cleaning.
- *Attainable*: I will set a daily reminder on my phone.
- *Realistic*: Spending this time every day will help me break my cycle of sitting in front of my computer, TV, or phone without a break and benefit my health through movement.
- *Time-bound*: I will start tomorrow and practice this habit for three months before considering continuing or changing it.

A S.M.A.R.T. Goal for Improving My Relationships

- *Smart*: Every Monday, I will list two friends or family members to whom I need to reach out this week by phone, not by text, email, or online messenger.
- *Measurable*: I will write my list on my phone on Monday and set a reminder for each person on my phone when I plan to call them.
- *Attainable*: Reaching out to two people per week will keep me connected to eight different friends or family members each month.
- *Realistic*: Reaching out to have a conversation will improve my relationships by showing value to the people that I care about and taking the time to call them and check in on their lives.
- *Time-bound*: My goal is to have a personal conversation with at least eight people each month and keep track of it through my Monday planning times.

Tools for Aiding Self-Efficacy Development

Understanding the importance of self-efficacy is helpful for all of us, but specifically for our young adults whose rocky childhoods have robbed them of the opportunity to have adults speak into their lives consistently and candidly to build their belief in themselves and help them try again for success. As I type this, I'm reminded of a video I just saw on Instagram this morning from a sweet young dad, Zach, who I know in Nashville. This young man is married to one of our pseudo-daughters (a kiddo that I watched grow up and to this day treat as one of my own), and they have three beautiful daughters. Not long after their first daughter, Aurora, was born, Zach's precious mom, Stephanie, passed from a long battle with cancer. Zach posted a video on his Instagram page of him speaking an affirmation over his daughters, a saying that his mom spoke over him as a child. He attributes his mom's affirmations to helping him become the man he is today, which is undoubtedly true. He's fantastic—just like his mom. The affirmation went something like this as he asked his daughter to look him "in his eyeballs"—"There's no one in the world like you, you're one of one, there's not another you, no one can do what you can do in this world, whatever you decide you want to do in here (pointing to her heart) we can make happen, whatever you want to do, that means if you want to live in Hawaii, you can live in Hawaii, if you want to be a police officer you can be a police officer, you can do anything that you want to do in here (pointing at her heart) as long as you put in the hard work up here (pointing at her head) you'll be able to do it." As their dad, Zach is actively building their self-efficacy, and, just like his mom did for him, he will do a variation of the speech for these sweet girls many times throughout their lives. Guess what? They will grow up believing their dad and knowing they can do anything they believe in their heart (expectations and attributions) and set their minds to (goals). Yet many young adults we work with and bring into our hearts and homes have never had a dad like Zach to speak into their lives. In most cases, they've had the opposite. But it's not too late. That's why I am doing this work and you're reading this book.

I want to share a few tools that I've personally used to help our girls as we've worked alongside them to develop self-efficacy so that they can use it as the foundation to generate the building blocks that they need to *thrive* and build their own *flourishing* lives—to believe in themselves (self-esteem), learn to use and express their power (agency), make choices and manage their own lives (self-determination), and to own their mistakes and make appropriate amends (personal responsibility).

A Sense of Responsibility

In the last chapter, I shared that a sense of responsibility (action) is important to belonging and an important tool for self-efficacy. A sense of responsibility, marked by acting responsibly, significantly enhances belonging because it demonstrates commitment, fosters cohesion, earns respect and recognition, and contributes to positive feelings of worth and self-image. When you fulfill responsibilities and are recognized and celebrated for your contribution, it deepens connection and reinforces a sense of ownership and accountability. Self-efficacy is reinforced and formed through these deep feelings of accomplishment and being trusted by others. Whether it's staying at home by themselves, having a phone bill that they are responsible for, taking care of an animal, taking care of younger siblings, or being a leader in a peer group, these types of opportunities not only reinforce belonging but they create healthy self-efficacy by proving to the young person that other people trust in and look up to them. Look for ways to give your young person a sense of trust and responsibility, say aloud to their eyeballs how proud you are, and constantly affirm their effort (even if they don't totally succeed).

Use Your Resources

"Use your resources…" is a phrase my girls probably still hear in their sleep. Most of them will say that it's the one thing that always goes through their head before they call me to ask something (good!). *"Mom, can you help me with this math problem?"* "Did you use your resources first?" *"Mom, how do you…."* "Did you use your resources first? We pay for you to have a walking resource library in your pocket (phone). Try to figure it out yourself first, and then I can help you if you still need me." While this may sound quite disconnected and often felt that way, it's an essential tool in developing self-efficacy. I'm not always going to be around to help them solve their problems, so they have to learn to research for themselves and find the help that they need. A resource might be another work colleague who can help them figure out how to do something correctly, a YouTube video to learn how to bake a loaf of bread, or a Udemy class to learn a whole new skill and start a new career. My husband has a degree in electronics and was a computer hardware technician. Yet, in the early 1990s, he taught himself the coding behind websites (to help me build a prettier GeoCities page—I know my age is showing), and that skill started an entirely new online engineering career path that he has followed to this day—completely self-taught. Many of the skills that I use in my day-to-day life are self-taught skills. I call Google my brother from another mother because it's so helpful to me daily. Now, when my young adult daughters call to ask me for help on something, they often start the request with, *"Okay, I've used my resources, and here's what I've found _____. Now I'm just confused or need help to understand _____."* Perfect. Let's figure this out together.

"Plan with a Capital P…"

This is a phrase that I learned that goes back to the skills of goal setting. I heard Dr. Jeffery Arnett use this phrase as he was teaching about Emerging Adulthood. He used it to describe young adults struggling to transition to adulthood because they have these giant goals but no real plan to accomplish them. *"I am going to be a rap star." "I'm going to own my own business!" "I'm going to the moon!"* Great! What's your "Plan with a Capital P?" How do you plan on doing that awesome thing? What skills are you developing? Do you even know what skills are needed/required? The most desired career path for graduating seniors in the past few years has been to be a social media influencer. Sure, still, at the time of writing this book, you can make pretty good money doing that. I wouldn't scoff at a young person with the drive and ambition to find a niche and make it work. The problem is that most young people who want that career path have no clue about the hours that must be devoted to figuring out your niche, planning your content, recording your content, editing your content, responding to your fans, exploring new ideas to keep things fresh, and being remarkably consistent to post. It's a full-time job that requires dedication, planning, skill, stamina, creativity, follow-through, and personality. It's achievable. But only if you "have a plan with a capital P."

"Your circus. Your monkeys."

"Your circus. Your monkeys." Or "Not my circus. Not my monkeys." We began using these phrases with our girls when they were older teens and heading into adulthood. It was our gentle way of saying, "I'm not going to help you or be responsible for that." Transitioning from someone taking total responsibility for you to take total responsibility for yourself is hard. It won't happen unless we, as parents, take our hands off and help our young people understand that they must begin to plan, prepare, own up to mistakes, take initiative, and work hard for their goals. We started this transition when we had girls in middle school with the simple instruction that if you leave it at home, it stays at home. We don't bring homework, coats, projects, or any forgotten item to school for you. If you get a failing grade, so be it. It's your grade (monkey) to worry about. We don't call into work or write school notes for irresponsibility on your behalf. That's your circus. Your monkey. We don't bail anyone out of jail. Your circus. Your monkey. Obey the law, and you never have to worry about that. (Caveat to that one – we did one time and one time only, and it was only because we had proof that our daughter was not involved/guilty, and the charges were dropped later because the evidence was clear). We don't get involved in relationship disputes that don't include us—especially marital ones. Your circus. Your monkey. We don't talk to teachers or bosses on your behalf to ask for leniency or grace for your irresponsibility. Your circus. Your monkey.

We always worked hard to send the message: "We believe in you, we know you are smart and capable, mistakes happen, and that's okay—you have the wisdom and resources to solve your problems. We are always here for you to talk through your solutions, ask our opinions/advice, or give input on your plan (with a capital P). But we will not solve it for you, do it for you, speak on your behalf, or show up where you need to. We love you too much for that." Is it hard? Yes. Is it helpful? Yes. Did they like it? No. Are they grateful now? Mostly.

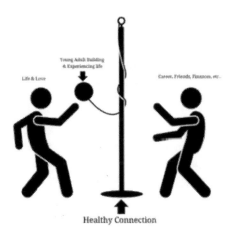

Figure 17 Drawing of the tetherball analogy for connection to young adults transitioning to adulthood

It's important to remember that all of this is done in equal combination with solid belonging. Both belonging & self-efficacy guide a young person into a *thriving* life. The Tetherball Analogy from Chapter 2 illustrates this perfectly. As a healthy connection (parent/mentor) for our young adults and older teens, it is important to allow them to go out and experience a world they actively build in love, friendship, career, education, providing for themselves, and more.

The Hardest Part

I can hear many of you as readers saying, "But I can't get my young person off their games to look for a job." Do they pay the internet bill? Change the WIFI passcode. The truth is that I can't give you answers to every situation that you will face with your young people. Still, I can tell you that the most challenging part is exercising the *authority* that you have to take meaningful action to move your young person forward—which often looks like inaction or *not doing*. For us, this has looked like not allowing a young adult daughter to live with us because she was using drugs, and that's a boundary in my personal life due to my childhood trauma. She lived in her car with her cat. It was heart-wrenching. But at the same time, it was also part of the rock bottom that she needed to experience to pick herself up and get her life back on track. It also looked like having another daughter who struggled greatly with drugs before she even came into our family and then continued to struggle for years. Every time she called in desperation, we responded with the same question: "Have you called Beth?" Beth is a friend who runs a beautiful ministry called Hoving Home for women to recover from addiction and find their identities in Christ. Beth herself was an addict and a Hoving Home participant nearly two decades before. Our daughter had Beth's cellphone number and had spoken with Beth several times. We had communicated to her, in total unity with Beth, that the next step for her was to choose recovery, and outside of that, we couldn't help her. For two years, every call ended with "No. I haven't called Beth." We assured her that we loved her and believed in her but that we couldn't solve her current crisis; only she could. To solve it, she needed to call Beth. After two years, we finally received a desperation call that started with, "I just talked to Beth. I need to be in North Carolina tomorrow. Can you come to get me?" One of her sisters immediately went and got her and brought her to our house, where she got a shower, some clean clothes, and a night of sleep. She was probably 80lbs soaking wet at that moment. The unhealthiest that I had ever seen her look. I put her on a bus to Beth at 6 am the following day. Today, she's two years clean and beginning to build and experience life for herself. Before that final call, she had spent three nights in a field beside a gas station, hallucinating. That's still heartbreaking to know. However, she would tell you today that three nights in a field woke her up, and she never wants to return to that state of being again. Anytime she feels tempted, she remembers the field. She doesn't remember the lectures I gave her. She doesn't remember the warnings that others gave her. None of those things motivated her to change. Her rock bottom was a field. Her "tetherball pole" knew she belonged to us even in the middle of that field, and we had provided a way out. It was time to take control of her monkeys.

*"The most terrible poverty is loneliness
and the feeling of being unloved."*
Mother Teresa

CHAPTER NINE

ISOLATION
VOID OF CONNECTION

The National Institute on Aging describes loneliness and isolation as the distressing feeling of being alone or separated. Social isolation is the need for more social contracts and having few people to interact with regularly. You can live alone and not feel lonely or socially isolated, and you can feel lonely while being with others." For many of our young people who've grown up in foster care or in homes where they suffered severe neglect, the feeling of isolation and loneliness is pervasive. In Chapter 2, I described the visual of being lost at sea without an orange life preserver or safety flag. There could be a million planes above, and none of them may be able to spot you because you're a tiny speck in the vast sea. Many of our youth describe a similar feeling of being in a vast world without a single person who truly sees them. How tragic. We've all experienced isolation or loneliness at some point in our lives. Yet, for the youth we love and serve, much of their lives have been marked by the fingerprint of feeling unseen, unloved, and unimportant.

For many years, as our family was growing, Steve and I were both staff members of Victory World Church, a large multi-cultural church in the Atlanta area. A Sunday morning could see nearly 15,000 people in attendance across multiple services and multiple campuses. Most Sundays were spent at the church, and I can recount numerous times that I would hear a specific voice call out, "Mom!" my head would turn because I recognized one of my girl's voices from across a very crowded sanctuary. As a mom, I knew the sound of their voices and would instinctively turn to find their face in a crowd of faces and set my eyes upon them. Every child deserves to feel belonging like that. The contrast between the experience of a young person with meaningful, supportive relationships that create a sense of belonging and safety to a young person alone in their struggles without a safe, stable, and available support system is profound. Walking alongside a young person to overcome the feelings of isolation through a *Redemptive Connection* requires a balanced approach of providing guidance and structure (*authority*) while being open, empathetic, and emotionally available (*vulnerability*). The transition from isolation to connectedness is not just about physical presence or superficial relationship; it's about deep, meaningful engagement that promotes healing, growth, and a sense of belonging. It's about creative restoration through sacrifice.[21]

Impact of Isolation and Loneliness

"At 12 years old, my biological mother passed away due to hypertension. My heart felt like it had shattered into a million pieces to where it was impossible to put it back together. I felt extremely depressed, and most importantly, I did not know what the future held for me.

Because no immediate family members could take custody of me, I was placed in the California foster care system.

When my social worker explained to me where I was going to live, I felt anxious, and without a doubt, afraid of entering a new environment with people I did not even know. I remember my first foster mother telling me to not be nervous or scared and to feel like I was part of their family. But did she really understand what emotions I felt, or what thoughts were running through my mind? Did she understand the intensity and how emotionally draining it was to feel like I was an outcast from the rest of the world?

As the state shuffled me through four different foster homes, those questions became more of a blur. I started thinking that the only person who could truly understand what I was going through was me. School was becoming more difficult. I moved to multiple middle and high schools, and I was experiencing more grief and loss. Throughout the six years I was in the foster care system, 11 other family members passed away. The rest of my family disowned me, and I felt that I was alone in the world, different from everyone else.

Questions seeped through my thoughts. Do other people experience trauma such as this? Do other people lose 12 family members consecutively? Why does everyone dislike and hate me?

I did not know how to feel anymore, nor how to express my emotions. I did not know who to turn to, and I did not know whether I would make it in life." This is an excerpt from a Children's Rights' *"Fostering the Future"* campaign article

---

[21] The Redemptive Frame, PraxisLabs.org

written by Child Welfare advocate John Devine[22], describing his history and story from foster care.

Social isolation is a remarkably damaging experience that leads directly to loneliness, depression, and lack of self-efficacy. It is a common marker of children who experience long-term foster care histories being bounced from home to home without ever experiencing true belonging. Often, feeling like they don't fit in, aren't wanted, and are different from their peers—leading to feelings of inadequacy and low self-esteem. Social isolation also impacts their ability to form healthy relationships easily and challenges their social and emotional development.[23] The American CDC (Centers for Disease Control & Prevention) links isolation and loneliness with increased risk for heart disease and stroke, type 2 diabetes, depression and anxiety, addiction, suicidality and self-harm, dementia, and early death. The cost of loneliness on the US economy is a staggering $406 billion a year![24] A clear sign that loneliness and isolation aren't just a foster care issue—it's a health crisis across our nation.

Before we move on, it's important to realize that loneliness and isolation can impact any child or adult. Loneliness is often a known outcome of children who experience the early childhood trauma of NICU, which is why so many advancements have been made in allowing parents and other caregivers into NICU to touch, hold, comfort, swaddle, and be *with* babies during those critical early days. In the mid-90s, however, that was not the case. Our daughter was born with Group B Strep and required a seven-day NICU stay. It was common during that time for NICUs to have strict visiting hours to allow the baby time to heal without being held and touched. However, extended parental separation and time alone send early messages to the developing brain that "I'm alone." I know this firsthand as our daughter has expressed many times in her childhood and throughout life that she has struggled with a profound sense of "being alone" even though she is keenly aware that she's deeply loved and cherished. Many things can be attributed to a sense of isolation and loneliness beyond early childhood trauma and a history in foster care. Certainly, the COVID-19 pandemic had an impact on children, youth, and

[22] Foster Care: The Feeling of Isolation and Overcoming. Written by John Devine May 6, 2016. Published by Childrensrights.org. https://www.childrensrights.org/news-voices/foster-care-the-feeling-of-isolation-and-overcoming

[23] Most Common Causes of Stress for Children in Foster Care. Fosteringpeople.co.uk Published June 2, 2023. https://www.fosteringpeople.co.uk/resources/blogs/latest-blogs/causes-of-stress-for-children-in-foster-care/

[24] Health Risks of Social Isolation and Loneliness. Published by the Centers of Disease Control and Prevention. https://www.cdc.gov/emotional-wellbeing/social-connectedness/loneliness.htm

especially among young adults, with 61% of 18–25-year-olds reporting high levels of loneliness[25]. In addition, studies from the Pew Research Center and others have linked an increasingly digital lifestyle and more screen time directly to loneliness, depression, anxiety, and less emotional connection with others[26]. There are many issues at work today beyond foster care history that result in what I would consider a pandemic of isolation and loneliness in today's society. It may even be impacting you personally right now, and I encourage you to seek professional guidance and deeper relational connection if you are experiencing loneliness. You are not alone; our young people shouldn't be alone either.

Isolation in the Redemptive Connection Framework

For most of the young people we work with, and my daughters who joined our family with broken family histories, their starting place is Isolation—feeling insecure, broken, and unwanted/unseen by anyone in their life. Their lives are void of meaningful connection; many articulate feeling invisible and unimportant to anyone. As a result of this inner sense of worthlessness, most have very low self-efficacy, which hinders them from curating the life they desperately dream of having. This is the place where our Mentoring Families *step into their story*. It's not an easy road for the young person or those stepping in to provide love and belonging.

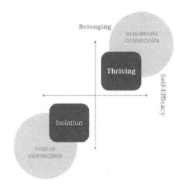

[25] Young Adults Hardest Hit by Loneliness During Pandemic. Written by Colleen Walsh. Published by The Harvard Gazette. February 17, 2021.
https://news.harvard.edu/gazette/story/2021/02/young-adults-teens-loneliness-mental-health-coronavirus-covid-pandemic/

[26] Is Your Phone Making You Lonelier? Written by Anthony Silard Ph.D. Published by Psycohology Today. September 8, 2020. https://www.psychologytoday.com/us/blog/the-art-living-free/202009/is-your-phone-making-you-lonelier#:~:text=Both%20studies%20found%20that%20more,is%20actually%20making%20us%20Olonely.

Figure 18 The Redemptive Connection Framework illustrates Isolation as Void of Connection.

For youth and young adults, the journey toward forging healthy, meaningful, safe, and stable connections from a place of isolation— whether they chose the relationship or a social worker chose it— is excruciatingly difficult. Even though they desperately want connection and success, they are often terrified of another letdown and afraid of failure. This is why finding ourselves and being acutely aware of our authority and vulnerability as mentors, parents, and caregivers is critically important. Nearly every piece of research lists safe connections as a primary way to combat isolation and loneliness. So, suppose we will be those safe connections and help our young people move out of isolation through Redemptive Connection. In that case, we must examine the role our own *authority* and *vulnerability* play.

Isolation: Balancing Authority & Vulnerability

Being a *Redemptive Connection* to a young person who is struggling with isolation and loneliness can sometimes feel overwhelming. We want so desperately to give them the *belonging* and love that we know they need and to fill all those gaps of loneliness in their lives. On the other hand, we also see that they are responsible for shaping and living out their own life and need to build some *self-efficacy*. It's hard to push responsibility and independence when there's a massive void in their life of never being truly cared for or able to be safely dependent on someone else to care for them. It feels so disconnected and harsh. The difficulty that this puts many parents and Mentoring Families in can cause us to become either overbearing and distanced because they *"need to build and be responsible for their own life"* or overly generous to help them out because they *"never had anyone to just love on them and do for them."* Let's explore the vital role of authority and vulnerability in combating isolation.

Healthy Authority in Combating Isolation
- **Structure & Safety:** We can provide our young adults with a structured and safe environment. A sense of predictability and stability is comforting and can help to reduce feelings of isolation. This can be especially helpful for youth who've experienced a chaotic or neglectful childhood. Routines, traditions, and clear expectations (I'll call you at 6:00 tomorrow – and then you do) are all helpful tools to create good structure in your relationship, providing a sense of safety.

- **Guidance & Limits:** It's healthy to set guidelines and limits. Helping our young people understand expectations and boundaries is particularly helpful for those who haven't experienced consistent rules or consequences. The "Have you called Beth" story from the last chapter exemplifies a healthy limit we set with one of our daughters.

- **Role Modeling:** Being a role model is critically important to showing our young people how to navigate life responsibly and make healthy decisions. Allowing them to observe your decision-making or to work alongside you to solve a problem also guides them away from isolation toward more engaging and productive behaviors.

Healthy Vulnerability in Combating Isolation
- **Building Trust:** Openness and vulnerability go a long way toward building trust, which is an essential component of any relationship and particularly important for a young person feeling isolated. Slow down and show your genuine emotions, share personal experiences, and admit your mistakes.

- **Encouraging Expression:** Being a safe place for young people to express their feelings and thoughts can help reduce feelings of loneliness and disconnection. Our young people aren't always going to express thoughts that we agree with or align with, but we must keep communications open. Open dialogue is a hallmark of our family gatherings. Usually, every gathering ends up in some vigorous debate (politics, religion, sports, you name it…we've likely argued about it) because we all have differing opinions. We encourage this type of expression because we want all our girls to feel seen and safe with the feelings and ideas they are working out and working through. We don't have to agree to love each other, and the fun part is that vigorous debate requires that we defend our positions, which involves research, listening, and learning. All self-efficacy skills. Yet it feels very vulnerable to hear your young person share a feeling or thought that might be scary or worrisome to you. We must remember that we also saw the world differently in our 20s. Life is long. They can work it out just like we did.

- **Emotional Connection:** Many parents/mentors feel like I did early on — *"never let 'em see you sweat."* I needed to always show my best side so my kids would respect me. One day, I was on the phone with one of our girls, asking about her week (she was away at school) and generally catching up. She asked me how I was, and I gave the usual, "I'm fine. Just busy," to which she replied, "Mom, you know you don't always have to have it all together. You can share your problems with us; maybe we can help you too." Wow. And ouch, again. She was right. As I've practiced being more emotionally available and transparent, I've watched my relationships with our girls *flourish* because it makes me more relatable to them and bridges the gap between us.

For our relationships with our young adults to flourish in ways that empower them to thrive in life, we must balance authority and vulnerability. A balanced approach includes clear guidance and structure while being open, empathetic, compassionate, and understanding. This balance helps to create a supportive relationship where young adults can feel secure about themselves while feeling connected to people who care about them enough to hold loving boundaries.

Behavioral Outcomes & Responses to Isolation

When a young person is experiencing isolation and is without safe, stable support systems in their lives, they can exhibit behaviors as a response to the pain of their emotional state. As with our innate fight, flight, freeze, or fawn response to fear stimuli, these behaviors often serve to escape or cope with the inner turmoil of their lives. Although it can be challenging to experience as a parent or a mentor, it's important always to take time to understand the "why" behind the "what" of behaviors so that we can be an effective ally to our young adults in their battle for normalcy, connection, and interdependent life. Below are four categories of behavior & experiences common to youth with low self-efficacy and low belonging:

Numbing Behaviors

- Engagement in Risky Behaviors: This can include alcohol or substance abuse or other dangerous activities used as a means to escape or numb feelings.
- Digital or Online Escapism: Excessive use of the internet, social media, or video games can be a way to distract from or numb emotional pain.
- Changes in Eating Patterns: Overeating or loss of appetite can also be a form of numbing or coping with emotional distress.

Addressing numbing behaviors in a young person experiencing isolation requires a tactful and empathetic approach, utilizing a balance of our authority and our vulnerability. A balanced approach is essential because it establishes a trusting and safe environment conducive to open communication. It allows for deeper understanding between you and your young adult, strengthening your relationship, even in difficult circumstances.

Young Person in Isolation   Our *Flourishing* Response

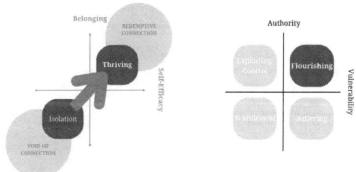

Figure 19 This graph of the Redemptive Connection Framework and Authority/Vulnerability matrixes side-by-side illustrates the desire to move our young person into a balance of belonging and self-efficacy using a balanced approach of authority and vulnerability,

A Balanced Approach Using Authority and Vulnerability:

- **Healthy Authority:** Establish boundaries around behaviors that are numbing or harmful, such as excessive screen time, substance use, or unhealthy eating patterns. Create and maintain a structure that encourages healthier activities, like physical exercise, hobbies, or social interactions. Enforce the boundaries consistently while explaining their purpose is for the young person's well-being.
  - o Boundaries can seem complicated with young adults no longer living under your roof. You can't hold them accountable to your boundaries when they aren't around you—nor should you—it's their life to live how they want to—their circus/monkeys. However, you can set boundaries regarding your home and help (money, time, etc.). Our girls know that excessive drinking and drugs are not allowed in our home. Smoking and vaping have to be done outside; it doesn't matter how cold it is. If you're here, you help; no lazy bones allowed. And, back to the "Have you

called Beth" story in the last chapter, that was our boundary.

- **Healthy Vulnerability:** Openly discuss your concerns regarding their numbing behaviors and how they affect them and the family/relationship. Share your experiences with coping strategies and how you have managed challenging emotions. Show empathy and understanding for their feelings of isolation and reassure them of your support.

Young Person in Isolation   Our *Control* Response

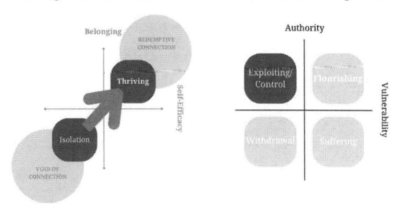

Figure 20 Graph of the Redemptive Connection Framework and Authority/Vulnerability matrixes illustrate the desire to move our young person into a balance of belonging & self-efficacy using an unhealthy use of Authority/Control.

Unbalanced/Unhealthy Use of Authority

- An unhealthy use of authority might involve imposing strict rules without understanding or compassion, such as abruptly removing devices, forbidding certain activities without providing alternatives or punishing the young person for their coping mechanisms.
  - o "You can't smoke at all on our premises" might be a perfect boundary for some. We live on 45 acres, so it's punitive for us to say that. If we lived in a neighborhood with a house next to us, we might personally feel different. "You can't smoke near our house or in our vehicles, and you must pick up all butts from the ground and dispose of them" is

perfectly balanced and acceptable, and it is, in fact, our boundary.

o "Until you get a job, we will stop paying for your cell phone." Again, this might be acceptable (we quit paying for phones at 18). What we must be careful of is whether or not this is a purely punitive response instead of a balanced one.

o "Until you are off of drugs, you are not welcome at our house." This is a perfect example of an unhealthy boundary because it inhibits Belonging rather than encourages it. "We love you and would love to see you. However, we can't have you here if you're high/drunk, etc." "It is hurtful when you come to our house and sit on your phone or play video games because we want to interact with you. We need you to put your device down and join us in our family activity." These are more balanced boundaries.

• What are we feeling in these moments? We often feel frustrated, anxious about the young person's well-being, or desperate to see immediate changes. These feelings can drive a more authoritarian and less empathetic approach, focusing on stopping the behavior rather than understanding its underlying causes.

Young Person in Isolation   **Our *Suffering* Response**

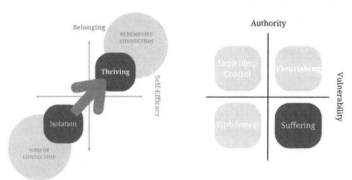

Figure 21 The graph of the Redemptive Connection Framework and Authority/Vulnerability matrixes illustrates the desire to move our young people into a balance of belonging and self-efficacy by using an unhealthy use of Vulnerability/Suffering.

<u>Unbalanced/Unhealthy Use of Vulnerability</u>
- Unhealthy vulnerability could manifest as over-sharing distress about the situation, making the young person feel responsible for our emotions. It might also involve enabling the numbing behavior out of fear of confrontation or a desire to avoid exacerbating the young person's sense of isolation.
  - "I'm so stressed out and worried because of your behavior. It keeps me up at night." This places an emotional burden on the young person to manage our emotions.
  - Oversharing can also make our young people feel like they need to be more concerned about our needs than the issues they are struggling with, such as sharing our financial worries or other relationship issues.
  - "You're making me depressed with your actions." This is a form of shame, guilt, and blame.
  - Saying things like, "I need you to be okay so that I can be okay" puts a young person who is already struggling with their emotions into the position of an emotional anchor for our own emotions. Those are our circus and our monkeys.
  - Using phrases like, "If you cared about me, you wouldn't do this," can manipulate a young person's feelings to elicit certain behaviors, making them feel responsible for our happiness.
- How do we feel in these moments? We are likely feeling overwhelmed, guilty, or overly responsible for the young person's unhappiness. These feelings might lead to self-pity, a sense of helplessness, or a martyr mentality where we neglect to set necessary boundaries for fear of harming or losing the relationship.

As you walk alongside your young person experiencing isolation, it is important to recognize that we all have emotions that come into play when we observe something hurting someone we love. It's super easy to get into an unhealthy place in either authority or vulnerability—trust me, I've been there countless times. I still must coach myself out of unhealthy places over and over. As we strive for a balanced approach that addresses our young person's underlying needs while maintaining healthy boundaries, we become safe *redemptive* connections who can actively help our young person develop healthier coping mechanisms and a stronger sense of self-efficacy.

Mental Health Challenges

- <u>Withdrawal from Social Situations:</u> Often a symptom of deeper mental health issues like depression or social anxiety.

- <u>Emotional Disturbances:</u> Signs of depression, anxiety, or mood swings can indicate underlying mental health challenges.

- <u>Changes in Communication Patterns:</u> Reduced communication can be a symptom of mental health issues, such as depression or anxiety.

- <u>Changes in Sleeping Patterns:</u> Patterns like insomnia or excessive sleeping are common in various mental health conditions.

Supporting a young person who is struggling with mental health challenges can leave us feeling helpless, especially if we've never had experiences or education around these issues. I grew up with a mom who suffered from severe mental health challenges and used numbing behaviors as her way to cope. Of course, that didn't make me an expert, but it gave me a sense of calm in knowing that there is outside help available and in understanding my feelings as I watched someone I dearly loved struggle. It also gave me a good perspective on the need for the individual to own their healing. No matter how much I loved my mom or needed her to show up for me, it was her decision whether to get help, act, or succumb to her illness. Unfortunately, my mom spent most of her life succumbing. This taught me compassion, boundaries, and balance early in my life as a young married woman seeking to build a life while feeling all the feelings of needing to also care for my mom. I can look back and see when I operated with too much authority or *vulnerability*. It was a learning and leaning (on my God & my husband) process for me to learn how to take a balanced approach.

<u>Balanced Approach Using Authority and Vulnerability</u>

- **Healthy Authority**: Provide structure and support that addresses the young person's mental health needs, such as helping to facilitate access to therapy or counseling and encouraging routines that promote mental well-being. Set boundaries around harmful behaviors while explaining the reasons behind these limits.
  - o "Let's arrange an appointment with a counselor together. Maybe we can look to find someone who specializes in young adult mental health because I believe having someone professional to talk to can be helpful for you. Would you like my help with this?"

- o "Let's work together to create a daily schedule that includes time for activities you enjoy, like drawing or playing music, as well as consistent meal and sleep times to help you feel more balanced."
- o "I understand that gaming can be a way to relax, but too much screen time can affect your sleep and mood, so let's agree on a time limit that allows for other activities that are good for your well-being."
- o "We've agreed that using substances isn't a healthy way to cope with stress. If this happens, we'll need to discuss the reasons behind the choice and consider additional supports and boundaries that might be helpful."
- o "We understand that you are struggling with some mental health challenges right now, and we've offered to help. It's okay if you don't want our assistance. While you're working it out, we need to ask that you show respect in our home by not screaming and yelling at us, showing up and banging on our doors, or cursing. We love having you here, but we may have to meet in public if you can't control those things while you're healing."

- **Healthy Vulnerability:** Share your feelings of concern in a supportive manner. Be open about the challenges of dealing with mental health issues, sharing your own experiences to normalize their struggles. Listen actively and empathetically to their experiences and feelings.
    - o "I want you to know I'm here for you, and it worries me to you struggling. It's okay not to be okay, and it's important to me that we work through this together."
    - o "When I was your age, I also went through a period where everything felt overwhelming. Talking to someone about it was one of my best steps, and it helped me learn a lot about myself."
    - o "Many people face challenges with their mental health, including me at times. Seeking help is strong and brave—it is not a sign of weakness."
    - o "Tell me more about how you're feeling. I'm here to listen and understand, not to judge or jump to conclusions. Your feelings are valid, and I appreciate you sharing them with me."

o   "It's frightening to us to hear you scream and yell, bang on doors and curse. We love you and are always here for you."

Unbalanced/Unhealthy Use of Authority

- Unhealthy authority might involve dismissing the young person's mental health struggles as a phase or a minor issue, enforcing strict rules without understanding the mental health context, or demanding quick fixes or immediate improvement in their mental state.
    - o   "You're just going through a phase; you'll get over it. You don't need a therapist; you need to be stronger and stop being so sensitive."
    - o   "I don't care how you feel; these are the rules of the house, and you will follow them. You will no longer sit in the other room while everyone else is playing games and interacting."
    - o   "I expect to see an improvement in your attitude soon, or there will be consequences. You can be happy; you're just not trying hard enough."
- The parent or mentor might be feeling fearful for the young person's future, frustrated by what they perceive as a lack of progress, or overwhelmed by the severity of the mental health challenges. These feelings can lead to a controlling approach focused on behavior modification rather than emotional support and understanding.
    - o   "What if I'm failing as a parent or mentor because my children aren't improving? I need to do something drastic to fix this immediately."
    - o   "If I don't control this situation, they may never recover, and it'll be my fault."
    - o   "I've tried being understanding, but it's not working. It's time to lay down the law and see some results."
    - o   "We can't keep going like this; things need to change now, and if that means being tougher, so be it."
    - o   "I don't understand all this therapy talk; in my days, we just got on with it. Maybe they need a good dose of reality check instead of all this coddling."
    - o   "This isn't how I imagined parenting/mentoring would be; maybe I'm too soft, and that's why they are struggling."

Suicidality & Self-Harm

- <u>Self-harm or Suicidal Ideation:</u> These are critical behaviors that often indicate severe emotional distress and the need for immediate professional intervention. Addressing self-harm or suicidal ideation in a young person is a sensitive and vital issue that requires immediate attention and a careful balance of authority and vulnerability.

<u>Balanced Approach Using Authority and Vulnerability</u>

- **Healthy Authority:** Ensure the young person's safety first and foremost. This might involve removing harmful objects from their environment and immediately seeking professional help. Establishing a safe environment is crucial. Setting up appointments with mental health professionals and accompanying them to these appointments can provide structured support.
  - o Locking away medications, sharp objects, and firearms.
  - o Partnering to make and attend appointments with mental health professionals.
    - Maybe coming to a mutual agreement that attending therapy sessions is non-negotiable (only if the young person also agrees that it's non-negotiable) while allowing the young person to have a say in their treatment plan.
  - o Discussing a safety plan with the young person and professionals.
    - Setting boundaries around medication management, if applicable, to ensure proper usage.
  - o Establishing an explicit agreement that the young person will reach out to a trusted adult or emergency services if they have urges to harm themselves or worse.
    - "Ensuring your safety is my top priority. We can work through the underlying issues once we know everyone is safe. I need to call 911." Sometimes, a call to emergency services is the right thing to do. Most of us are not trained in this area, and we must get them the fastest response and best help we can—and that is not us (unless you're a trained professional, but even then, you might be too close to the situation and need to allow a third party to assist).

- o It's essential to show your young person that you take them seriously. Setting up appointments shows that we take their feelings seriously and that there are professional ways to help.
- o Creating an open line of communication where the young person can talk about their feelings without fear of judgment, but also making it clear that certain behaviors are ineffective ways to communicate their pain or needs.
- o Designating times for checking in to discuss emotions and experiences while respecting the young person's need for privacy and space.

- **Healthy Vulnerability:** Openly express your concern and care for the young person compassionately and non-judgmentally. Share your feelings about wanting to support and understand them, acknowledging the seriousness of their feelings and the situation. It's important to listen actively and empathetically.
  - o Sitting with the young person and holding space for their feelings.
  - o Sharing our emotions about the situation without overwhelming them or making it about us.
  - o Demonstrating our willingness to listen and be there for them.
  - o "I'm worried, but we must stay calm. You are not alone, and I am here to support you."
  - o It's okay to let your young person see that you are concerned and care deeply about their well-being.

Unbalanced/Unhealthy Use of Authority

- An unhealthy use of authority might involve responding with anger, frustration, or panic, potentially leading to punitive measures or overly restrictive controls. This could include reacting harshly to the self-harm or suicidal thoughts or attempting to force the young person into treatment without their input.
  - o Yelling or expressing anger about the self-harm.
  - o Implementing strict rules or ultimatums without support.
  - o Forcing the young person into treatment without considering their feelings.
    - ▪ Note: regarding suicidal ideation and calling 911. This is often the best approach, and the authorities will take this seriously, as they

should, and will usually force a 72-hour mental health stay at a hospital. This is okay. It's the professional's call to make, and in a suicidal state of mind, this is often what the young person needs.

- The parent or mentor might feel scared, overwhelmed, or angry. These intense emotions can lead to a desire to quickly regain control over the situation, focusing more on stopping the behavior immediately rather than understanding its root causes.
  - o "I can't believe they would do this! This needs to stop immediately or else."
  - o "They're just doing this for attention; they need to learn the hard way that this isn't acceptable."
    - Note: As we will see in the next section, this can sometimes be the case, but that doesn't mean we shouldn't take appropriate and loving actions in partnership with a professional because their desperate need for attention is a cry for help in and of itself.

Unbalanced/Unhealthy Use of Vulnerability

- An unbalanced use of vulnerability could manifest as the parent or mentor expressing excessive distress, guilt, or despair to the young person, potentially making them feel responsible for the adult's well-being. This could also include not setting necessary boundaries due to fear of upsetting the young person further.
  - o Breaking down and crying frequently in front of the young person.
  - o Sharing fears and anxieties in a way that puts pressure on the young person to be responsible for their emotions.
  - o Neglecting to enforce any boundaries because of fear or guilt.
- The parent or mentor may feel helpless, desperate, or personally responsible for the young person's actions. These feelings might lead to a victim mentality, where the focus shifts to their suffering, or a martyrdom complex, where they neglect their own needs and boundaries to 'save' the young person.
  - o "I can't handle this. Their pain is too much for me, and I don't know what to do."

    o "If something bad happens to them, it's my fault. I should have been a better parent/mentor."

In both unbalanced authority and vulnerability, it is crucial to prioritize the young person's immediate safety and mental health. In both unbalanced scenarios, the focus becomes skewed towards punitive measures that lack empathy or an overburdening emotional expression that places undue stress on the young person. Maintaining a balance where the young person's immediate safety is secured, and their emotional needs are met with understanding and support is critical, paving the way for professional intervention and healing. Professional help from therapists, counselors, or crisis intervention services should be sought immediately. Self-harm and suicidal ideation are serious matters that often require the guidance and support of mental health professionals.

Relational Challenges

- <u>Trust Issues and Relational Challenges:</u> Difficulty forming or maintaining relationships can sometimes lead to attaching to unsafe people or groups to seek connection.
- <u>Attention Seeking & Relational Sabotage:</u> Using disruptive or inauthentic means to fit in or gain attention such as talking loudly, talking incessantly, fishing for compliments, feigning helplessness, exaggerating, pretending to be ill, interrupting, creating drama, playing the victim, or exaggerated emotions are all actions that, while seemingly directed towards gaining attention, can harm relationships and lead to further isolation. This pattern can result in a cycle where the young person's actions push others away, the opposite of what they want.

<u>Balanced Approach Using Authority & Vulnerability</u>

- **Healthy Authority:** Set clear guidelines and expectations for respectful and healthy interactions with others. Provide opportunities for young people to engage in social activities to practice and develop relational skills in a safe environment. Encourage participation in group activities or therapy sessions focusing on building skills and understanding relationship dynamics.
  - o Organizing a family game night to foster casual, stress-free interaction. Encouraging participation in activities where the young person can receive attention in positive ways.

- o Offering to help the young person enroll in a social skills workshop or group therapy.
- o Collaboratively create rules for respectful communication when you're together and consistently enforce the agreed-upon rules for interaction while being flexible and understanding.
- o Offering praise when the young person engages socially or handles a relationship challenge well.
- o Setting up an accountability system for honesty, such as verifying stories if doubt arises. Engaging the young person in open discussions about the consequences of lying and drama creation. It's important to enforce boundaries to teach them healthier ways to communicate their needs.

- **Healthy Vulnerability:** Share your experiences with relationship challenges, including what you've learned and how you've grown from them. Listen to the young person's feelings and experiences without judgment, showing empathy and understanding. Validate their feelings and encourage open discussion about their fears and desires regarding relationships.
  - o Sharing a personal story of when you struggled to make friends, maintain a relationship, or felt the need for more attention, highlighting what you learned and how you handled or mishandled it.
  - o Sitting with the young person to listen to their concerns about friendships or social interactions without interrupting or offering unsolicited advice.
  - o Responding to the young person's relational fears with empathy and relating them to your own experiences constructively and not burdensomely. Acknowledging the young person's feelings and needs that might be driving their behavior without condoning the behavior itself.
  - o Showing patience and understanding when the young person experiences setbacks in their social relationships.
  - o "I feel for you and understand your need for attention, but there are better ways to get it. Let's work on this together."

Unbalanced/Unhealthy Use of Authority

- An unhealthy use of authority could manifest as forcing the young person into social situations that they are uncomfortable with or punishing them for their struggles in forming and maintaining relationships. It might also involve setting unrealistic expectations for social interactions or dismissing their concerns about relationships.
    - Demanding the young person attend social events without considering their comfort level or readiness.
    - Punishing the young person for wanting to spend time alone or not having a certain number of friends.
    - Punishing the young person harshly without seeking to understand the underlying reasons for their behavior.
    - Criticizing the young person for not being more like siblings or peers in terms of social engagement.
    - Issuing ultimatums about social behavior that may be unrealistic or insensitive to the young person's struggles.
    - Dismissing any claim or concern they express, assuming it is always a lie or an exaggeration.
- A parent or mentor might feel anxious about the young person's social development, frustrated by their apparent lack of progress, or worried about their future. These feelings can lead to a more controlling approach, focusing on changing behaviors without addressing underlying emotional needs.
    - Assuming they are just "doing this to manipulate."
    - Feeling like you can't show any weakness or they'll keep lying.
    - Deciding that they need to "learn this the hard way."

Unbalances/Unhealthy Use of Vulnerability

- Unhealthy vulnerability could include the parent or mentor oversharing about their relational disappointments or using the young person's challenges to focus on their feelings of failure or sadness. It might also involve not setting boundaries or effectively addressing negative behaviors due to fear of causing further emotional harm.
    - Breaking down in front of the young person because of their social withdrawal makes them feel responsible for their emotional state.

- o Confiding in the young person about your fears and anxieties regarding their future in a way that adds to their stress.
- o Overreacting emotionally to the young person's lies or manipulations potentially reinforces the behavior.
- o Consistently giving in to the young person's feigned helplessness, thereby enabling dependency.

- The parent or mentor might feel guilty, helpless, or personally responsible for the young person's relational struggles. These feelings might lead to a victim mentality, focusing more on how the situation affects them or on self-sacrificing behavior that overlooks the need for healthy boundaries and structure.
  - o Becoming overly emotional or tearful every time the topic of the young person's social life is discussed.
  - o Consistently stepping in to solve the young person's relational problems instead of allowing them to navigate these independently, thereby inhibiting their growth.
  - o "Every time they lie, it feels like a personal attack on me. I can't seem to get through to them at all."
  - o "Maybe if I just do what they want when they pretend to be sick, they'll eventually feel secure enough to stop."

In both cases of unbalanced authority or vulnerability, striving for a balanced approach that provides support and guidance while allowing the young person to express their feelings and work through their relational challenges at their own pace is important. In each scenario, the key is to address the behavior constructively while guiding the young person toward understanding the importance of honesty and direct communication. It's about reinforcing positive behaviors and providing appropriate attention while discouraging manipulative tactics in a firm but understanding manner. Professional guidance from a therapist or counselor, especially one specializing in adolescent and young adult development, can be highly beneficial.

A G.R.A.C.E. Response to Isolation
In confronting the multifaceted challenges of isolation in our young people, the G.R.A.C.E. Response provides a holistic approach combining firm guidance and empathetic support. It recognizes that the path to healing is not through authority or vulnerability alone but through a careful blend of both. In this section, we'll explore how the G.R.A.C.E. Response

can be applied to nurture a sense of belonging and self-efficacy in young people, empowering them to step out of the shadows of isolation and into the light of *Redemptive Connection* and personal growth.

G: Get to Why

Understand the underlying reasons behind the young person's isolation. Is it due to feelings of inadequacy, past traumas, or difficulties in socializing? By identifying the root causes, we can tailor our approach to meet their specific needs.

R: Rally Around Realistic Goals

Set achievable goals with the young person that address aspects of their isolation. Whether it's initiating one social interaction per day or attending a therapy session each week, these goals should be measurable and meaningful.

A: Affirm Redemptive Positives

Focus on the young person's strengths and the progress they make, no matter how incremental. Highlight their resilience and celebrate their steps toward overcoming isolation and fostering a positive self-image.

C: Cultivate Resilience

Encourage the development of coping skills that allow the young person to deal with setbacks and challenges. Resilience is critical to moving past isolation and toward a more engaged and interdependent life.

E: Engage Supportive Community

The support of a caring community can combat isolation. Involve friends, family members, mentors, and mental health professionals who can offer the young person a support network, reflecting the multi-dimensional nature of the G.R.A.C.E. Response.

By applying the G.R.A.C.E. Response, we offer a framework that addresses the immediate and long-term needs of young people grappling with isolation. It's a compassionate and structured approach that holds space for a young person's autonomy while providing the consistent and nurturing guidance they need to thrive.

For a parent or mentor walking alongside a young person in isolation, promoting healthy belonging & self-efficacy can happen in the context of healthy authority and healthy vulnerability: *"We love you." "We're here for you." "I'm sorry we can't solve that for you, but we can help you think through some solutions if you'd like." "We believe in you." "You're stronger/ better than this. Would you like to have coffee and chat about it?"* The road to healing for our young people is not solitary but a shared venture paved with empathy, understanding, and mutual respect. Every young person's story is unique, and their pathway out of isolation will also be unique. Our role isn't to walk the path for them but to help light the way, offering support and guidance each step they take.

"The opposite of fear is felt-safety, and we know how to promote felt-safety; through connection."
Dr. David Cross

CHAPTER TEN

HARMFUL FELT-SAFETY
EXPLOITATIVE CONNECTION

A TBRI concept that was pivotal to my personal growth in understanding trauma and trauma responses is "Felt-Safety.[27]" A strategy described as "... adults arrange the environment and adjust their behavior so children can feel in a profound and basic way that they are truly safe in their home and with us. Until a child experiences safety for his or herself, trust can't develop, and healing and learning won't progress." The Connected Child, Chapter 4.

There is a difference between being safe and feeling safe. What is going on in our physical or relational environment can be the safest place in the world, but we may feel unsafe or anxious due to our past experiences. Instead, we may feel anxious, wary, unsettled, or untrusting. Despite the absence of direct danger, our past is coloring our perception, making it difficult to feel emotionally secure. This is what the term *felt safety* is describing.

> *"We're always going to be your family."*
> *"You don't have to worry about what you're going to eat for dinner."*
> *"It's safe to sleep with the lights off and your door open."*
> *"You can feel comfortable here; treat this like it's your home."*

It didn't matter that I said any of those things; what mattered was whether they could feel them. In nearly every case, it took months... years...for some of our girls to accept and relax into family and feel safe in some areas. Food was a big issue in our home that I didn't understand soon enough. Some of our girls were food hoarders, stealing and hiding food constantly. I remember pulling out a towel from the linen closet once and discovering a nasty, moldy bowl of ravioli that had been "stored away" for safekeeping. Hiding and knowing that you have a stash of food to eat provides a great sense of felt safety, especially if splitting dinner between

---

[27] Purvis, K.B., Cross, D.R., & Sunshine, W.L. (2007). Disarming the fear response with felt safety. The Connected Child (pp. 47-72). New York: McGraw-Hill.

you and your biological sister as a kid sometimes consisted of dividing the spice package you saved from yesterday's ramen noodles—a harsh reality for one of our sweet girls in her childhood.

Our home, at the time when most of our girls lived with us, had an open-concept kitchen/dining/living room combination. When we were sitting on our sectional watching TV, our backs were to the kitchen. One night, Steve and I were sitting on the couch watching some show, and we heard the pantry door open behind us. After several minutes, we realized that we never heard it close back, so we looked back to find one of our girls staring into the pantry. I asked, "Why are you standing there staring into the pantry?" Our sweet girl said, "I was just remembering that as a kid, when I would go to other people's houses and see that they had food in the pantry, I thought they were rich. We never had food in our pantry. I can't believe I live in a house with so much food in the pantry." This was a heart and brain making sense of safety and learning how to feel it.

As parents and mentors, we must understand felt-safety and ways to partner with our young people to create a sense of emotional and physical security. We do this not just through the provision of physical things like home, transportation, clothing, etc.... but also through consistent, nurturing, and understanding interactions. Building trust, reducing anxiety, providing felt-safety, and disarming fear responses are critical elements in establishing felt-safety and fostering a positive and impactful relationship. We will discuss those in more detail as we explore some suggestions for helping your young person when dealing with Harmful Felt-Safety or Exploitative Connections.

Harmful Felt-Safety in the Redemptive Connection Framework

Harmful Felt-Safety, particularly in the context of older teens and young adults with histories of trauma and unstable adult support, can be defined as a state where young people feel a deceptive sense of security or belonging in environments or relationships that are damaging or exploitative. Driven by a primal need to belong, youth are enticed into exploitative connections, which often lead them into totality entanglements—*belonging with the primary outcome of creating unhealthy dependency.* Seeking belonging, they cling to felt-safety, even if it's harmful or exploitative. Rather than finding the authentic safety and belonging they crave, youth often find themselves trapped in lifestyles and difficult situations. This false sense of security usually arises because the environment or relationship superficially meets some immediate emotional or physical needs, masking underlying harmful dynamics. It's a particularly challenging and precarious situation where the young person feels secure but is at risk.

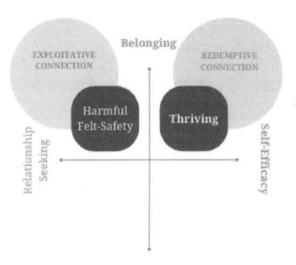

Figure 22 Harmful Felt-Safety as relationship seeking is illustrated in the Redemptive Connection Framework.

Below are some examples of *Exploitative Connections:*

- **Exploitative Relationships:** A common scenario is where a young adult, craving affection and belonging, becomes involved in a relationship that appears caring but is manipulative or abusive. They may "feel safe" because their need for belonging is seemingly met, but the relationship damages their well-being.

- **Risky Peer Groups:** Young adults might find a sense of belonging in a peer group that engages in risky or illegal activities. This group provides a sense of identity and community, but their activities are harmful.

- **Cults or Extremist Groups:** Young adults may be drawn to cults or extremist groups that offer a strong sense of community and purpose. However, these groups often employ manipulative tactics and exploit members, compromising their autonomy and safety.

- **Driven to Create Their Own Permanent Connection:** A young person, particularly a young woman, might get pregnant to maintain a relationship with a toxic partner or create a bond with someone that they believe will offer unconditional love. The young person may believe that having a child will secure the affection, connection, or stability they desperately seek. However, this decision is often based on a misguided sense of

148

security and can lead to further complications and challenges, both for the young adult and the child.

- **Overdependence on Technology:** Excessive reliance on social media or online communities for social interaction while feeling safe and unjudged in the virtual environment can lead to isolation from real-life connections and hinder the development of social skills.

- **Enabling Environments:** Sometimes, a well-intentioned but overprotective caregiver or environment may create a sense of safety but prevent the young adult from learning essential life skills, fostering dependency and hindering growth.

In each scenario, the key aspect of Harmful Felt-Safety is the illusion of security and belonging, which masks the detrimental effects on the individual's mental, emotional, or physical well-being. Recognizing these patterns and understanding their impact is crucial for supporting young adults in moving towards healthier, more genuine forms of safety and belonging.

We call these *exploitative connections* because, fundamentally, they involve a form of exploitation—taking unfair advantage of someone's vulnerabilities, needs, or circumstances. In the context of young adults with histories of trauma and lack of stable adult support, their innate needs for belonging and security make them particularly susceptible to situations where they might be exploited, often without their full awareness. Here's why these connections are labeled exploitative:

- **Manipulation of Needs:** These connections often arise because someone or something manipulates the innate human need for belonging, affection, or stability. For instance, an abusive partner might initially provide affection and support to the young person, fulfilling their deep-seated need for connection, but later use this as leverage for manipulation or control.

- **Exploitation of Vulnerabilities:** Exploitative connections prey on the vulnerabilities of young adults. Due to their traumatic histories and lack of stable support, they might not readily recognize or defend against manipulative or harmful behaviors.

- **Imbalance of Power:** Such connections often involve an imbalance of power, where one party has more control or influence. This power may be used to maintain the connection, even when it harms the young adult.

- **False Pretense of Safety and Support:** While these connections provide a superficial sense of safety and support, they endanger the young person's emotional, mental, or physical well-being. The 'safety' felt is not based on genuine care or healthy relationship dynamics but rather on fulfilling immediate needs or desires in a way that ultimately harms.

- **Long-term Detrimental Impact:** The impact of exploitative connections can be profoundly damaging in the long term, affecting trust, self-esteem, and the ability to form healthy relationships. The young adult may continue to seek similar connections, perpetuating a cycle of exploitation.

Exploitative connections describe the essence of these harmful relationships or environments—they exploit an individual's need for belonging and safety, often leading to a cycle of dependency and harm rather than genuine support and growth. Identifying and addressing these patterns is crucial in helping young adults heal from trauma and build healthy, supportive relationships.

Belonging & Ostracism

Research has shown that our human need to belong is one of our most vital needs. It is so strong that threats to belonging have genuine and devastating consequences to the individual, both psychologically and physically[28]. Being ignored, excluded, or ostracized causes significant suffering, and we go to great lengths as humans to avoid it[29]. Enduring as little as 2 to 3 minutes of ostracism will produce strongly negative feelings, especially sadness and anger[30]. Furthermore, self-reports of belonging, self-esteem, control, and a sense of meaningful existence—the four psychological needs theorized to be threatened by ostracism—consistently show the negative impact. We are predisposed to respond to ostracism at a fundamental level. Because of this primal need to belong, many youth and young adults are prone to becoming entangled in *exploitative connections*. In their drive for *belonging*, they find themselves trapped in *harmful felt-safety*, and their fear of feeling ostracized makes it difficult for them to escape.

For youth and young adults setting out to build their own lives, the desperate search for *belonging* is a critical step. In Chapter 2, we reviewed

---

[28] Baumeister, R.F., & Leary, M.R. (1995). The need to belong: Desire for interpersonal attachments as a fundamental human motivation. *Psychological Bulletin, 117,* 497-529

[29] Williams, Kipling & Nida, Steve (2011). Ostracism: Consequences and Coping. *Association for Psychological Science. Purdue University & The Citadel.*

[30] Williams, K.D. (2009). Ostracism: A temporal need-threat model. In M. Zanna (Ed.), *Advances in Experimental Social Psychology.* (41, pp. 279-314). New York, NY: Academic Press

Maslow's Hierarchy of Needs[31] (pictured again on the next page), which lists belonging needs above physiological and safety needs. Yet, many of us, as parents and mentors, anticipate a much faster track to accomplishing and developing potential from our young people. However, the truth is that without safe, stable, and secure belonging, that path is nearly unachievable because the need for belonging is so intense a massive amount of mental, emotional, and physical effort will be placed on securing it *before* their psychological processes are free to consider the other important parts of their lives. And, for us, this quadrant can particularly cause us to struggle to balance our *authority* and *vulnerability* as we seek to be *Redemptive Connections* to young people we love dearly.

Maslow's Hierarchy of Needs

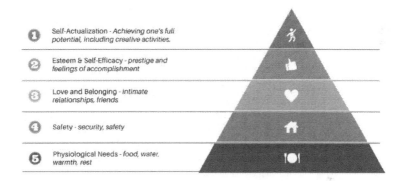

1. Self-Actualization - *Achieving one's full potential, including creative activities.*

2. Esteem & Self-Efficacy - *prestige and feelings of accomplishment*

3. Love and Belonging - *intimate relationships, friends*

4. Safety - *security, safety*

5. Physiological Needs - *food, water, warmth, rest*

Harmful Felt-Safety: Balancing Authority & Vulnerability

Being a *Redemptive Connection* for a young person who is in the midst of toxic, exploitative, and harmful relationships can be challenging—especially when we're able to see clearly how damaging the relationship is, but our young people can't see it. We may repeatedly try to tell them how bad the relationship or group is for them, and, in many cases, all this accomplishes is to push them further away from us and potentially further entrench them in poor relationships. Or we may try to ignore the situation and let their monkeys play in their circus, but this leaves us feeling guilty and thinking/worrying about the problem all the time. With eight daughters, you can bet your bottom dollar that we've had our fair share of experiences with toxic relationships and poor friend groups. You can also bet your next dollar that we've handled it poorly in most cases and gotten it right a couple of times. It's hard. Very. I wish someone else had written

---

[31] Maslow, A.H. (1943). A theory of human motivation. Psychological Review, 50(4), 370-96.

this book years ago so that "years ago Pam" could benefit from these strategies.

As parents or mentors, we must remember that you may feel like your opinions, presence, and thoughts don't matter. The contrary is true: they matter greatly. Whether your young person admits it or not, they are keenly aware of the difference in the environment when they are engaging with you versus when they are engaging with their exploitative connections. We can offer our young people a stable and nurturing alternative by providing consistent care, understanding, and a secure environment. Over time, this builds significant trust and fosters a sense of genuine safety. We can also guide our young people toward healthier relationships and coping strategies through positive role modeling, empathetic listening, a curious approach, and straightforward yet kind communication. Our presence and patience in their lives offer a supportive foundation, allowing our young people to discover who they are and build self-efficacy from the safety and security of relationships with committed and loving people who care deeply about them. Let's explore the role of balanced *authority* and *vulnerability* in combating Harmful Felt-Safety.

Healthy Authority in Combating Harmful Felt-Safety

- **Setting Clear Boundaries:** Establishing and enforcing reasonable limits while ensuring the young person understands why they are in place. If a young person is living in your home, one example might be enforcing a curfew and explaining that it's for their safety and well-being, not just a rule for the sake of having a rule. When your young person isn't living with you, healthy boundaries might be around appropriate times to call, show up, or expect a reply from a text—or which "friends" are or are not invited to visit your home.

- **Providing Structure:** Creating predictable anchor points and routines fosters stability and security. Establishing routines like shared meals, regular check-ins, and traditions creates a sense of predictability and stability. For us, holiday celebrations— especially Thanksgiving and Christmas—are HUGE deals. We shower our young adult girls and their spouses with gifts because almost none of our girls experienced this in their childhoods. We save all year to make this happen, and we go all in with Elf on The Shelf, matching PJs, stockings, blankets, books, and more. It's an exhausting extravaganza (for me). But it's full of so much joy as I watch my adult girls experience a piece of childhood over again. One of our girls told me this year, "Thanks, Mom, you always make me feel like a kid at

Christmas time." That's my goal, my dear. This is an important anchor point in our year; it's structured, and our girls know what to expect and look forward to.

- **Guidance & Support:** We can offer advice and support while allowing young people to make decisions within safe boundaries. We can also help our young people analyze the dynamics of their current relationships using a curious approach and gently guiding a conversation toward what *they* consider a healthy versus unhealthy relationship. As the conversation progresses, we might encourage them to reflect on how their current relationships measure up to *their* standard (not yours). By doing this, we are respecting their autonomy by not dictating what they should do but instead helping them develop some analysis tools and insight.

- **Role Modeling:** Demonstrating healthy behaviors and decision-making as a guide for the young person to emulate. We aren't immune from poor relational choices ourselves, and, like me, you've probably made some bad decisions. Using our own lives and openly discussing our past mistakes and challenges can help our young people grow as we share how we overcame or walked away from toxic relationships. Modeling how to handle conflict and challenging conversations is also an excellent skill to build with your young person. Many of our youth were never given a *voice and a choice* in their relationships or lives, so they have never really learned to express their opinions, needs, and wants.

Healthy Vulnerability in Combating Harmful Felt-Safety

- **Openness and Emotional Sharing:** Being open about your feelings and experiences shows that vulnerability is a strength, not a weakness. It's okay to share how you feel about their relationship choices with a young person if the sharing is done in a non-judgmental and understanding way. For example, *"I am happy to see you making your own decisions in life and relationships. It does make me a little nervous when I think about your relationship with _____. I see some negative patterns there and don't want you to get hurt. If you ever wanted to hear my observations, I would happily share them."* Also, be willing to acknowledge that your observations may be off the mark because you may have limited visibility into the situation. You may also have examples of relationships in your life that you thought were supportive but later realized that they were manipulative or controlling. It can be powerful to describe your emotional journey of recognizing the exploitative nature of the relationships, the struggles in leaving them, and how you learned to establish healthier relationships.

- **Active Listening & Empathy:** Genuinely listen to the young person's concerns and feelings, showing empathy and understanding. There's a concept that I learned from Jim Burn's book, Doing Life with Your Adult Children, called "Door Open. Mouth Shut" that's an expression of always being welcoming to your adult children but learning to keep your mouth shut on your opinions, ideas, and thoughts about *their* life. This is critically important when your young person is in a relationship you view as harmful. A better approach would be to take the curious route and listen to them as they describe their relationship without interrupting or rushing to conclusions on their behalf. You may even reflect on what you've heard to show understanding, "It sounds like you feel connected to this person, but also sometimes unsure about how they treat you." This approach validates the young person's feelings and experiences, creating a safe avenue to explore their thoughts and concerns more deeply.

- **Encouraging Expression:** Providing a safe space for the young person to express their thoughts and emotions freely, without fear of judgment. Speaking with a therapist, keeping a journal, finding an artistic expression that they enjoy that allows them time to think, long walks or any activity specifically centered around time and space to express their thoughts and emotions or think through them. There are even lists of prompt questions online that you could use to help a young person begin to journal their experiences and feelings. These activities lead to insights into the nature of their current circumstances.

- **Admitting Mistakes:** Acknowledging and owning up to your own mistakes, demonstrating that everyone is fallible and that growth comes from learning. There are going to be times that you inevitably overstep—especially when it comes to harmful and toxic relationships. Even though your motives are from a place of love and protection, it is important to quickly acknowledge that it's wrong of you to overstep and that their relationships and lives are theirs to live. This is the most critical when talking about young adults who don't live with you. Youth in your home is a different story, but even then, there's only so much control you can have over the friend choices they make when they are not near you. You might also have stories of failure related to your mistakes in choosing relationships. Most importantly, our ability to own our mistakes is a critical step in modeling for our young people how to repair fractures in relationships.

Behavioral Outcomes & Responses to Harmful Felt-Safety

When a young person is in harmful felt-safety relationships, it can be challenging to see them as such. This requires a lot of patience (and prayer) from parents and mentors who love them and are worried about how their young person might be hurt or at risk in these relationships. This is hard to walk through as a parent or mentor, but just like our other quadrants, it's essential to try and take a step back from your emotions to see the "why" behind the "what" so that we can be influential allies to our young adults in their journey toward *thriving*. We will dive into six prominent categories of behaviors and experiences of youth with high belonging needs and low self-efficacy.

Exploitative Relationships

- Affection is a tool for manipulating relationships: A friend or partner may use affection to grant or withhold love based on the young person's compliance with their demands.
- Imbalanced Investment: Is a relationship in which one person is significantly more invested or involved than the other, leading to an imbalance in which one party exploits the other's emotional or financial resources.
- Controlling Relationships: Are those in which one partner dictates the other's actions, isolating them from friends and family to maintain dominance.
- Exploitative Power Dynamics: Are relationships in which one individual uses the other's naivety or lack of experience to their advantage, often in deceitful or unethical ways.
- Illegal or Unethical Relationships: Are situations where a young person is coerced into illegal or unethical activities under the guise of love or loyalty.

I've answered the phone more times than I can count from one of our girls who finds herself in harmful relationships where her trauma reactions and poor self-awareness/control are triggered, and a significant altercation occurs. It's tough as a parent to see what's happening and be unable to move the needle or make a difference. What I can tell you from personal experience is this: it does change, but it takes a long time. Your young person must see it for themselves, which can take a while. I watched our girl grow and mature, and the exploitative relationships had less and less control over her as time went on because we have consistently spoken kind and loving truth to her yet allowed her to care for her monkeys. It's not easy, but it *is* possible. We must own our feelings and actions and try to take a balanced approach as often as possible.

Young Person in Harmful Felt-Safety **Our *Flourishing* Response**

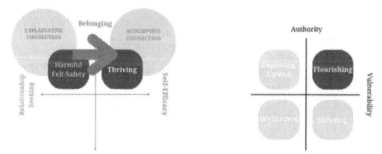

Figure 23 This graph of the Redemptive Connection Framework and Authority/Vulnerability matrixes side-by-side illustrates the desire to move our young person into a balance of belonging and self-efficacy using a balanced approach of authority and vulnerability, leading to flourishing.

A Balanced Approach Using Authority & Vulnerability

- **Educating:** Offering information about the characteristics of healthy vs. exploitative relationships without being judgmental. Sharing articles or resources on healthy relationships and red flags of manipulation or control during a scheduled meet-up.
  - o It's essential to ask your young person if they would like to learn about this with you. This gives them *a voice and a choice* in participating in this learning. They may say no. It's okay; they could always come back later if they know you're always open to conversing and learning when they are ready.
- **Empowering:** Encouraging young people to recognize their value and equipping them with the skills to set boundaries. You can offer role-play exercises they may be experiencing in their relationship so they can practice with you and learn how to set and say safe boundaries while they feel safe with you.

     o One of the most empowering things you can do is to continually speak life-affirming words to them. Let them know that they have worth, potential, and promise. Eventually, they will believe it with you, and as they grow, they will grow out of the toxic relationship that they are in.

- **Supporting:** Being present as a reliable source of emotional support, letting the young person know they are not alone. Offering to be there for the young person to talk after a problematic encounter, providing a compassionate and listening ear without pushing for action.

- **Collaborating:** If the situation is beyond your expertise, work with other professionals, such as counselors. Introduce the young person to a trusted therapist or counselor specializing in relationship dynamics.

- **Modeling:** Demonstrating healthy relationships in your interactions with others and with the young person. Invite the young person to family events where they can observe and interact with the family in a healthy, respectful, and loving manner.

- **Communicating:** Maintaining open lines of communication, showing that you are a safe and non-judgmental resource for discussion. Setting up a weekly coffee date where the young person knows they can openly discuss their life and relationships, with the assurance of confidentiality and support.

Young Person in Harmful Felt-Safety   Our *Control* Response

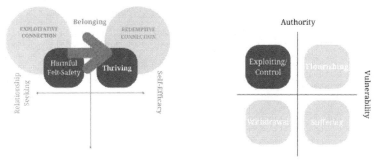

Figure 24 Graph of the Redemptive Connection Framework and Authority/Vulnerability matrixes illustrate the desire to move our young person into a balance of belonging & self-efficacy using an unhealthy authority.

<u>Unbalanced/Unhealthy Authority</u>

- **Imposing Strict Rules Without Discussion:** Strict rules without explanation can make young people feel like they have no personal agency or freedom and are not a good tool for building self-efficacy. Overly punitive measures can breed resentment rather than compliance or understanding.
  - o Examples: Forbidding the young person from seeing their partner without trying to understand the relationship. | Implementing a blanket ban on certain friends without discerning individual influences. | Enacting curfews or communication blackouts without considering the young person's need for autonomy.
  - o As mentors or parents, we often feel frustrated or anxious about our young person's safety and overcompensate with control. We may often believe that strict rules are the only way to protect our young person. We need to balance and authority, and we have a responsibility to help protect our young people. However, we must be thoughtful and approach our authority with vulnerability in seeking to understand. Setting a curfew or saying no to an outing with bad friends (if your young person lives with you) may be perfectly correct if the decision is made thoughtfully and in connection and relationship with your young person – not simply a hammer coming down from our fear.

- **Making Decisions for the Young Person:** Not feeling heard or having their feelings validated can lead to feelings of isolation, especially when our young people feel they have no autonomy over their lives to make good and bad decisions.
  - o Examples: Choosing who the young person can socialize with without their input. | Dictating how the young person should respond to interactions within these relationships. | Handling conflicts on behalf of the young person instead of teaching conflict resolution skills.
  - o It's natural to feel protective, but we must recognize that we risk becoming overbearing in our efforts to protect. We may also clearly see that our young

person isn't using the best judgment and feel it's up to us to steer them in the right direction. Using a G.R.A.C.E. Response, curiosity, and suspending our judgment can help us step back and be more balanced, allowing our young person some room to make decisions and figure out how to solve things independently.

- **Withholding Support as Punishment:** Withdrawing support or affection can lead to a sense of isolation and reinforce the felt-safety they find in the unhealthy relationship.
  - Examples: Withdrawing emotional support if the young person refuses to end a relationship; threatening to revoke privileges or support services because of the young person's relational choices; using 'silent treatment' to show disapproval of their relationship choices.
  - We can sometimes feel desperate to see change and will use punitive measures to 'move the needle.' Waiting is so hard when it comes to giving our young person time to work things out, and I sometimes resort to 'tough love' as the only solution to what I see as self-destructive behavior. I can tell you from experience that it doesn't work.

Young Person in Harmful Felt-Safety   Our *Suffering* Response

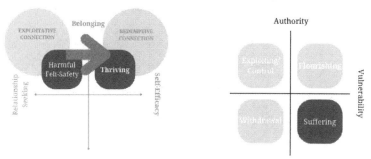

Figure 25 The graph of the Redemptive Connection Framework and Authority/Vulnerability matrixes illustrates the desire to move our young people into a balance of Belonging and self-efficacy by using unhealthy Vulnerability/Suffering.

<u>Unbalanced/Unhealthy Use of Vulnerability</u>

- **Oversharing Personal Struggles:** Oversharing our struggles can leave our young people feeling like they need to be confidants or caregivers, which reverses the roles. They may also feel like their own needs are being sidelined or that they must protect the parent/mentor's feelings.
    - o Examples: Frequently discussing our own past relationship failures, shifting focus from our young person's needs. | Using our time with our young people to vent about our current relational issues. | Constantly comparing our young person's situation with our past.
    - o It's easy to get overwhelmed by our emotions and unconsciously seek support from our young person, even if only to validate our relationship. We can think that by sharing our pain, we are creating a bond without realizing how much of a burden we're putting on our young person.

- **Taking on a Victim Role**: Taking on a victim role or having a victim mentality when you feel helpless that your young person is engaging in exploitative relationships and not listening to your advice may lead to the young person feeling like they need to change, not for themselves, but to alleviate our suffering. They may also feel guilty for causing you so much distress, which can be emotionally manipulative rather than healthy and balanced. We must remember that our goal isn't for immediate behavior change, which can make us feel better but may not fully address the underlying issue in the young person. Our goal is for *them* to develop self-efficacy and take authority in their own life to recognize patterns and get out of them. This takes longer initially, but it lasts a lifetime.
    - o Examples: Expressing how much we have sacrificed to help the young person, implying an obligation for them to change *because they owe us.* | Frequently lamenting the hardships we've endured because of the young person's choices. | Insisting that our suffering results from helping the young person—rather than because we're not choosing a balanced approach and letting the young person's problems

160

become *our* problem (that monkey is on the wrong back).

- o In this place, we may feel unappreciated and think we must suffer or aren't dedicated. This isn't true. We can be happy and fulfilled even if our young person makes poor choices. We are responsible for keeping the lines of communication open, the relationship healthy from our side, and being a sounding board if they need it and want it. The rest is on them. We don't have to suffer for their decisions or be torn down because they aren't showing the gratitude we think they should (how many of us did in our late teens/the early twenties?). We also may believe that we can motivate them to change if we demonstrate sacrifice. Again, not only is this manipulative, but it's also not producing the right change for the right reasons.

Risky Peer Groups | Cults or Extremist Groups

I've included Cults or Extremist Groups with Risky Peer Groups because many of our responses and engagements will look the same. As an overview of what a Cult/Extremist Group might look like, generally, such groups share common characteristics, such as having a charismatic leader, promoting an "us vs. them" mentality, demanding loyalty and conformity, and using manipulative tactics to control members' thoughts and behaviors. They offer a strong sense of belonging or a clear purpose or mission, which can appeal to young people looking for direction or a sense of community. However, these groups often compromise individual autonomy, leading to unsafe situations for their members. Many of the same approaches that are helpful and harmful if your youth is in a Risky Peer Group also apply to Cults or Extremist Groups.

Here are some examples of Risky Peer Groups:
- Gangs: Groups that engage in illegal activities such as vandalism, theft, or violence.
- Substance Abuse Circles: Peers who regularly use drugs or alcohol and encourage others to do the same.
- Illegal Street Racing Groups: Those who participate in or encourage unsafe driving and street racing.
- Groups Engaged in Cybercrime: Peers involved in hacking, illegal downloads, or other forms of cybercrime.

- **Radical Groups**: Organizations that encourage extreme behaviors or ideologies, often against societal norms.

It can often be challenging to strike the right balance of oversight and trust with our young people when they are engaging in risky and sometimes illegal behaviors. We fear the consequences of their actions, and we also fear pushing our young person away by being too distant, too controlling, or too judgmental. When we're feeling this tug-of-war within ourselves, we must remember that our goal is for our young person to learn to stand on their own two feet with healthy belonging & self-efficacy in equal measure. This means that we must keep our relationship open and understanding (even if we disagree – we can still understand that they have the power over their own choices and the consequences of those choices). It also means that we do have to let them make mistakes (big and small) and experience success from *their own* decisions. Our goal is for our young person to feel cared for and respected (in their autonomy), fostering trust and openness. When we have a mutual understanding that our boundaries and support are in place because we want the best for them and their growth, we can become a trusted resource rather than an adversary. To do this well requires an intentionally balanced approach of authority & vulnerability from us.

Balanced Approach Using Authority & Vulnerability
- **Setting Boundaries:** Clearly articulating expectations about behavior and the consequences of engaging with risky groups.
  - Establishing a curfew (if applicable). *"We care about your safety and well-being, so we think a curfew is important. Let's agree on a time you'll be home. It's not about distrust but ensuring your safety. What do you think is a fair time?" "We've been thinking about how we can both feel comfortable with your evening plans, and we feel setting up a curfew is a step in the right direction. We want you to have your evenings, and we also want to know when we can expect you home so that we know you're safe and okay. What time do you think is reasonable for weekdays and weekends? We would like to hear your thoughts."*
  - Discussing legal ramifications of illegal activities. *"Getting involved in illegal activities has serious consequences, not just now but for your future too. It's important to think about how certain actions can impact your life in the long term. We're here to discuss any questions or pressures you might be feeling." "I want to have an open conversation about the risks of getting involved in illegal stuff. It's not just about the law but*

how it affects your future opportunities, like jobs or college. Let's talk through any peer pressure you're facing."

- o Encouraging participation in positive group activities. *"We've noticed that you have a lot of potential and energy. Why don't we look for a club or activity that aligns with your interests? It could be a great way to meet new friends who share your passions. What do you think?" "Have you ever considered joining a group or activity that matches your interests? It's a fantastic way to channel your energy positively and meet people with similar interests. Let's explore some options together and find something that excites you."*

- **Monitoring:** Keeping an open line of communication about the young person's activities without intruding on their privacy and autonomy.
  - o Regular check-ins about their day. *"How was your day today? Anything interesting happening or anything you want to talk about?" "I'd love to hear about what you did today. Did you discover anything new or meet someone interesting?"*
  - o Knowing who their friends are. *"I noticed you've been spending time with new friends. I'd love to learn more about them. What are they like?" "Tell me about the friends you're hanging out with these days. What do you guys usually do together?"*
  - o Being aware of where they spend their time. *"Where do you all usually hang out after school? I'm always here to give you a ride if you need one." "I'm curious about the places you like to go with your friends. Maybe we can visit together sometime, or I can help you find new spots."*

- **Guidance:** Offering advice on how to recognize and avoid negative influences.
  - o Talking about peer pressure resistance techniques. *"If you're ever feeling pressured to do something you're uncomfortable with, it's okay to say, 'I'm not into that,' and change the subject. Have you thought about how you might handle a situation like that?" "Remember, having a few 'exit strategies' up your sleeve for uncomfortable situations is powerful. How do you think you could politely decline something you don't want to do?"*
  - o Role-playing responses to offers of risky behavior. *"Let's try a quick role-play. I'll pretend to be someone offering you a cigarette. How would you respond to keep the situation light but firm?" "Imagine I'm a friend trying to convince you to*

skip class. How would you react? Practicing out loud can help prepare you for the real thing."

- o Providing literature or resources on the impact of risky behavior. *"I found this article about how risky behaviors affect your health and future. Would you be open to reading it together and discussing your thoughts?" "There's a book I read about young people overcoming challenges that I think you might find interesting. It covers some of the risks you might face and how to deal with them. How about we check it out together? I would be happy to reread it with you."*

- **Open Dialogue:** Sharing your concerns without judgment, encouraging the young person to talk about their experiences and peer relationships.

  - o Sharing personal stories of overcoming negative peer influence. *"There was a time I felt pressured to fit in with a group that didn't align with my values. It was tough, but I realized that being true to myself brought me closer to friends who genuinely cared about me. It's okay to feel torn, but remember, true friends will respect your choices." "When I was your age, I faced something similar with friends who didn't always make the best choices. It was tough to step back, but it taught me a lot about who I am and the kind of life I want to lead. It's okay to balance fitting in and standing up for what you believe is right."*

  - o Acknowledging the challenges of fitting in while staying true to oneself. *"I understand how hard it can be to feel like you're on the outside looking in. Wanting to belong is natural, but staying true to who you are is also important. How do you feel when you're with your friends? Do you feel like you can be your real self? Trying to fit in while staying true to who you are is hard. It's like walking a tightrope sometimes, isn't it? How have you been navigating that?"*

  - o Reflecting on the difficulties of making good choices under peer pressure. *"Making decisions can be hard, especially when being pulled in different directions. I've been there. It's important to take a step back and think about what's best for you in the long run. What's one choice you're proud of making recently?" "Making decisions under peer pressure is incredibly tough. I remember going along with something I wasn't comfortable with just because I didn't want to be left out. Looking back, I wish I had trusted my gut. Have you ever felt torn like that?"*

- **Support:** Offering emotional support and understanding for your young person's challenges.
  - o Being present for them after a negative peer encounter. *"I'm here for you to talk about what happened. Would you like to share how you're feeling?" "It sounds like today was rough with your friends. Let's sit down, and you can tell me about it, okay?"*
  - o Providing reassurance of their worth irrespective of peer group affiliation. *"Remember, your value isn't defined by who you hang out with. You're important to me no matter what." "You are valued for who you are, not the people you're with. I hope you always remember that."*
  - o Celebrating their individuality and positive choices. *"I've noticed you made a tough but good decision today. I'm proud of you for that." "Your choice to stay true to yourself in that situation shows a lot of strength. Let's celebrate your courage."*
- **Collaboration:** Working with your young adult to find alternative social groups and activities.
  - o Help them explore clubs or teams that align with their interests. *"I saw a flyer for a local science club that meets weekly. It sounded like something up your alley. Do you want to check it out together?" "You've mentioned wanting to get more involved in sports. Let's look at what teams are available in our community.*
  - o Co-organizing community service projects to meet new people. *"What do you think about organizing a community clean-up? It could be a great way to meet others who care about the environment like you do." "Let's plan a charity event together. It's a good chance to do something positive and connect with like-minded individuals."*
  - o Encouraging hobbies that build a sense of accomplishment and community. *"Have you ever considered joining a photography class? It might be a fun way to express yourself and meet new friends." "Starting a book club could introduce you to others who love reading as much as you do. Shall we give it a go?"*

Responding with a balance of authority and vulnerability fosters a nurturing and supportive environment that allows the young person to feel understood and guided without feeling pressured or judged. As our young people get older our role becomes less parenting and more coaching and prompting to help them as they make significant life moves, decisions, and choices.

Unbalanced/Unhealthy Use of Authority
- **Forbidding Association:** This includes outright bans on interaction with certain friends and monitoring social media, which may lead to rebellion and feelings of being misunderstood by the young person.
  - o Examples: Prohibiting any contact with specific friends without discussing the concerns. | Blocking the young person's social media interactions with those friends. | Insisting on choosing who the young person can or cannot hang out with.
  - o You may feel concerned about your young person's safety and frustrated about your inability to control the situation. That's normal. Yet, we must be careful not to become overly harsh in these moments. Some of these approaches *could* be reasonable if they balance authority/vulnerability while respecting the young person's autonomy and dignity. When we become dictators of their lives, we cross the line into unhealthy authority.
- **Imposing Harsh Penalties:** Enforcing strict punishments for associating with these groups can result in resentment and a sense of isolation from the young person, undermining your intention to protect.
  - o Examples: Grounding the young person for extended periods for associating with those groups. | Taking away personal items or privileges as a form of punishment. | Enforcing unrealistic restrictions on personal freedom.
  - o As parents and mentors, we can feel desperate to deter our young person's behavior, especially when we sense danger. Yet imposing harsh penalties doesn't stop the situation; it temporarily delays it and may open resentment and bitterness that drive the young person to worse behaviors in the future.
- **Invasive Monitoring:** Excessive surveillance of the young person's communications and movements fosters distrust and frustration, damaging your relationship.
  - o Examples: Overly scrutinizing the young person's communications (texts, social media, etc.) |

Demanding constant updates on whereabouts without trust. | Following or spying on the young person without consent.

o We may rightly feel some anxiety and distrust about what our young person is doing, but we can't control them forever, and we can't control them at all when they don't live under our roof. It's their life and their choices. As tetherball supporters, we must stay connected and keep speaking the truth.

These approaches can strain relationships, fostering mistrust and resentment rather than promoting safety and wise choices. At this point in our young person's life, we are moving from having total authority to having only influence. They can choose whether to listen to us based on how they feel about our relationship with them. Healthy influence requires healthy relationships and trust. The strategies we naturally want to employ—control—are driven by fear and a desire to take charge. But they risk alienating our young people, which is the opposite of what we want.

Unbalanced/Unhealthy Use of Vulnerability

- **Expressing Excessive Worry:** This involves overwhelming our young person with our anxieties about safety, resulting in guilt and pressure for the young person to change behaviors primarily to alleviate our worries.
  - o Example: Constantly expressing fears about the young person's safety, leading to heightened anxiety for both you and your young person.
- **Over-Relating Personal Sacrifices:** Frequently reminding our young people of the sacrifices made to support them can make them feel like a burden and potentially rebel against this guilt.
  - o Example: Frequently reminding the young person of the sacrifices made to support them, implying they owe good behavior in return.
- **Emphasizing Our Own Suffering:** By focusing on how the young person's actions negatively impact us, we may inadvertently make the young person feel responsible for our well-being, fostering resentment and a communication breakdown.
  - o Example: Highlighting how the young person's actions are causing your personal distress or health issues.

When we operate from an unhealthy vulnerability, we risk creating a dynamic where our young person may feel more inclined to hide their actions and feelings, leading to a breakdown in communication and trust.

Driven to Create Their Own Permanent Connection:

- <u>Seeking a Partner:</u> Pursuing romantic relationships with an intense desire to escalate the commitment level, often overlooking red flags quickly.
- <u>Rapid Family Formation:</u> Moving quickly into starting a family or cohabitation to cement a relationship.
- <u>Social Media:</u> Creating extensive online presences to cultivate relationships and communities that provide a sense of permanence and identity.

Each of these stems from a fear of abandonment, a deep desire for belonging, and the desire to create lasting bonds. I phrase it this way, *"If I can't get someone to love me unconditionally—I'll create someone who will."* Falsely placing their feelings of being loved and need to belong on an unborn child or romantic partner overburdens the relationship and will likely eventually lead to massive disappointment. We know that all relationships are messy. It doesn't matter how much you love someone. Yet many young adults may not understand that their expectations and fantasies about relationships and family are too idealistic.

<u>Balanced Approach Using Authority & Vulnerability</u>

- **Guided Conversations:** Facilitate discussions about the realities of long-term commitments and parenting, highlighting the joys and challenges. *"Let's talk about what it means to be in a committed relationship. It's about more than just feeling secure; it's a partnership and sharing responsibility." "I understand wanting to feel loved unconditionally. Let's discuss how healthy relationships grow over time and why building a strong foundation is important first."*
- **Resource Planning:** Offer educational materials or workshops on relationships and family planning. *"I found this workshop on understanding relationships that I thought we could check out together. It might offer some good insights." "There's a lot to consider before starting a family. I've got some books and resources that we can go through to help you think about all aspects."*
- **Future Planning:** Help them set personal and professional goals emphasizing the importance of self-sufficiency before taking on the responsibility of caring for another. *"What are*

your dreams for the next five years? Let's make a plan that includes those personal goals alongside any thoughts about family." "Before we add new responsibilities, let's see how we can work towards your independence. What steps do you think we should take?"

- **Sharing Personal Insights:** Without oversharing, relate your understanding of their need for connection, perhaps by discussing times when you sought stability through others. *"I remember feeling a strong need to be connected when I was younger. Sometimes, it led me to make hasty decisions. It's okay to take your time." "I've also felt the fear of being alone. It's hard but also an opportunity to discover what makes us happy, apart from others."*

- **Emotional Support:** Provide a nonjudgmental space for them to express their fears and desires for connection. *"I'm here for you, no matter what. You can always talk to me about your feelings, even the hard ones, and we'll work them out together." "It's natural to want a lasting bond. Let's talk about your feelings, and we can figure out healthy ways to fulfill those needs."*

- **Encouraging Self-Reflection:** Compassionately guide them to explore their motivations and the potential outcomes of their choices. *"It's brave to look inward and ask why we feel the way we do. Have you thought about why these connections feel so important right now?" "Understanding our motivations can be tough but rewarding. What do you think you're looking for in these permanent connections?"*

As a parent or mentor, we can feel empathetic and try to support without imposing. We want our young person to feel understood and guided rather than judged and controlled, leading to a more open and trusting relationship. Yet, as with everything else, we cannot prevent them from making poor choices. One of our girls was pregnant at 17, and I remember feeling overwhelmed by the news but also knowing that many young moms make it with proper support. So, we worked hard to support her without owning her responsibilities. It certainly wasn't always easy, but taking the approach that it was her life and her choices gave us some freedom to continue living our lives without becoming overburdened by hers. This approach fostered a much better relationship, producing an adorable grandson we treasure. By taking a balanced approach with authority & vulnerability, we can show understanding and provide guidance (belonging) while promoting the young person's self-growth and informed decision-making (self-efficacy).

Unbalanced/Unhealthy Use of Authority

- **Excessive Control Over Choices:** We might insist that our young person end a relationship or demand that they use contraception, fearing the responsibility of an unplanned child.
  - o We may feel anxiety over potential financial and emotional burdens and fear the inadequate preparation of our young adults. Those are all typical concerns that expose us to vulnerability. Excessive control may prolong the time, but it will likely only be effective at preventing the behavior if the root belonging need is addressed. Addressing that root need becomes more complex as our young person will likely resist our control, be disempowered, and distrustful.
- **Threats of Withdrawal of Support:** We threaten to cut off support if the young person doesn't comply with our expectations regarding relationships and family planning.
  - o We're desperate to prevent an outcome that we may feel unprepared to handle, so we resort to threats as a last resort. This can backfire on us because it can cause our young person to resort to secretive behavior out of increased pressure and fear of abandonment.
- **Criticizing Decisions:** Persistent criticism of our young person's relationship choices, perhaps driven by the fear of dealing with the consequences of those choices.
  - o We will naturally feel frustrated and concerned about the future and possibly even feel responsible for preventing what we see as a mistake. In becoming critical, however, we can leave our young person feeling judged and unsupported, reinforcing their desire to meet their belonging needs elsewhere.

In an unhealthy authority approach, we can dismiss our young person's desire for connection and belonging and unwittingly belittle their feelings. This leaves the young person feeling invalidated, lonely, and increasingly hungry for belonging, which drives the behaviors we're fighting so hard to prevent. Our reactions stem from fear and a feeling of responsibility to protect our young person. Yet, they are counterproductive to the outcome that we're hoping for.

Unbalanced/Unhealthy Use of Vulnerability

- **Over-identification with the Young Person's Situation:** We may project our fears and experiences onto the young person, overwhelming them with anxiety about future difficulties.
  - o We may feel an overwhelming sense of personal anxiety or déjà vu about our own stories and fear that our young adults' potential mistakes reflect our pasts. This may make our young people feel smothered by our intense identification with their situation and lead to a lack of true individuality.
- **Overwhelming Emotional Response:** We may express distress or disappointment so intensely that it overshadows the young person's feelings and experiences.
  - o We might experience feelings of panic or despair, fearing that our guidance and influence have been ineffective and that our young person's choices will lead to a challenging future (and they might – but isn't every future challenging?). In turn, our young person might feel responsible for our well-being and withdraw from the relationship out of guilt.
- **Catastrophizing the Future:** Painting a dire picture of the future where we see ourselves bearing the responsibility of the young person's potential child, which can create an oppressive atmosphere.
  - o I'm no different than you, and fear can sometimes consume me. I no doubt struggled with these feelings myself in this situation. Feeling a fear of additional responsibilities and potential financial strain, if I had let myself, I could have easily given into feeling helpless and trapped by a choice that wasn't mine. Thankfully, I didn't want our daughter to feel like I thought she had no hope for a future because that is utterly not true. If she had felt that I didn't have faith in her to grow and handle it—even though I knew it would be hard—it would have destroyed our relationship, my relationship with my grandson, and possibly the future of the sweet little family she has now.

In all these scenarios, our intense emotional involvement and projection of our fears can create an environment where our young person feels pressured and unsupported, exacerbating the issues we're trying to prevent.

Overdependence on Technology:

- <u>Social Replacement:</u> Preferring to interact with friends exclusively through social media rather than in person.
- <u>Gaming Excess:</u> Spending excessive time on video games, especially multiplayer online games, at the expense of offline activities.
- <u>Online Persona Focus:</u> More concerned with maintaining and curating an online persona than developing real-world skills or relationships.
- <u>Virtual Escape:</u> Using virtual reality platforms or chat rooms as a primary means of escape and spending a disproportionate amount of time in these worlds.
- <u>Information Overload:</u> Constantly browsing the internet to the point where it interferes with daily responsibilities like schoolwork or job duties.

There's no question that overuse and overdependence on technology are chronic problems for us and the young people in our society. For our young people seeking to escape feelings of isolation and loneliness, technology provides an easy way to meet their belonging needs in a seemingly safe and protective environment. Social media and online communities offer a place where young people can find like-minded people or express themselves in ways they might not be comfortable doing in person. This virtual belonging meets a fundamental human need for connection and recognition, providing a sense of community and identity, even if it sometimes comes at the cost of developing real-world social skills and relationships. In these scenarios, the young person may retreat further into unhealthy digital worlds, especially when faced with real-world challenges, reducing their engagement with direct personal experiences and possibly stunting their social development.

<u>Balanced Approach Using Authority and Vulnerability</u>

- **Technology-Free Zones:** Establish areas or times when technology is not allowed in the home or with others and encourage face-to-face interactions.
  - *"Let's make dinner time a phone-free zone so we can all share our day and enjoy the meal together." "How about we keep bedrooms tech-free after 9 PM to help us all unwind and get better sleep?"*

- **Structured Tech Time:** Designate specific times for technology use, balancing online and offline activities.
  - *"You can have screen time after homework and chores are done, as long as it's not during family time." "Let's set a schedule that includes tech time and activities like sports or reading to keep a good balance."*
- **Realistic Career Path Discussion:** Engage in conversations about the viability and challenges of becoming an influencer as a career path.
  - *"It's impressive how some influencers manage their careers. Let's investigate what it takes to succeed in that space." "Being an influencer can be a real job, but it requires hard work and business savvy. How do you feel about exploring this together?"*
- **Sharing Personal Experiences:** Talk about your struggles with technology balance, showing it's a common challenge.
  - *"I've noticed I feel more relaxed when I take breaks from my phone. Have you felt something similar?" "There was a time I found myself checking emails too often. It's tough, but setting limits helped me."*
- **Expressing Concerns and Listening:** Voice your concerns about technology overuse in a caring way while inviting them to share their views.
  - *"I'm worried we might miss fun family times because of our phones. What do you think?" "I've read that too much screen time can affect sleep. Have you noticed this? Let's talk about what we can do."*
- **Acknowledging the Appeal:** Share an understanding of the allure of being an influencer while guiding towards a realistic understanding of the effort involved.
  - *"I see why becoming an influencer is appealing. It seems like a fun way to earn a living, but it's also a lot of work behind the scenes. What part of it interests you the most?" "The success of influencers can be inspiring. It makes me wonder about all the planning and learning they had to do. Would you like to research what goes into it with me?"*

Addressing overdependence on technology through a balanced approach involves setting clear guidelines (healthy authority) and showing understanding and support (healthy vulnerability). These approaches help to create a supportive environment that encourages the young person to practice self-awareness and develop healthier habits without imposing strict control. It's also important to recognize that just like the internet changed the world for many of us who lived through it, this digital age of social media and emerging tech is changing the landscape for our young people. The rise of AI, Cryptocurrency (Digital Assets & Blockchain Infrastructure), Metaverses, and more create not only an opportunity for distraction but also opportunities to develop new careers in emerging technology fields that we may never fully understand. We don't want to be so afraid of our young people's exploration of technology that we stand in the way of their unique gifts and talents. Yet we do need to also promote *in real life* (irl) communication and engagement.

<u>Unbalanced/Unhealthy Use of Authority</u>

- **Blanket Ban on Technology:** Implementing total bans on the use of technology without exploring its potential benefits can leave our young people feeling frustrated and confused, feeling like we're causing them to lose opportunities for learning and growth to keep up with their peers by being so heavily restricted.
  - o There's no question that technology comes with risks, including being exploited, losing money, becoming an escape mechanism for real life, and more. This can leave us feeling very fearful and overwhelmed, unfamiliar with the speed and change of technology our youth have access to. It can easily cause us to overreact and come down with an iron fist rather than proper structure and healthy boundaries with understanding.
- **Uninformed Criticism:** Dismissing a young person's interest in technology as mere distractions or timewasters without seeking to understand its value or potential can leave our young people feeling dismissed and undervalued, which can drive potentially secretive behaviors and distance in our connection with them.
  - o If you see the technological landscape as "the Wild West," you wouldn't be far from the truth. It's vast and largely unexplored, and its impact and consequences can't be fully known for years. Because of this, it feels so much safer to steer our young people toward more traditional approaches to life and work—and it certainly helps us sleep better at night. But it's not the world they will live in within just a few decades, so we must take a balanced approach and

seek to understand what they find fascinating. We may discover that in the middle of "the Wild West," our young people are building greatness and conquering new territory.

- **Overemphasis on Negative Aspects:** Focusing solely on the risks of technology (e.g., scams in digital assets) without acknowledging the innovative and positive aspects they offer can leave our young people feeling underestimated. It can also cost us an opportunity for open dialogue and learning from our young people.
  - o It's natural to want to protect our young people from potential harm, but every great exploration comes with significant risk. Our focus should always be on real-life engagement and healthy guardrails for our young people, teaching them how not to get lost in an online world and forget that a real one exists around them.

When addressing overdependence on technology, unhealthy authority can manifest as a fear of the unknown without understanding technology's potential benefits. Taking such a rigid and uninformed approach may cause frustration and a feeling of being undervalued by our young person. While it might be overwhelming, and we need to protect, we should also not miss the opportunity to build self-efficacy in our young person by allowing them *to teach us* something about the emerging digital world.

Unbalanced/Unhealthy Use of Vulnerability

- **Excessive Emotional Investment in Tech Usage:** Being overly empathetic with our young person's engagement in technology while ignoring its negative consequences or aspects. This could confuse and frustrate our young person because they sense our disapproval of their level of technological engagement, but we never address it or give clear guidance.
  - o We may feel anxious and helpless, fearing that addressing technology use might push the young person away.
- **Projecting Personal Anxieties:** Projecting our fears about technology onto our young person, discouraging the exploration of digital opportunities and environments. This can stifle our young people because their interests are dismissed or misunderstood. Out of this feeling of being

unfairly judged and restricted based on our fears (founded or unfounded), our young person could potentially use secretive technology. This comes with a measure of risk and danger because we have no visibility into it due to our refusal to engage.

- o Giving completely into our fears about technology leads us to projecting our concerns onto our young person.

- **Avoiding Discussions on Technology's Impact:** Avoiding conversations about technology's role and impact out of fear of conflict. This can leave our young people without the necessary guidance on balancing technology use, which can cause them to feel like we don't support their need to understand how to properly engage in the digital world, leading to unguided exploration or misuse.

In managing overdependence on technology, unhealthy vulnerability can stem from our fear of emerging technology, dangers lurking online, and feelings of helplessness in navigating and keeping up with digital trends. I get it. It's a lot. I've spent more than four years studying blockchain, digital assets, and Web 3.0 to speak intelligently to the young adults around me. I am just now at a place where I can converse with an expert on the topics. Yet, there's so much I still don't understand how to use, access, or anticipate. We can't project our lack of understanding onto our young people growing up in a world that is rapidly moving to digital. Who knows, maybe they can teach us a thing or two.

Enabling Environments:

- <u>Doing All Tasks & Financial Rescue:</u> Continuously paying for the young person's expenses rescues them from financial accountability. Taking care of household chores prevents them from acquiring basic life management skills.
- <u>Extended Living Arrangements Without Independence Goals:</u> Allowing young people to live at home into late adulthood without encouraging steps toward independence or contributing to household expenses and responsibilities.
- <u>Excessive Intervention in Personal Affairs:</u> Calling a young adult's manager or college to address disputes or desires hinders the young person's ability to advocate for themselves and manage conflicts.
- <u>Making All Decisions:</u> From small daily choices to significant life decisions, we cannot direct our young people's lives. This

will limit their ability to think and act independently and greatly impact their self-efficacy.

It's hard to imagine ourselves as *exploitative connections,* yet when we allow our fear of conflict, fear of losing our young person, or confidence that we know best to create an environment where we are *doing for* our young people rather than letting them do things for themselves then we are *exploiting* our relationship with our young person because the need being met is ours and not theirs. While it might feel like we're protecting and providing for our young person, we're actually fostering dependency that makes us feel better. Still, it inhibits personal growth and self-reliance for our young people. Our youth, especially as they enter adulthood, need *interdependency.* They need to know that we are there for them and that they can depend on us for advice and guidance, but that we cannot live or do their life for them.

Balanced Approach Using Authority & Vulnerability

- **Guided Financial Independence:** Gradually introduce financial responsibilities, like budgeting or contributing to household expenses. *"Let's work together to create a budget that includes saving a little from your weekly earnings." "How about you take over the payment for your cell phone bill? We can discuss the best way to manage this expense."*
- **Encouraging Problem-Solving:** Encourage young people to think through solutions instead of immediately intervening in challenges. *"I understand you're having a tough time at work. What do you think is the best way to handle it?" "That sounds like a challenging situation at college. Let's brainstorm some ways you might address this."*
- **Sharing Personal Challenges:** Open up about your own experiences with independence or problem-solving to model resilience. *"When I first started managing my finances, I made mistakes too. It's part of learning." "There was a time I had to deal with a difficult coworker. It wasn't easy, but I learned a lot from handling the situation."*
- **Expressing Support While Promoting Autonomy:** Make it clear that while support is always available, the goal is for them to grow into self-reliance and build self-efficacy. *"I'm here to support you, but I believe you have the skills to navigate this challenge." "It's important to try and solve these problems independently, but I'm always here if you need guidance."*

Taking a balanced approach to authority and vulnerability is crucial because it helps our young people develop essential life skills, fosters interdependence, and builds self-efficacy. It ensures they feel supported yet encouraged to solve problems independently, promoting healthy emotional and psychological growth. This approach prepares them for the complexities of adult life, ensuring they can navigate challenges effectively while knowing they have a supportive safety net if needed. It also gives me, personally, peace of mind in knowing that if something were to happen to me tomorrow, I've done my part to ensure that my girls can navigate life successfully without me.

Unbalanced/Unhealthy Use of Authority

- **Dictating Every Decision:** Making all choices for our young people, from minor daily to significant life choices, leaves them without the skills to make informed decisions.
- **Shielding from Consequences:** This involves constantly rescuing the young person from the natural consequences of their actions, which prevents them from learning accountability and resilience.
- **Dismissing Opportunities for Growth:** Discouraging our young people from engaging in activities or jobs that promote independence due to our anxieties.

In all these scenarios, we are likely overprotecting our youth due to our fears that they can't manage alone. And for most of the mentors and parents I work with (me included), this is an understandable fear. We know that for most of our young people, their cognitive and social abilities might be half of their chronological age due to their experiences with trauma. While that's true, the world will still tell that precious 20-year-old who acts and reacts like a 13-year-old that they are adults and, therefore, can do things independently. So, the risk we take is that we overcompensate for them to such a degree that when they decide at 18 and above that they are moving out, we've impeded their ability to succeed. It's much easier to give more autonomy while we still can than watching them flounder away from us. And it's *our responsibility* to help them become responsible in healthy ways.

Unbalanced/Unhealthy Use of Vulnerability

- **Over-sharing Personal Fears:** Expressing our anxieties about the world excessively makes our young people overly cautious or fearful.
- **Expressing Helplessness:** Frequently discussing our feelings of helplessness in guiding our young people, which could discourage them from seeking solutions or taking risks.

- **Victimizing Ourselves:** Portraying ourselves as victims of the young person's choices potentially leads to guilt-induced compliance rather than healthy decision-making.

Acting out of unhealthy vulnerability as a mentor or parent can hinder our young person's growth toward interdependence and self-efficacy. It can create a dynamic where the young person feels responsible for our emotional well-being, leading to guilt and inhibiting their ability to make autonomous decisions. Avoiding such behavior encourages a healthier relationship, creating an environment where our young people can learn to navigate life's challenges confidently and interdependently.

A G.R.A.C.E. Response to Harmful Felt-Safety

The G.R.A.C.E. Response confronts the many scary and harmful outcomes of a young person engaged in Harmful Felt-Safety relationships, providing a narrative that embodies grace, understanding, and empowerment. Through its use, we help provide our young person with the tools and support needed to navigate away from exploitative situations toward genuine safety and belonging, reinforcing the idea that growth and healing are possible with the proper support and understanding.

G: Get to Why

Explore underlying reasons for your young person's attraction to harmful felt-safety scenarios, understanding their need for belonging and safety. Practice accepting and acknowledging the young person's feelings and experience. Accepting that a young person feels a certain way doesn't mean you must agree with those feelings.

R: Rally Around Realistic Goals

Set achievable goals with your young person for developing healthier relationships and self-sufficiency. Goal setting can empower young people to make choices that lead to genuine safety and belonging.

A: Affirm Redemptive Positives

Highlight your young person's strengths and positive steps they've taken—focusing on effort, not outcomes—reinforcing their value and potential for growth. Guidance with compassion toward understanding the difficulty of navigating away from harmful connections alongside the hope and benefits of having the strength to make the right choice.

C: Cultivate Resilience

Encourage strategies for coping with setbacks and building emotional strength and flexibility. Healthy resilience uses our innate strengths to overcome adverse situations. Help your young person discover their strengths and learn to leverage them to build a thriving life.

E: Engage Supportive Community

Connect the young person with supportive networks and resources that offer genuine safety and belonging. Helping young people build healthy relationships and community support fosters their ability to choose and maintain *Redemptive Connections.*

"A journey of a thousand miles begins with one step." This Chinese proverb is highly appropriate for us as mentors and parents for young people navigating their way toward healthy belonging from harmful felt-safety relationships. It is not going to happen overnight. But it can happen if we continually show up with love and belonging to help our young people feel genuinely safe, seen, and valued. Our goal is not to yank them out of harmful relationships but to equip them with the courage, resilience, and autonomy to envision a better life for themselves and take the steps to make it happen. We will cheer them on every step of the way.

"Survival mode is supposed to be a phase that helps save your life. It is not meant to be how you live."
Michele Rosenthal

CHAPTER ELEVEN

SURVIVAL
FORFEITING CONNECTION

"I don't care how many hours I have to work. I'll work my whole life away if I have to, but I never want to be hungry and not have a home again." This was a statement made to me by one of our precious daughters after I asked her to consider not working so many hours so that she could be at more family events. It tore my heart open. I *knew* that she desperately needed a break for her health. I also *knew* that she needed to experience the true belonging of family. She *knew* the pain of hunger, the failure of the people who were supposed to protect her, and extreme loneliness. At this moment, what I *knew* would naturally lose to what she *knew* and *felt* overwhelmingly in her body, mind, and emotions. All I could do was share an understanding and choose to stay the course in my outreach to her heart. I understood her because I've lived much of my life in this quadrant. I'm still growing and learning in relationships, and slipping into *survival* mode by overworking, disconnecting, avoiding emotions, and other maladaptive strategies. *Survival* mode is still super easy for me to do when I'm not aware of myself. Of all the quadrants, this one is the easiest and the hardest for me to write.

Survival in the Redemptive Connection Framework
Avoidant Attachment, Dismissive Attachment, or Counter-dependency can all describe the relational difficulties for a young person in the Survival quadrant who chooses to self-protect by forfeiting the possibility of healthy connections. Instead, they tap into their internal resilience structures and messages of brokenness, deciding that there's no one else to depend on or trust. Rather than suffer more hurtful relationships, they pull themselves up by their bootstraps and "make it on their own"—getting by on their limited resources and abilities. While this strategy may work for part or much of their life, a young person may experience many relational difficulties, loneliness, and a hard time experiencing failures and setbacks.

Defining Counter-dependency[32]

Counter-dependents lack trust in others and fear the consequences of doing so. They resist asking for help, even when it is reasonable, and seek to become completely self-reliant. They operate with an "avoidance mindset," which manifests as steering clear of conflict by taking care of things themselves, having difficulty relaxing, constantly needing to stay busy, and struggling to form deep bonds with others due to fear of intimacy. Counter-dependents are often intensely hard on themselves and can feel an extreme sense of loneliness and depression. They can also have a disrupted sense of self due to constantly managing their personalities, and they should never appear weak or needy. They may struggle with anxiety, continually second-guess the motives of those in their lives, and feel a constant push to be capable of everything and never make mistakes. They crave connection but feel a sense of shame for needing it.

Harley Therapy's Mental Health Blog[33] says: Counter-dependents can often come across as vibrant, "life of the party" sorts or as the kind with many friends and relationships. The difference is that those relationships will not be deep and trusting and might not last. So, one of the main signs of counter-dependency is an inability to have connected and authentic relationships. Here are a few signs that they list as not being connected:

- Seeming good at relating but having a point or wall where it stops.
- Feeling 'trapped' in relationships.
- Pushing people away or going cold without warning.
- Fear of abandonment or rejection (so abandon or reject first).
- Tendency to date needy 'over-givers' (codependents).
- Are always 'busy' (might even overwork or have too many hobbies to avoid intimacy).
- Anxiety and fear arise if relationships get too deep.
- Instead of seeking support in relationships, they are prone to complaining and suffering.

Healthy Autonomy & Counter-Dependency. What is the Difference?

Psychology Today[34] says: The key to understanding counter-dependency is differentiating it from healthy autonomy. Healthy autonomy is a state of confident self-reliance in which an individual a) recognizes

---

[32] https://www.ashleytreatment.org/rehab-blog/what-is-counter-dependency/

[33] https://www.harleytherapy.co.uk/counselling/what-is-counterdependency.htm

[34] https://www.psychologytoday.com/us/blog/theory-knowledge/201404/signs-counter-dependency

their interdependency with others, b) has an agentic sense of self (i.e., a sense that one can effectively control one's destiny), and c) is not fully controlled or influenced by others. The primary defining feature of healthy autonomy is first that the autonomy motive is an "approach mindset," meaning that the individual desires to be (relatively) self-reliant because they want to recognize their full potential as an individual, but one who is simultaneously and securely interconnected with others. Second, healthy, autonomous individuals can regularly form effective, meaningful, intimate, long-term relationships with others. They can share, be vulnerable, and are comfortable relying on others when it is reasonable.

On the surface, counter-dependency may look like a healthy autonomy. For example, both involve the capacity to separate from others. However, what drives counter-dependency is an "avoidance mindset," namely the avoidance of relying on others because of a fundamental mistrust of the dependability of relationships. In addition, although these individuals might have superficially positive relationships because they fundamentally fear intimacy, even in marriage, a counter-dependent will hide core aspects of their experience, resist showing dependency needs, and be reluctant to open up. Instead, they will often offer a superficial confidence and/or separate and avoid whenever a need or opportunity for deep emotional connection surfaces. It can be very frustrating for their partners and those who love them and desire connection.

In this book, I've quoted Karyn Purvis as saying, "What was broken in relationship can only be healed in relationship." There isn't a quadrant that so perfectly fits this statement as the Survival quadrant. In survival, a young person, or even me, desperately longs for connection, belonging, and intimacy. Still, because it's easier to be self-reliant, they will create space between themselves and others to self-protect and feel a sense of control.

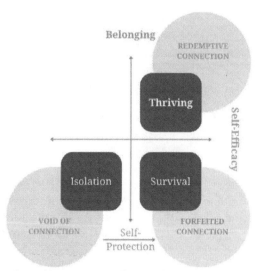

Figure 26 Survival as self-protection is illustrated in the Redemptive Connection Framework.

Below are some examples of *Survival*:

- **Conflict Avoidance:** Young people may physically leave or emotionally withdraw during arguments or confrontations.

- **Communication Evasion:** Ignoring or avoiding responses to direct communication attempts such as emails, calls, or messages.

- **Tension Shutdown:** Becoming emotionally non-responsive or detached during tense or stressful situations.

- **Disassociation & Overcompensation:** Mentally detaching from immediate surroundings or emotions. Or manifest a mental detachment during stress while also overcompensating by being the planner and caretaker, constantly staying busy with tasks to avoid facing their own needs or vulnerabilities.

- **Activity Distraction | Overworking/Success Drive:** Filling time with activities or noise to avoid silence or dealing with troubling thoughts and channeling energy into continuous work or the pursuit of success, often using these achievements to avoid emotional engagement or introspection.

- **Blame Shifting:** Tending to assign fault to themselves or others in a rigid, black-and-white thinking pattern.

In each scenario, self-protection is prominent with strong self-efficacy, while distrust of relationships shows extremely low belonging. This can be one of the easiest quadrants to overlook as a mentor or parent because the traits can superficially resemble positive autonomy. Our young person may succeed in their career or education goals with a strong work ethic and high levels of independence—every parent's dream, right? However, success at independence can mask an underlying fear and lack of vulnerability to develop deep, safe, and connected relationships.

This tendency to *forfeit connection* can easily be overlooked or misunderstood as simply part of being a driven and self-sufficient young person. However, this would be a mistake on our part due to the risk associated with leaving *survival* unaddressed in our young person's life.

Below are the risks associated with *survival*:

- **Emotional and Psychological Distress:** Persistent isolation may lead to mental health issues like chronic loneliness, depression, or anxiety.
- **Economic Vulnerability:** A lack of stable connections can result in financial instability, chronic poverty, or homelessness.
- **Health Neglect:** Without a supportive network, a young person may struggle with untreated physical and mental health issues, as there's no one to encourage care.
- **Relationship Strain:** Difficulty in forming lasting, intimate connections could lead to a pattern of shallow relationships.
- **Stress and Burnout:** Intense focus on work and personal achievement may cause emotional and physical exhaustion.
- **Growth Inhibition:** A reluctance to be vulnerable and connect deeply with others can hinder personal and emotional development.

Understanding the risk involved with the *survival* quadrant helps us as mentors and parents to see the behaviors and the importance of addressing them. Because a young person in this quadrant is so self-sufficient, getting them to slow down, listen to the risk, and act can be challenging. It takes consistent reassurance of a deep connection to them over a sustained period to help the young person relax and begin to repair. Transparently, in my case, it took parenting young adults from hard places and needing to "succeed" for me to see my own need for connection and tendency toward survival. It was only out of my drive to succeed and feelings of failure that my eyes were opened to my dismissive attachment or counter-dependency—only then was I ready to put in the work to heal myself.

As mentors and parents, it's critical to recognize these risk factors because identifying them early can prevent longer-term negative impacts. Understanding these risks enables us to provide targeted support, guidance, and resources to help our young people build better coping mechanisms, develop and maintain meaningful relationships, and take advantage of the services they need to heal. Our support and encouragement can improve mental, emotional, and physical health and improve young people's social and economic outcomes.

Survival: Balancing Authority & Vulnerability

Being a *Redemptive Connection* to a young person in the *survival* quadrant can, on the one hand, seem super easy because they don't need much from us regarding money, advice, or planning. They already know where they are headed and are taking the steps necessary to make it happen. On the other hand, it can also feel like we're not needed, and we can question whether the young person values us. This can cause us to harbor some resentment as it draws out our inner insecurities. This quadrant can be especially hard on our attempts at a flourishing relationship because the young person may continually not need or turn away our attempts at authority while leaving us vulnerable, wondering if the relationship matters. Yet balancing authority and vulnerability is just as crucial in this quadrant as in any other because it creates a safe environment for open communication and growth.

When used compassionately, authority provides the structure and guidance that the young person still needs—whether they admit it or not. Vulnerability models trust and openness that young people desperately need to master, and it encourages them to share their struggles and fears as they see us sharing ours. This balance helps build a strong, trust-based relationship where the young person feels supported and understood, which is crucial for moving beyond survival mode and thriving with genuine connection and belonging.

<u>Healthy Authority in Survival</u>
- **Establish Relational Structure:** A clear relational structure can help a young person in survival by providing them with a sense of security and predictability in an otherwise chaotic or uncertain world. Providing a structured environment helps the young person learn to trust, understand relational expectations, and navigate their relational responsibilities more effectively. This structure is essential for their emotional and psychological development, allowing them to focus on healing and growth.

- **Active Listening:** Practicing active listening with a young person in the survival quadrant helps to build trust and validate their thoughts and feelings. By being attentive when we listen and responding with empathy, we can communicate that their feelings are important and that we respect them. This supportive method can help break down their barriers (walls), encourage them to be open, and promote a deep connection, which is essential for their emotional recovery and healthy relational skills.

- **Guidance with Independence:** It's important to remember that independence is valued highly by our young people, and to a large degree, they *can* do it. We should empower young people to make decisions, boosting self-confidence and resilience. While valuing the young person's capacity for independence, offering support and sharing wisdom is equally essential, helping them refine their problem-solving and critical-thinking abilities. This balanced approach nurtures growth, ensuring the young person feels capable yet supported as they navigate life's challenges.

- **Responsible Modeling:** Modeling healthy relationships and intimacy, such as showing respect, being responsive, demonstrating empathy, and understanding others and allowing our young people to observe us constructively as we handle conflicts (especially with them), maintaining open and honest communication, and exhibiting emotional support and affection appropriately. This modeling teaches our young person the importance of healthy emotional connections. It sets a positive example for building and maintaining meaningful and respectful relationships, which is vital for their emotional growth and development.

Healthy Vulnerability in Survival

- **Respectful Communication:** Actively listening, validating their feelings, speaking calmly and clearly, and ensuring our language is free of judgment and criticism. This approach may feel risky because you may want to push harder for a better relationship. Yet a respectful approach builds trust and reinforces the young person's value and worth.

- **Conflict Resolution:** Teaching our young people how to understand the other person's perspective, calmly discuss concerns without assigning blame, and collaboratively seek solutions are essential conflict resolution skills that help them stay in relationships rather than walk away.

- **Emotional Support:** We can offer emotional reinforcement by affirming their emotions and encouraging them to share instead of hiding them. A young person in the survival quadrant finds it challenging to express emotions. As a parent or mentor, we should gently encourage expression without pressure, offer a consistent, non-judgmental presence, and validate their shared emotions. Acknowledging their strength and resilience is as important as showing appreciation for their experience and struggles.

- **Honesty & Integrity:** Consistently telling the truth, following through on promises, admitting mistakes, and showing consistency between words and actions are all ways we can show up with honesty and integrity in our relationship with our young person. Demonstrating these qualities teaches the importance of trustworthiness and reliability in building and maintaining healthy relationships. It sets a strong example for our young person to emulate, emphasizing the value of living with honesty and integrity in their own life.

- **Healthy Intimacy:** We can demonstrate healthy intimacy to our young person by regularly showing emotional warmth, engaging in open and honest conversations about feelings, respecting their boundaries, and being reliable and present. Creating a safe and trusting environment can teach young people the importance of close, caring relationships and how to express affection and vulnerability healthily, fostering a sense of security and belonging.

Behavioral Outcomes & Responses to Survival

Many things in our young person's life are useful during trauma. Survival is one of those categories where the skills they developed may have kept them safe, out of harm's way, and possibly even alive. In clinical terms, they would be called *adaptive* skills, defined as "the ability to effectively meet social and community expectations for personal independence, physical needs, and interpersonal relationships expected for one's age and cultural group.[35]" In other words, they are behaviors that help them adapt to their current environment. Those adaptive behaviors

---

[35] Brown, McDonell, Snell, 2016. Definition taken from Human Kinetics article titled, "Adaptive and Maladaptive Behavior" https://us.humankinetics.com/blogs/excerpt/adaptive-and-maladaptive-behavior

can become *maladaptive* as they enter adulthood and try to build a life, career, relationships, and social skills. Behavior that interferes with everyday activities is called *maladaptive behavior* or, more often, problem behavior. It is often undesirable, socially unacceptable, and interferes with acquiring desired outcomes, skills, or knowledge[36]. As a child, I learned early on to keep to myself and stay out of the line of fire if my parents were fighting or alcohol was involved. This created a fierce independence and autonomy in me. Admittedly, I was a firstborn, and some of that came with the territory, but I was also hypervigilant and ready to flee the war zone instantly. Carrying that into marriage and parenting was not healthy. The behavior that was highly adaptive growing up became maladaptive as I became an adult. And it took me many years to realize it. So, I can tell you from firsthand experience that it can be very difficult to move out of survival behaviors because, in many ways, they are a security blanket that we've held onto for our entire lives. It's a very vulnerable feeling to lay them down, and it takes people we trust implicitly to give us the safe space to do that. Trust takes time and builds over a lifetime. You can't rush many things in this quadrant.

Conflict Avoidance:
- <u>Room/Communication Exit:</u> To avoid confrontation, the young person walks out of the room or hangs up the phone during discussions on sensitive topics.
- <u>Subject Change:</u> Quickly changing the subject to avoid engaging in conversations about personal issues or conflicts.
- <u>Silent Response:</u> Responds with silence or evasive answers like "I don't know" when inquiring about feelings or needs.
- <u>Meeting Avoidance:</u> Skips family meetings or activities involving discussions of behavior, feelings, or conflicts.
- <u>Deflecting Humor:</u> Uses humor to deflect serious conversations about personal issues or family dynamics.

---

[36] Bruininks, Woodcock, Hill, 1996. Definition taken from Human Kinetics article titled, "Adaptive and Maladaptive Behavior" https://us.humankinetics.com/blogs/excerpt/adaptive-and-maladaptive-behavior

Young Person in Survival

Our *Flourishing* Response

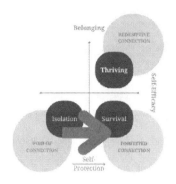

Figure 27 The graph of the Redemptive Connection Framework and Authority/Vulnerability matrixes side-by-side illustrates the desire to move our young person into a balance of belonging and self-efficacy using a balanced approach of authority and vulnerability, leading to flourishing.

A Balanced Approach Using Healthy Authority & Vulnerability

- **Engage with Empathy:** Approach the young person with understanding and patience, acknowledge their discomfort with conflict, and gently encourage open dialogue. *"I understand that talking about this can be tough. It's okay to feel uneasy. What can I do to make this easier for you?" "I've noticed you seem uncomfortable when we discuss certain topics. It's completely normal to feel this way. I'm here to listen whenever you're ready to share."*

- **Reassure Safety:** Reiterate that their thoughts and feelings are valid and that the family space is a safe environment for honest conversations. *"I want you to know that your thoughts and feelings are always respected here. It's safe to share, even if we disagree." "This is a safe space for you to express yourself. Nothing you say will change how much we care about you."* And make sure you mean that for real.

- **Model Vulnerability:** Share personal experiences with conflict to show it's normal and manageable, demonstrating vulnerability as a strength. *"I remember feeling similarly when I was your age. It was hard, but sharing helped me through it. It's okay to be vulnerable." "I've had times when I was scared to open too. It's tough but also a step towards understanding each other better.*

- **Consistent Presence:** Maintain a consistent presence, showing that avoidance doesn't affect the stability of their

190

relationship with the young person. *"Even if you don't want to talk right now, I want you to know I'm here for you, always ready to listen." "Remember, I'm here for you, whether you want to talk or sit silently. You're not alone."*

- **Positive Reinforcement:** Recognize and reinforce any efforts towards engagement, however small, to build confidence in communication. *"I appreciate you sharing that with me, even if it was difficult. It means a lot." "Opening up about how you feel is a big step. I'm proud of you for that, and we need to understand you better."*

Young Person in Survival   **Our *Control* Response**

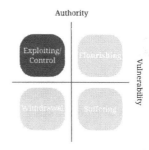

Figure 28 The graph of the Redemptive Connection Framework and Authority/Vulnerability matrixes illustrates the desire to move our young person into a balance of belonging and self-efficacy using unhealthy authority.

Unbalanced/Unhealthy Use of Authority

- **Demanding Conformity:** Insisting the young person in engaging in conversations or attending meetings without considering their comfort or readiness.
- **Minimizing Feelings:** Dismissing the young person's emotions or concerns as overreactions or irrelevant, undermining their feelings.
- **Forced Disclosure:** Pressuring the young person to share their thoughts, story, life history, or feelings before they are ready, violating their sense of privacy.
- **Ignoring Boundaries:** Overstepping our young person's boundaries to control or influence their actions.
- **Punitive Measures:** Using punishment or the threat of punishment in response to avoidance or silent treatments rather than seeking understanding.

As mentors or parents, we might feel frustrated, anxious, or powerless, which leads us to exert more control through authority. This reaction can stem from our desire to resolve issues quickly or our discomfort with conflict and uncertainty. However, for our young person, this approach can evoke feelings of being misunderstood, trapped, rejected, or bullied, which can further hinder their ability to open up and possibly lead to even more withdrawal or resistance.

Young Person in Survival   Our *Suffering* Response

Figure 29 The graph of the Redemptive Connection Framework and Authority/Vulnerability matrixes illustrates the desire to move our young people into a balance of belonging and self-efficacy by using unhealthy vulnerability.

Unbalanced/Unhealthy use of Vulnerability.

- **Over-Sharing:** Disclosing personal problems or insecurities inappropriately, seeking comfort from the young person.
- **Seeking Approval:** We look for validation from the young person for our actions or decisions, reversing roles.
- **Emotional Dependency:** Relying on the young person for emotional support, burdening them with adult concerns.
- **Lack of Boundaries:** Failing to maintain a professional or parental boundary, confusing the relationship dynamics.
- **Avoiding Decisions:** We hesitate to make or enforce decisions because we fear upsetting the young person and undermining our authority.

It's easy to feel insecure in our relationship with a young person in the survival quadrant. Their fierce independence and confidence can make us feel like we aren't needed. This may cause us to seek validation and support from our young people to draw them into the relationship, reversing the typical support dynamic. This dynamic can make the young person feel burdened, responsible for our emotional well-being, and confused about the proper roles in the relationship.

Communication Evasion:

- <u>Unanswered Messages</u>: Consistently not replying to texts, emails, or direct messages, leaving communications unacknowledged.
- <u>Delayed Responses</u>: Waiting excessively long to reply, often when urgent decisions or input are needed.
- <u>Selective Responding</u>: Only answering certain parts of a message or questions while ignoring others that might require deeper engagement or disclosure.
- <u>Ghosting</u>: Ceasing all communication suddenly and without explanation, especially after a period of active interaction.
- <u>Excuse Making</u>: Frequently citing reasons or excuses for not responding, such as being too busy, even when patterns suggest avoidance.

In Chapter Six, we talked a lot about emerging adulthood and that the late teens to late twenties are years of a young person's life where they may be self-focused in healthy ways. We must distinguish between healthy self-focus on building a life for themselves and unhealthy communication avoidance. Most days, I talk to one or more of my girls, but I may not speak to them every day. That's okay. They are all busy building their lives, working jobs, having relationships, parenting kids, and focusing on marriages.

<u>A Balanced Approach Using Healthy Authority & Vulnerability</u>

- **Open Dialogue:** Invite discussions about communication preferences and express the importance of timely responses for mutual understanding. *"I've noticed some of my messages haven't been answered. Can we talk about how we communicate? It's important to me that we understand each other." "I understand everyone gets busy, but I worry when I don't hear back from you. How can we make our communication work better for both of us?"*
- **Empathetic Inquiry:** Show understanding of possible reasons behind evasion while highlighting the value of honest communication. *"Is there a reason you've been unable to respond to messages? I want to make sure you're feeling okay and not overwhelmed." "If*

responding feels difficult, could you let me know? Even a short message helps. I'm here to support you, not to add pressure."

<u>Unbalanced/Unhealthy Use of Authority</u>

- **Demanding Replies:** Insisting on immediate responses without considering the young person's context or feelings. *"Why haven't you answered my messages? You need to reply as soon as you see them." "It's disrespectful to ignore my calls. I expect an answer every time I reach out."*

- **Punitive Measures:** Implementing consequences for not responding, such as restrictions or ultimatums, without seeking to understand underlying reasons. *"If you continue to ignore my messages, we must reconsider our relationship or your privileges." "Every message you ignore will result in a consequence. Communication is not optional here."*

When frustrated, ignored, and worried, it's easy to default to "bringing the hammer down" to evoke a response. We feel a sense of responsibility for our young person's well-being and safety, which can grow when we don't hear from them. I don't know about you, but in 10 seconds, I can go from "they're alright and just living their life" to "they've been kidnapped, wrecked their car, been arrested, lost their job, are living in a van down by the river…" I think, as parents, our brains are just wired that way. Our young person, on the other hand, may feel pressured, misunderstood, or overwhelmed by our expectations. This dynamic can lead to feelings of rebellion or further withdrawal, making the communication gap even wider than it already was.

<u>Unbalanced/Unhealthy Use of Vulnerability</u>

- **Over-Personalizing:** Interpreting the lack of response as a personal rejection or failure may lead to the young person expressing feelings of hurt or inadequacy. *"I feel like you don't value our relationship when you don't reply. It really hurts me." "Your silence makes me feel like I'm failing you as a mentor. What am I doing wrong?"*

- **Seeking Validation:** Looking for reassurance from the young person that they are still valued, potentially reversing the roles, and placing an emotional burden on them. *"Please just let me know you're okay. I worry you're upset with me." "I need to hear from you. It's the only way I know you still care."*

In this emotional state of heightened vulnerability, we are driven to seek affirmation and validation from our young person to build our worth and feel like our role matters. However, this dynamic puts undue strain on the relationship and can lead to the young person feeling overburdened with emotions.

Tension Shutdown:
- Emotional Withdrawal: Pulling back from conversations or interactions, often resulting in silence or minimal engagement.
- Physical Disengagement: Leaving the room or creating physical distance when discussions become intense or uncomfortable.
- Flat Affect: Displaying little to no emotional response when a reaction is typically expected, appearing indifferent.
- Selective Mutism: Choosing not to speak in certain stressful situations despite being physically capable of communication.
- Distraction Engagement: Turning attention to unrelated tasks or activities to avoid dealing with the present tension.

Tension shutdown can occur based on a fight, flight, or freeze response—flipping their lid (see Chapter Five). Several of our girls have shut down when they've experienced tension, especially during conflict. I remember one of our girls in her late teens sitting on the couch with a blanket over her head as we tried to engage with her over a point of mutual conflict. She refused to look at us. We asked her if she would rather take some time and write us an email, to which she huffily replied from under her cocoon of protection, "Yes!" Then promptly got up and stomped out. We received the most articulate email an hour later, which surprised us both. Her brain needed space to form its thoughts. Letting her respond via email was the game-changer. One of our other girls needed to run before the conflict. This would lessen her temptation to rage during a complicated conversation. Running it off allowed her to get some pent-up emotions out before engaging in conversation. While I can give you some suggestions and ideas in this book, remember that every young person is unique, and you may have to experiment to find what their brains, bodies, and hearts need.

A Balanced Approach Using Healthy Authority & Vulnerability
- **Patient Inquiry:** Gently ask open-ended questions to encourage communication without pressure. *"I've noticed you seem quiet. Would you like to talk about what's on your mind when you're ready?" "It's okay if you're not ready to talk now. How can I support you in this moment?"*
- **Validating Feelings:** Acknowledging the difficulty of the situation and their response without judgment. *"It seems like this is*

tough for you. I'm here to listen whenever you feel like sharing." "I understand that sometimes it's hard to express our feelings. I want you to know it's okay to take your time."

Unbalanced/Unhealthy Use of Authority

- **Forcing Communication:** Demanding immediate discussion despite the young person's discomfort or unwillingness to engage. *"We're talking about this now, whether you like it or not. You can't just shut down on me."*

- **Dismissing Emotions:** Minimizing or invalidating the young person's feelings by telling them to "get over it" or criticizing their response as overly sensitive. *"Stop being so dramatic. It's not that big of a deal. Just get over it and move on."*

- **Punitive Actions:** Implementing consequences for not engaging in conversation, such as taking away privileges or issuing ultimatums. *"If you're not going to talk to me and tell me what's wrong, then you can forget about our plans this weekend; they're canceled."*

Unbalanced/Unhealthy Use of Vulnerability

- **Emotional Coercion:** Expressing personal hurt or disappointment to guilt the young person into opening up, which burdens them emotionally. *"When you don't talk to me, it really hurts my feelings. I'm trying so hard to help you."*

- **Over-Reliance for Comfort:** Seeking comfort from the young person for your feelings of failure or frustration due to the communication breakdown, reversing the support dynamic. *"I feel like I'm failing as a mentor/parent when we can't communicate. I need to know you still value this relationship."*

Disassociation & Overcompensation:

- Zoning Out: Frequently appearing lost in thought or unresponsive during conversations, indicating mental disengagement from the present.

- Hyper-Activity: They immerse themselves in tasks or projects, often discussing more responsibilities than necessary to avoid idle time.

- Controlled Environment: Obsessively organizing or planning every detail of personal and family life, seeking to maintain control over external circumstances.

- <u>Caregiver Role:</u> Consistently putting others' needs before their own, often to the detriment of personal well-being or ignoring their own needs.
- <u>Emotional Numbing:</u> Showing little to no reaction to events that would elicit a strong emotional response, indicating detachment.

Disassociation can sound pretty scary, and in some ways, it is, but it's also an effective and adaptive survival skill for young people in an abusive environment. The ability to "go somewhere else" in your mind provides protective endurance through the abuse. That's tough to hear, and it's tough to watch with our young people who we're walking alongside toward healing. Still, it's essential to understand so that as we approach this behavior, we have an empathetic and understanding point of view.

<u>A Balanced Approach Using Healthy Authority & Vulnerability</u>

- **Empathetic Engagement:** Openly discuss the behaviors without judgment, showing understanding and concern for their underlying causes. *"I've noticed you've been taking on a lot lately and seem distant. How are you feeling about everything?" "It's okay to step back and not handle everything alone. What's one thing you wish you could let go of?"*
- **Supportive Guidance:** Offer support and resources while encouraging young people to explore feelings and needs they may neglect. *"Let's find a way together to balance your commitments so you have time to focus on yourself. What's something you enjoy doing just for you?" "I'm here for you, not just to help with tasks but to support you emotionally. Would you like to talk about what's on your mind?"*

<u>Unbalanced/Unhealthy Use of Authority</u>

- **Demanding Stoppage:** Insisting the young person immediately ceases their coping mechanisms without understanding the underlying issues. *"You need to stop zoning out and overdoing it with the planning. Just focus on what's important."*
- **Minimizing Concerns:** Disregard the reasons behind their behaviors as unimportant or an overreaction. *"I don't see why you're making such a big deal out of this. You're just avoiding what you need to do."*

<u>Unbalanced/Unhealthy Use of Vulnerability</u>
- **Self-Blaming:** Blaming ourselves for the young person's behaviors, expressing personal distress or failure. *"Seeing you like this makes me feel like I've failed you. What am I doing wrong?"*
- **Emotional Dependence:** Seeking emotional support from the young person, reversing roles and responsibilities. *"I need you to be okay for me to feel okay. Your actions are making me worried all the time."*

Activity Distraction | Overworking/Success Drive:
- <u>Non-Stop Scheduling:</u> Filling every moment of the day with tasks, meetings, or projects, leaving no downtime.
- <u>Perfectionism in Tasks:</u> Obsessing over details to ensure every project or task is completed to an unrealistic standard of perfection.
- <u>Avoiding Quiet Moments:</u> Seeking out constant noise or activity, like always having music or TV on, to prevent quiet reflection.
- <u>Multitasking Excessively:</u> Juggling multiple activities at once to stay busy, often beyond what is reasonable or productive.
- <u>Relentless Goal Setting:</u> Continuously setting and pursuing goals without reflecting on achievements or personal well-being.

Many of these behaviors are healthy and should be celebrated when balanced. The challenge for our young people in the survival quadrant is that these activities are used to mask their underlying need for healthy relationships and the hurt that is associated with it. As parents and mentors, we must walk gently and supportively alongside them as they navigate their hurt and become ready to relax and relate meaningfully. This can take a long time, but the level of trust and connection secured along the way is truly priceless.

<u>A Balanced Approach Using Healthy Authority & Vulnerability</u>
- **Encourage Mindful Breaks:** Suggest specific times for breaks to relax or engage in leisure activities without a productivity goal. *"How about we set aside time this weekend for something fun, just to unwind? It's important to recharge." "I've noticed you're working non-stop. Let's take an evening off to do something you love. What do you say?"*
- **Promote Self-Reflection:** Facilitate discussions that encourage reflecting on personal goals and the reasons behind the drive to overwork. *"Let's talk about what's driving you to stay*

so busy. Do you feel it's helping you achieve what you really want?" "I'm proud of your dedication but also concerned about your well-being. Have you thought about why you're pushing so hard?"

Unbalanced/Unhealthy Use of Authority

- **Enforced Downtime:** Imposing strict limits on work or activities without understanding the young person's needs or motivations. *"You're working too much. I'm deciding now that you cannot work after 8 PM. That's final."*

- **Mandatory Leisure Activities:** Forcing participation in specific leisure activities without consideration for the young person's interests or state of mind. *"I've signed you up for painting classes on the weekends. You need a hobby that isn't work-related."*

- **Work Restrictions:** Setting arbitrary limits on work hours or activities that ignore the young person's sense of responsibility or commitment. *"You are no longer to work on projects after dinner. Your focus should be on family time only."*

Unbalanced/Unhealthy Use of Vulnerability

- **Emotional Guilt-Trip:** Using personal feelings of distress or disappointment to manipulate the young person into changing their behavior. *"You're always busy working. It makes me feel like you don't value our time together. Can't you see how this affects me?"*

- **Sharing Personal Stress:** Relaying personal stress about the young person's future as a way to make them slow down, creating undue pressure. *"Seeing you this driven makes me worried about your health, and that stress keeps me up at night. Can you take it easier for my sake?"*

Blame Shifting:

- <u>Immediate Deflection:</u> Quickly redirecting blame to others when criticized or confronted with a mistake.
- <u>Self-Criticism:</u> Harshly blaming themselves for any problem, even when factors are beyond their control.
- <u>Absolutist Thinking:</u> Viewing situations as entirely someone's fault or not at all, without acknowledging shared responsibility.
- <u>Avoiding Accountability:</u> Shifting responsibility to avoid facing the consequences of their actions or decisions.
- <u>Rationalizing Mistakes:</u> Justifying actions that led to negative outcomes instead of acknowledging fault.

Young people in the survival quadrant are likelier to be hard on themselves and blame themselves for relational failures and mistakes. This becomes a defense mechanism to protect themselves from further emotional pain or vulnerability. Having experienced situations in their lives where they felt powerless or exposed, they shift blame to others or themselves to regain a sense of control or avoid confronting painful truths about their circumstances and stories.

<u>A Balanced Approach Using Healthy Authority & Vulnerability</u>

- **Promoting Self-Reflection:** Encourage young people to reflect on their role in conflicts or issues, fostering a sense of personal accountability. *"Let's think about what happened together. Can you see any way your actions might have contributed?" "It's okay to make mistakes. What's important is learning from them. What do you think you could do differently next time?"*
- **Modeling Accountability:** Demonstrate taking responsibility for one's actions, showing that admitting fault is a strength, not a weakness. *"I realize I might have contributed to this misunderstanding by not being clear. I'm sorry for my part." "When I overlook things, I try to acknowledge my role. It helps us move forward. Let's try to do that together."*

<u>Unbalanced/Unhealthy Use of Authority</u>

- **Forced Apology:** Demanding an immediate apology without understanding or addressing the underlying issues. *"You need to apologize right now, regardless of how you feel about the situation."*
- **Dismissive Correction:** Quickly shutting down their perspective, emphasizing fault without fostering understanding. *"Stop blaming others; it's your fault. Just accept it and move on."*

- **Unilateral Decision-Making:** Making decisions on fault and consequences without involving the young person in the reflection process. *"I've decided you're to blame, and you'll be grounded for this."*

Unbalanced/Unhealthy Use of Vulnerability

- **Emotional Manipulation:** Using personal feelings to guilt the young person into taking or shifting blame. *"You saying that hurts me. Do you want to be the one who's always in the wrong?"*
- **Over-Identification with Blame:** We take on the blame to shield our young people, avoiding teaching responsibility and accountability. *"It must be my fault then; I probably didn't teach you right."*
- **Seeking Sympathy:** Sharing personal distress about the situation to shift blame away from the young person. *"Look how upset this is making me. Maybe we should forget about finding fault."*

The G.R.A.C.E. Response to Survival

Using the G.R.A.C.E. Response when working with our young people in the Survival quadrant can help them feel seen, valued, and supported, which fosters healthy belonging and self-efficacy. By focusing on understanding, goal setting, affirmation, resilience, and community support, we can help guide our young people toward healing and trust in themselves and in others around them.

G: Get to Why

Understand the motivations of the youth's fierce independence and offer suggestions with understanding. *"I've noticed you're often staying busy to avoid downtime. Can we talk about what's driving this need to always be doing something?"*

R: Rally Around Realistic Goals

Set some achievable goals to help your young person learn to relax and relate. *"Let's work together on finding a balance between work, relaxation, and relationships. How about starting with one hour a week dedicated to an activity or relationship you enjoy that's not work-related?"*

A: Affirm Redemptive Positives

Recognize the incredible strength young people have to work hard and build a life for themselves. *"Your ability to work hard and stay focused is impressive. Imagine using those strengths not just for survival but for thriving in areas you're passionate about."*

C: Cultivate Resilience

Help your young person foster coping skills for areas they feel uncomfortable or want to check out. *"When things get tough, remember how you've overcome challenges before. Let's think of strategies to help you face stress without hiding in work or excess busyness."*

E: Engage Supportive Community

Encouraging your youth to involve others in their life. *"I think connecting with others who understand what you're going through would be helpful. Let's look into groups or activities where you can share experiences and get support."*

While it can be exhilarating and satisfying to watch our young people succeed in caring for themselves, displaying a good work ethic, and being responsible, it can also be lonely when they feel like we don't desire or have time for a relationship. It's apparent that balancing healthy authority and vulnerability requires a nuanced approach. Yet, when we get it right, we can effectively and lovingly help our young person address their survival mindset. This balance is imperative as we seek to build a relationship with our young person where they feel supported and encouraged in their strong self-efficacy skills while inviting them into a deep, meaningful connection that promotes healthy belonging.

"Generous listening is powered by curiosity, a virtue we can invite and nurture in ourselves to render it instinctive. It involves a kind of vulnerability—a willingness to be surprised, to let go of assumptions and take in ambiguity. The listener wants to understand the humanity behind the words of the other, and patiently summons one's own best self and one's own best words and questions."
Krista Tippett

CHAPTER TWELVE

HOLDING PAIN

As I tell this next story, I realize that many of my most profound understandings have revolved around food-related instances with our girls. Food, smell, touch, and sensation are powerful activators of memory. Our reactions to those things are often visceral. We walk by a bakery with fresh cinnamon rolls baking, close our eyes, breathe deeply, and are transported back to our childhood kitchen on a Saturday morning with Smurfs playing on the TV. My dad was a mechanic, and to this day, when I walk into any tire shop, I love the smell. It immediately transports me back to my childhood hanging out in Daddy's garage as he worked on someone's car or visiting my grandfather at the tire recapping place, playing on the giant Michelin man as I wait for Daddy & Papaw to finish whatever current conversation they're having. I almost immediately smile when I open the door of a tire shop, and the smell wafts out. I never mind sitting and waiting for my car to be finished because the waiting room of a tire shop feels like a warm hug for me. If the memory is good, the reaction is good. The opposite is also true; if the memory is bad, the reaction is bad. When we understand this, it's easier to hold onto our patience and approach reactions and behaviors with our young people from a place of curiosity rather than control.

I still vividly remember the first time that I encountered this with one of our girls. I was busy at the stove making dinner—spaghetti with meat sauce. One of our girls had the chore of unloading the dishwasher so she was in the kitchen with me. She suddenly cops a huge attitude and says, "I don't know why I'm the only one who has to unload the dishwasher. It's unfair and stupid. I just think y'all like to play favorites." Whoa Nelly! I spun around, stirring spoon in hand, with all the force of a momma about to take down a youngling and put her in her place "Excuuuuuuse me?" I said—clearly, it was way before I had any trauma training. As soon as I made eye contact, she crumpled to the floor in a bundle of tears. I turned down the heat on my skillet, sat on the floor next to her, and said, "What's going on?" Her response broke my heart, "I got mad when I smelled the spaghetti. My mom always made me spaghetti on my birthday when she was around." I immediately understood—without fully understanding trauma, sensory reactions, etc. I saw brokenness and my heart knew. I said, "I'm sorry you're mad because I'm making spaghetti. That's a pretty special memory that you shared with me about your mom. I imagine you think about that a lot." We talked for a few more minutes, and I assured her it was okay to have heavy feelings when you remember things that hurt your heart. Then I said, "I love you. Thank you for sharing. It's okay to be mad. It's not okay to speak to me disrespectfully like that. Don't do that again, okay?" She said, "Okay." And we both got up and returned to getting spaghetti dinner on the table. At dinner, she shared with the family that spaghetti was her favorite birthday meal made by her mom, and we all celebrated what a good memory it is to have.

Of course, it was not okay for her to speak to me so disrespectfully, and the accusation that we were being unfair or playing favorites hurt my feelings. But there was a *why behind the what*—she was feeling angry. And there was a *why behind the why*—the smell of spaghetti reminded her that she missed her mom. At that moment, when I realized that something deeper was going on, I was practicing *holding pain*. I intentionally put aside my hurt and anger to see hers and, for a moment, held them both simultaneously. Where the smell of a tire shop is a warm hug for me, the smell of spaghetti is a harsh reminder of her loss. Her anger and bad attitude were just as much a visceral reaction to her stimulated senses as my immediate smile opening the door.

Defining Holding Pain

"Holding Pain" came out of the initial conversation that Andy and I had in L.A. After we had sketched out an initial 2x2 for belonging and self-efficacy, Andy asked, "What would you say is the one thing that determines the success or failure of a Mentoring Family?" I remember thinking there are so many factors I didn't know how to boil it down to one. Finally, I said, "Holding pain. Both theirs and their young adults." In typical Andy fashion, he leaned back in his chair and said, "Wow. Explain that to me a little more." I explained to him that so many of our most successful families have the capacity to endure hurt or disrespect from their young person, take time to understand the why behind the young person's behavior, and respond with compassion and curiosity rather than react out of their discomfort and frustration. For Connections Homes, the definition of holding pain is now, "Those who have the greatest ability to help a youth *thrive in life* and *impact their world* have one primary characteristic: the capacity to hold pain—both theirs and their youth's."

Our calling to step into the story of broken lives isn't a calling to come alongside a young person walking into adulthood and link arms. It's a calling to come alongside a young person limping out of brokenness and help to bear their weight to provide the support they need to enter adulthood and thrive. Our *Redemptive Connection* is intended to provide the scaffolding they need to stand on while deeply and meaningfully connected to someone who is their biggest cheerleader, most fierce advocate, and challenging coach.

My friend David Hennessey says, "We've all heard about people that want to "rescue children." I don't like the phrase "rescue" because it doesn't truly reflect the experience of working with children from hard places. The reality is that these children are stuck in a pit swirling with chaos, pain and trauma all around them. We don't simply pick them up and pull them out of the pit, miraculously rescuing them. Rather, we enter that pit -- with the chaos, pain and trauma swirling around both of us -- with an outstretched hand. Continually reaching toward them, we strive to develop trust and connection until they, finally, grasp our hand (which may take years). Only then may we begin to guide them out of that pit, walking alongside one another for as long as it takes (maybe a lifetime). In the process, we must continually guard ourselves against the chaos, pain and trauma, for we are not immune to their effects. Defending ourselves with healthy spiritual, emotional, and relational disciplines is absolutely required to journey together out of that pit." I love this outlook because it implicitly means that we take on a little dirt and mud as we wait patiently *with* our young people. It's a perfect visual for *holding pain*. We're willing to be uncomfortable *with* them.

Holding pain doesn't mean you're a doormat. Quite the opposite, as we've covered in this book, our job is to love them, help them feel safe, and hold them accountable. You can hold pain in both belonging and self-efficacy. It's being able to see the sadness caused by the smell of spaghetti, sit *with* your young person at that moment, ask kindly that they not behave in the way that hurt you again, and finally get up and get back to the business of life. Rinse and repeat… more times than you can count.

Some Additional Tools for Holding Pain

Chapter Five covered a lot of really good tools and practices to help with Holding Pain, including suspending judgment, taking a curious approach, and the G.R.A.C.E. Response. I encourage you to bookmark that chapter and refer to those tools as needed. I will add a few more tools to your toolkit for you to understand and practice as you walk *with* your young person.

How to Respond to Your Young Person's Trauma Story

First, I'll say that you should never, ever push for a young person to tell you "what happened" to them. Sometimes, as mentors and adoptive/foster parents, we may know a little. But I can promise you that even if what we know is well documented in a 10-inch-thick binder, we still don't know and never can. The only person who can honestly know your young person's story is your young person, and they may never disclose any of it to you or even to themselves. Pushing them to tell you any part of their trauma story is deeply damaging to your relationship and to them. Telling their story, in most cases, means reliving their trauma again. And, as we've already discussed, relived trauma can result in a visceral reaction.

There are other times when a young person tells everything over and over. This is also something that should be treated with a lot of respect and a lot of listening. Dr. Di Young, a senior psychotherapist at Sydney's South Pacific Private Treatment Centre, says it this way, "Often a person who has disclosed a traumatic event, whether recent or a long time ago, wants to be heard. It takes courage to tell their story. They will hope that you can sit with their pain, but unfortunately can't fully trust that you will." The telling of their story is highly vulnerable and requires a lot of trust; trust that has likely been broken by other people who came before us, over and over. Trust that we will treat their story respectfully, hold space for them in healthy ways, and hold their pain. Unfortunately, hearing the stories can be hard, and it's easy for us to focus on our discomfort instead of hearing what our young person is saying, moving the focus of the interaction off them and onto us. I've learned over the years to keep my responses simple and compassionate, "I'm sorry that happened to you." "That must be hard to think about." "I'm so glad you trusted me with knowing that." "Is there anything that you need from me right now? Anything I can do?" These responses and holding back our thoughts and feelings can be hard, especially when you're a world-class fixer like me. We must remember that healing takes a lifetime, and in many cases, just feeling heard helps. It's not something we can or should solve. It just is. And that's okay.

The key to holding pain while knowing (or not knowing) your young person's trauma story is to practice compassion, which includes both concern for your young person's suffering and a desire to help. Help, in this case, looks like being *with*, listening well, and differentiating yourself from their pain and suffering. Too often, we have a misconception that we must put ourselves in their shoes, take on their burdens, or share their suffering. All of those are good things and have their place in good relationships, but when it comes to our young person's trauma story, we will never have the capacity to feel their feelings, burdens, or suffering, and trying to will only push us further apart. Their story is about them. It has nothing to do with us.

Generous Listening

The Wellbeing Project defines generous listening as "The practice of listening to oneself, one another, and nature—with an open mind, compassion, and without prejudice or agenda."[37] Generous listening takes being a deep listener to another level because it requires an awareness of what is being said and a deep self-control with how we hear and respond to what's being said—suspending our judgment, being curious, and being quiet. We generously and genuinely set aside ourselves to be present and entirely *with* our young person.

To listen generously, we must practice noticing. Noticing our young person as they are speaking and picking up on what their body language, tone of voice, facial expressions, and overall demeanor are communicating. It's letting our young person talk it through, verbally process, and solve their own problem. We can't fix it for them, and we won't try. But we will hold space for them as they work it out. We don't try to fill the silence; if we have input, we focus on open-ended curiosity. "How did that make you feel?" "Do you feel like you understand why that happened?" "How are you thinking about working on that?" "What do you think is a good next step?"

Self-Care

You cannot sit with brokenness without feeling its sting on your heart and mind. That is normal. This is why it's so important that we don't build our lives and identities around those of our children. We are an individual human, and so are they; our failures aren't their failures, and their failures aren't ours. We both need to have autonomy and take responsibility for ourselves. I don't know how this looks for you, but when my children were all home, it looked like long runs, long baths, going to bed early to watch TV in my room, early mornings reading the Bible and prayer, dates with my husband, and girls' nights with my friends. One of my favorite t-shirts when training for my first half marathon read, "13.1 Miles of Peace & Quiet." It was perfect and true. I also made it a point to discover and do things I enjoy, like reading, crocheting, baking, and playing games.

---

[37] https://wellbeing-project.org/generous-listening-for-wellbeing/

Finding a good counselor to talk to while walking with your young person is also helpful. I learned not to hesitate to pick up the phone to call one of my friends who was trauma-trained and ask for their advice and encouragement. I needed it more than I can count, and I still do. Holding pain doesn't mean we bury it. It means we hold onto it long enough to bear with and be with our young person as they journey toward a thriving life. Along the way, we find places to empty our hearts and minds of the hurt so that there's space to return and do it again. I've emptied lots of hurt over tear-stained Bible pages or on long, sweaty runs where tears mixed with sweat and the beating of my heart wasn't just from running.

Being a *Redemptive Connection* isn't easy. As a matter of fact, it requires great sacrifice. The gift is that through our sacrifice, we may make just a little bit of life right and whole again for our young person. And, in doing so, we can one day look back with hearts full of gratitude and fulfillment as our young people truly thrive in life. If you're like me, you may be wondering if you can do this work and hold this kind of pain. You can. The good news is that you can build it if you don't have the capacity right now. Many resources are at the back of this book to help you. But the best news is that Jesus left us the greatest example in the world of how to hold pain. He held his and the entire world's. We'll talk about this in our final chapter.

"During the days of Jesus' life on earth, He offered up prayers and petitions with fervent cries and tears to the one who could save Him from death, and He was heard because of His reverent submission. Son though He was, He learned obedience from what He suffered and, once made perfect, He became the source of eternal salvation for all who obey Him."
Hebrews 5:7-9

CHAPTER THIRTEEN

OUR GREATEST EXAMPLE

It is an immense understatement to say that I couldn't have made it through all I've walked through without Jesus. In 11 years, our family grew from a family of three to a family of 10 (not counting sons-in-law and grandbabies); I wrote three devotionals and pioneered a unique nonprofit model. And if that wasn't enough to wade through, one and a half years after starting Connections Homes, the most brutal season of my life began. From the fall of 2015 to the spring of 2017, over 17 months, I lost 12 of my closest family and friends to death, including both my mother and my father, one of my best friends, and my grandmother. I went to so many funerals that I ultimately threw away my black dress. I couldn't stand to look at it again. Amid it all, we still had girls at home and in crisis; I was trying to be faithful with Connections Homes and more. I look back on those years and honestly don't know how I made it through. It was my *footprints in the sand*[38] season, for sure. These words from the final stanza of the poem ring so true for me, *"He whispered, "My precious child, I love you and will never leave you, never, ever, during your trials and testings. When you saw only one set of footprints, it was then that I carried you."*

That season taught me that you know God best in your greatest suffering and love God best in your greatest triumph. He truly walked alongside me and gave me a sense of peace and strength that I didn't know was possible. This is why it's so important to me to end this book focusing on Jesus as our greatest example of the capacity to hold pain—both his and the entire world's. No one has suffered pain, betrayal, and loss more than Jesus. The scripture at the start of this chapter says it all: he pleaded

---

[38] https://www.crosswalk.com/faith/spiritual-life/beautiful-ways-footprints-in-the-sand-offers-solid-hope.html

with God through tears to rescue Him from death on the cross yet, in obedience, loved humanity and honored His Father. He died a painful and gruesome death so that we could be redeemed and have eternal life. *This is creative restoration through sacrifice. This is what redemption looks like.*

He has called you and me to be like Him, to lay down our lives so that another can be restored through us. God, in His infinite love, has chosen us as His creative agents in the brokenness of this world to take part in redemption through creative restoration (reclaiming, renewing, returning to rightful order…). Restoration, in this sense, takes place as we take our place as image-bearers of our redemptive Savior and lay down our lives on behalf of others. Through sacrifice, we choose to pursue, take risks, share burdens, and bear a cost. *Our journey is to be made into His image—image-bearers in action within a broken and hurting world.* And the Bible gives us a model for ministry and life in the hard places.

Redemptive Connection Through a Biblical Lens

As a mom and an organizational leader working with young people who've experienced extreme hurt, abandonment, abuse, and neglect, I've seen just about every type of young person and behavior. Many of our young people are youth of color who've experienced racism and rejection because of the color of their skin. We serve LGBTQ+ youth, youth who drink or use drugs to self-medicate, youth who self-harm, youth who lie (a lot!), youth who create drama, youth who rage, youth who are atheists, youth who reject religion due to religious abuse, youth who cuss, youth on the autism spectrum, and more. Our families are Christians who deeply love Jesus and believe He has called them to serve young people without a family by becoming lifelong, safe, and trusted people. For me and the families we serve, our faith compels us into this work and sustains us through hard times. And that's the point—it's *our* faith. It doesn't have to be our young person's faith. It's *our* lifestyle. It doesn't have to be our young person's lifestyle. Before you get your feathers ruffled too bad, let me explain.

I'm not saying that we must "sign off on sin." Not at all. But "not signing off on sin" doesn't mean we never encounter it with love. If that's what it means, then Jesus did it all wrong. And since we know He didn't, we are compelled, again, to look at Him as our greatest example. He loved the sinner, He dined in their homes (gasp!), and ultimately, Jesus died for the sinner—among whom are you and me. I don't remember Jesus asking me to clean up the sin in my life before accepting me into His family; if He had—well, I'd still be an outsider.

Furthermore, Jesus gathered the riffraff and outcasts of society—the fishermen, the tax collector, the thief, the zealot—and *walked with them* for three years. Through many miles of miracles, turmoil, conflict, and toil, He transformed their life by speaking truth and *being* The Truth in love. Life on life, love on display. To the world's brokenness, Jesus brought love instead of judgment, gentleness instead of shame, and connection instead of rejection.

"But how can we ever get them to accept Jesus if we never address their sin?" First, it's not our job to get anyone to accept Jesus. That job belongs to the Holy Spirit, period. I'm not saying that you have to change who you are or ignore your beliefs; far from it. My girls have experienced and experimented with all kinds of things in the list above. They *know* where I stand on things because I tell them. I do have boundaries that I expect them to honor, such as not asking to stay all night at our house with their unmarried love interest. Or not smoking in our homes or doing drugs on our property or in our vehicles. If you're messing with witchcraft or porn (yes, both of those have been things), I don't want it in my house, and I won't engage with it in any way. Whatever my girls decide to do with their lives outside of my home is their decision; I don't have to agree with it to love them.

I use a curious approach in asking why certain things or people appeal to them, especially when it's something that I may disagree with. And, sometimes, they will ask me for my opinion, and I'll say, "Well, you may not agree with me, and that's okay, but here's what I think/believe…" They know that I will talk about Jesus and that I am who I am today because I deeply value my relationship with Him and live my life according to Biblical values. It's, without a doubt, the cornerstone of my life. And, for our girls who are not believers, when a crisis hits—they call me to pray. Will I have dinner in their homes where they live unmarried with a love interest? Absolutely! What do you want me to bring for dessert? Disagreement shouldn't mean disconnection. This is why we value our candid family talks at the dinner table. Disagreeable topics come up all the time, and we debate. Honestly, my kids love to bring the most controversial topics possible to the table so that they can see if we get rattled. We don't—at least not yet. I listen just as much to their points of view as they listen to mine. It's not about who wins or loses; it's just about being seen, authentic, and honoring each other.

Do I ever say, "The Bible says…" Yes! But it's always in the context of a two-way conversation and never in judgment or to bring shame. I firmly believe that each person has to walk out on their path toward a knowledge of Christ and that Christ calls each of us differently. But on that path, the Bible clearly shows that love and kindness draw us from our sin, not judgment, condemnation, guilt, and shame. *"You may think you can condemn such people, but you are just as bad, and you have no excuse! When you say they are wicked and should be punished, you condemn yourself, for you who judge others do these very same things. And we know that God, in His justice, will punish anyone who does such things. Since you judge others for doing these things, why do you think you can avoid God's judgment when you do the same things? Don't you see how wonderfully kind, tolerant, and patient God is with you? Does this mean nothing to you? Can't you see that His kindness is intended to turn you from your sins?* Romans 2:1-4

Remember, we are His image-bearers, His hands and feet upon the earth. A life lived loving others will draw people to curiosity about Christ because they feel your love, observe your life, and want to experience the same peace. We do this like Jesus did—life on life, love in action. We fail if we push them away by being pushy and critical about who they are and how they live their lives. I believe that as people who are loved by Jesus unconditionally, we receive the greatest example of being loved where we are and as we are. So, we should go and do the same.

Belonging

"If we live, we live for the Lord; and if we die, we die for the Lord. So, whether we live or die, we belong to the Lord." Romans 14:8

My life is shaped deeply by knowing I belong to the Lord and am loved as His beloved daughter. It's out of my receipt of belonging in my own life that I can provide belonging to others. I want my girls and every young person we touch through Connections Homes to feel deeply and genuinely seen and loved, to feel the same deep connection to me that I feel to my Heavenly Father. This is my way of reflecting Him to them, a living testimony to my loving God.

Self-Efficacy

"I can do all things through Christ who strengthens me." Philippians 4:13

I walk in the confidence of who I am and *whose* I am. I know confidently that I can do anything God asks of me because it is in His strength that I do it, not my own. As I display that confidence in God, it is a light to those around me that they, too, can have that same assurance.

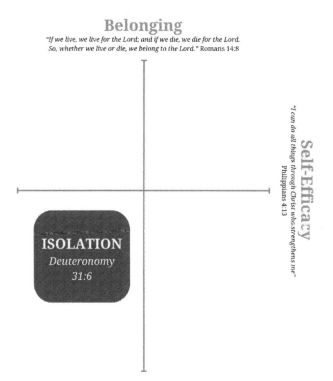

Belonging

"If we live, we live for the Lord; and if we die, we die for the Lord. So, whether we live or die, we belong to the Lord." Romans 14:8

"I can do all things through Christ who strengthens me". Philippians 4:13

Self-Efficacy

ISOLATION
Deuteronomy 31:6

Isolation

"Be strong and courageous; do not be afraid or terrified of them. For it is the Lord your God who goes with you; He will never leave you or forsake you." Deuteronomy 3:16

I have the assurance that I am never alone. He is by my side in my darkest days, in my most egregious sin, and in my deepest despair. That doesn't mean everything was over and okay in an instant. It wasn't. It just meant that He was walking alongside me—or, more likely, carrying me. I wasn't in it alone and didn't have to do it alone. The hard was still hard. The hurt still hurts. But He was near. In our young people's loneliness and isolation, they know we are there with them. And we will never leave them or forsake them.

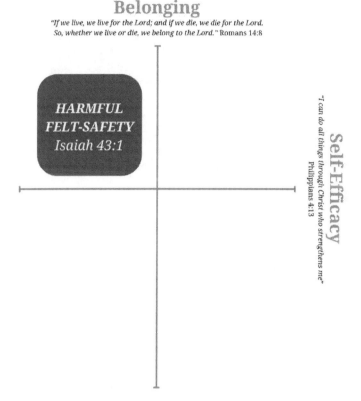

Belonging

"If we live, we live for the Lord; and if we die, we die for the Lord.
So, whether we live or die, we belong to the Lord." Romans 14:8

HARMFUL
FELT-SAFETY
Isaiah 43:1

"I can do all things through Christ who strengthens me"
Philippians 4:13

Self-Efficacy

Harmful Felt-Safety

"Do not fear, for I have redeemed you; I have summoned you by name; you are mine." Isaiah 43:1

When I stray, He calls my name. When I seek belonging in what I do, who I'm with, or how I'm perceived, He reminds me that, apart from Him, all else is a fading vapor. It is out of His perfect love for me, His patient kindness toward me, and His mercy and grace that I can chase unhealthy belonging and return to Him—time and time again. Isn't that the story of the whole Bible? A wayward people coming home to their God and then leaving in search of earthly belonging—time and time again.

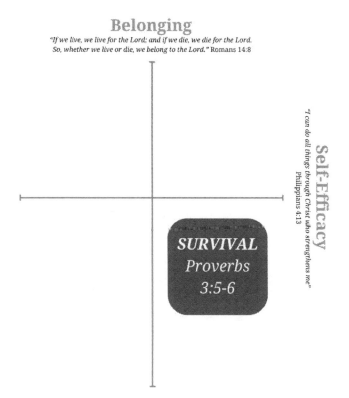

Belonging
"If we live, we live for the Lord; and if we die, we die for the Lord.
So, whether we live or die, we belong to the Lord." Romans 14:8

"I can do all things through Christ who strengthens me"
Philippians 4:13

Self-Efficacy

SURVIVAL
Proverbs
3:5-6

Survival

"Trust in the Lord with all your heart and lean not on your own understanding; in all your ways acknowledge Him and He will make your paths straight." Proverbs 3:5-6

How often have I taken my life into my own hands and tried to live according to *my* plans, understanding, and ways? Oh, too many to count. I am stubborn and full of great ideas. I don't always seek God first before barreling forward with whatever strikes my fancy. I don't always prioritize relationships and communion with Him over my work, leisure, and Candy Crush. We are all prone to survival mode, forsaking our belonging to God in favor of our ability to do it ourselves. It's out of our own humility that we acknowledge that we are also guilty of this and that we can have patience and understanding toward our young people who are making their way toward trust and confidence in relationships.

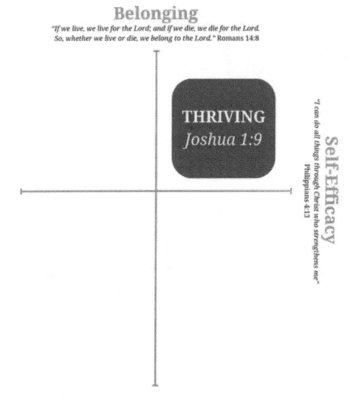

Thriving

"Be strong and courageous. Do not be afraid; do not be discouraged, for the Lord your God will be with you wherever you go." Joshua 1:9

Truly thriving in life has always been connected with who I'm connected with. This means I'm happiest and most confident when my family is in a good place. I'm fulfilled when I not only get to do good work but I'm also surrounded by good people to do the work alongside me. Our young people will thrive and learn to step out and be *strong and courageous* as they trust that we, among others, will always be there to encourage them in the way we see God encouraging Joshua. We can cheer them on, believe in them, and remind them that we are right here, in their corner—always.

Above All, Love

"Above all, love one another deeply because love covers a multitude of sins."
1 Peter 4:8

The book of Exodus Chapter 9 tells the story of Noah being found passed out drunk and naked in his tent by his son Ham. Ham leaves the tent after seeing his father's nakedness and sin to go and find his brothers and encourage them to look. Instead, the brothers went to Noah's tent and walked backward to cover their father's nakedness. Ham's descendants receive a curse for exposing his father's sin. The account doesn't say Noah's other sons thought his sin was okay. It just says they covered it. They didn't gossip, they didn't shame, they didn't even look. Noah's sin was between God and him. The same is true of our young people and their lives, including their sins. Loving deeply means forgiving as we've been forgiven; we reject gossip, condemnation, taking offense, or bringing shame.

Life is long and love never fails. It is not our responsibility to live our young person's life. Our job is to love them and live our messy, broken, and sinful lives alongside theirs, with humility acknowledging that we are also sinners in need of mercies anew each day. Proverbs 19:11 says, "A person's wisdom yields patience; it is to one's glory to overlook offense." And 1 Corinthians 13:4-7 says, "Love is patient, love is kind. It does not envy, it does not boast, it is not proud. It does not dishonor others; it is not self-seeking; it is not easily angered and keeps no record of wrongs. Love does not delight in evil but rejoices with truth. It always protects, always trusts, always hopes, always perseveres." I'm convinced that as we look upon the cross, we see the greatest example of love wrapping around our sins, the ultimate *Redemptive Connection*.

Belonging

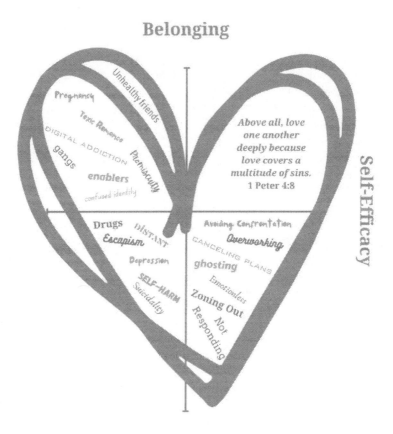

"But God shows his love for us in that while we were still sinners, Christ died for us." Romans 5:8

ADDITIONAL RESOURCES

The Whole Brain Child	Daniel J. J. Siegal, Tina Payne Bryson
The Connected Child	Karyn B. Purvis, David Cross
The Connected Parent	Lisa Qualls & Karyn B. Purvis
Reframing Foster Care	Jason Johnson
All In Orphan Care	Jason Johnson
Wounded Children, Healing Homes	Jayne Schooler, Betsy Keefer Smalley
Caring for Kids from Hard Places	Jayne Schooler, David Schooler
The Whole Life Adoption Book	Thomas Atwood, Jayne Schooler
Attaching in Adoption	Deborah Gray
Nurturing Adoptions	Deborah Gray
What Happened to You?	Oprah Winfrey, Bruce D. Perry
Anatomy of the Soul	Curt Thompson, M.D.
The Soul of Shame	Curt Thompson, M.D.
The Soul of Desire	Curt Thompson, M.D.
The Deepest Place	Curt Thompson, M.D.
Strong & Weak	Andy Crouch
The Body Keeps Score	Bessel van der Kolk, M.D.
How to Cultivate Belonging	Adele R. Ackert, LCSW
Childhood Disrupted	Donna Jackson Nakazawa
Rising Strong	Brené Brown
On Your Own Without a Net	D. Wayne Osgood, E. Michael Foster
The Resilience Edge	Christian Moore
Emerging Adulthood	Jeffrey Jenson Arnett
Attached (Adult Attachment)	Amir Levine, Rachel Heller
Brainstorm	Daniel J. Siegal, M.D.
Etched in Sand	Regina Calcaterra
Untangling Hope	Johnna Stein
Ready or Not	Pam Parish
Battle-Weary Parents	Pam Parish
The Gift	Pam Parish
Boy Who Was Raised as a Dog	Bruce D. Perry
A Child Called It	Dave Pelzer
Keep the Doors Open	Kristin Berry
Faith & Foster Care	Dr. John DeGarmo
Fostered	Tori Hope Peterson
Becoming Home	Jedd Medefind
Foster the Family	Jamie C. Finn

There are so many amazing resources that I couldn't possibly list all of them here. A quick Google / Amazon search of "foster care books" or "trauma"+ "foster care books" will provide you with an incredible list of resources.

ABOUT DON'T GO ALONE

Connections Homes created the Don't Go Alone (DGA) Program for young people aged 18 to 24 who have aged out of foster care or are homeless without family. The program matches them with a Mentoring Family who agree to be a part of their lives for the long term. The aim is to prevent poverty and homelessness and provide them with love and a sense of belonging through *redemptive connection*.

As of the writing of this book, the impacts of the program are:

- Less than 5% of girls connected to a Mentoring Family have become pregnant.
- 95% of youth who enter our program already pregnant or parenting have maintained care & custody of their children.
- Less than 1% of boys connected to a Mentoring Family have had any interaction with the law.
- 93% of youth are pursuing education goals with 53% pursuing post-secondary or skilled trade.
- At its current rate, the program saves our communities more than $22 million annually on welfare and social services costs.

Become a Mentoring Family

Throughout our lives, there are moments when we require someone to support us, lend a hand, walk alongside us, and celebrate our achievements with us. In most cases, we can rely on our family for all these things and more. They are our consistent, lifelong relationships that provide unwavering support. **But what about young individuals who do not have a family to depend on?** Can you be a *redemptive connection*?

Become an Affiliate

The DGA Program includes all of the critical systems, training, and elements needed for you to address the needs of young adults without a family in your community. Our team will provide training and support to your staff, enabling your organization to make a real difference in the lives of young adults. We also offer continuing partnerships and tools to help you manage the program effectively.

Become a Financial Partner

Connections Homes is a privately funded, faith-based nonprofit organization. We rely on donations from individuals, foundations, corporations, and churches who believe, like us, that no young person should have to do life alone. Please consider becoming a financial partner and helping every youth have a *redemptive connection*.

Made in the USA
Columbia, SC
30 June 2024

9a71f8b4-1c75-44bd-8af6-20249947ec8cR01